Discussions on War and Human Aggression

World Anthropology

General Editor

SOL TAX

Patrons

CLAUDE LÉVI-STRAUSS
MARGARET MEAD
LAILA SHUKRY EL HAMAMSY
M. N. SRINIVAS

MOUTON PUBLISHERS · THE HAGUE · PARIS
DISTRIBUTED IN THE USA AND CANADA BY ALDINE, CHICAGO

Discussions on War and Human Aggression

Editors

R. DALE GIVENS
MARTIN A. NETTLESHIP

MOUTON PUBLISHERS · THE HAGUE · PARIS
DISTRIBUTED IN THE USA AND CANADA BY ALDINE, CHICAGO

General Editor's Preface

This volume is a companion to *War, its causes and correlates*, two volumes published as one, which includes all of the papers which served as the basis for the brilliant discussion hosted by Notre Dame University and fully reported here. Thus, I need only repeat the comments made in introducing the book of papers.

Anthropologists tend to look at people and peoples positively, understanding widely differing cultural behaviors as contributing to survival. The societies we study have indeed survived; even those which we see only through archeology flourished long enough to be noticed. We do come to recognize cultural traps and even pathologies, but characteristically we do not start with or look for them. Hence we have looked at war only as we have looked at other secondary institutions displayed in some human societies sometimes. The change in recent years is that a small part of the species has weapons which, if they only continue to behave in ways well recognized in history, threaten the species itself. So it is that only now, in these volumes, anthropology provides its first treatment of the subject of war. And it is not surprising that its special occasion was a species-wide Congress.

Like most contemporary sciences, anthropology is a product of the European tradition. Some argue that it is a product of colonialism, with one small and self-interested part of the species dominating the study of the whole. If we are to understand the species, our science needs substantial input from scholars who represent a variety of the world's cultures. It was a deliberate purpose of the IXth International Congress of Anthropological and Ethnological Sciences to provide impetus in this direction. The *World Anthropology* volumes, therefore, offer a first glimpse of a human science in which members from all societies have played an active role. Each of the books is designed to be self-contained; each is an attempt to update its particular sector of scientific knowledge and is written by specialists from all parts of the world. Each volume should be read and reviewed individually as a separate volume on its own given subject. The set as a whole will indicate what changes are in store for anthropology as scholars from the developing countries join in studying the species of which we are all a part.

The IXth Congress was planned from the beginning not only to include as many of the scholars from every part of the world as possible, but also with a view toward the eventual publication of the papers in high-quality volumes. At previous Congresses scholars were invited to bring papers which were then read out loud. They were necessarily limited in length; many were only summarized; there was little time for discussion; and the sparse discussion could only be in one language. The IXth Congress was an experiment aimed at changing this. Papers were written with the intention of exchanging them before the Congress, particularly in extensive pre-Congress sessions; they were not intended to be read aloud at the Congress, that time being devoted to discussions — discussions which were simultaneously and professionally translated into five languages. The method for eliciting the papers was structured to make as representative a sample as was allowable when scholarly creativity — hence self-selection — was critically important. Scholars were asked both to propose papers of their own and to suggest topics for sessions of the Congress which they might edit into volumes. All were then informed of the suggestions and encouraged to re-think their own papers and the topics. The process, therefore, was a continuous one of feedback and exchange and it has continued to be so even after the Congress. The some two thousand papers comprising *World Anthropology* certainly then offer a substantial sample of world anthropology. It has been said that anthropology is at a turning point; if this is so, these volumes will be the historical direction-markers.

As might have been foreseen in the first post-colonial generation, the large majority of the Congress papers (82 percent) are the work of scholars identified with the industrialized world which fathered our traditional discipline and the institution of the Congress itself: Eastern Europe (15 percent); Western Europe (16 percent); North America (47 percent); Japan, South Africa, Australia, and New Zealand (4 percent). Only 18 percent of the papers are from developing areas: Africa (4 percent); Asia-Oceania (9 percent); Latin America (5 percent). Aside from the substantial representation from the U.S.S.R. and the nations of Eastern Europe, a significant difference between this corpus of written material and that of other Congresses is the addition of the large proportion of contributions from Africa, Asia, and Latin America.

"Only 18 percent" is two to four times as great a proportion as that of other Congresses; moreover, 18 percent of 2,000 papers is 360 papers, 10 times the number of "Third World" papers presented at previous Congresses. In fact, these 360 papers are more than the total of ALL papers published after the last International Congress of Anthropological and Ethnological Sciences which was held in the United States (Philadelphia, 1956).

The significance of the increase is not simply quantitative. The input of scholars from areas which have until recently been no more than subject matter for anthropology represents both feedback and also long-awaited theoretical contributions from the perspectives of very different cultural, social, and historical traditions. Many who attended the IXth Congress were convinced that anthropology would not be the same in the future. The fact that the next Congress (India, 1978) will be our first in the "Third World" may be symbolic of the change. Meanwhile, sober consideration of the present set of books will show how much, and just where and how, our discipline is being revolutionized.

Other *World Anthropology* volumes related to the subject matter treated here and in *War, its causes and correlates* include those volumes on primatology and evolution; cultural and comparative history; and ethnological, psychological, political, economic, and social anthropology.

Chicago, Illinois   SOL TAX
February 25, 1976

Preface

This volume is the result of a three-and-a-half-day conference on "War: Its Causes and Correlates" held at the University of Notre Dame in August 1973. The symposium was one of several pre-Congress sessions organized under the aegis of the IXth International Congress of Anthropological and Ethnological Sciences (the IXth ICAES).

The Conference was both international and interdisciplinary. Participants came from ten nations: Egypt, Germany, Great Britain, Israel, Kuwait, Mexico, the Netherlands, New Zealand, Norway, and the United States. Although anthropology was more heavily represented than other academic fields, members of eleven other disciplines participated in the sessions. There were even two businessmen, two housewives, and an industrialist.

Where possible, the formal papers were reproduced and made available prior to or upon the arrival of the participants. Only brief summaries were presented during the sessions, the rest of the time being devoted to open discussion.

The formal papers are presented in *War, its causes and correlates*, edited by Martin A. Nettleship, R. Dale Givens, and Anderson Nettleship. As with the other symposia and sessions of the IXth ICAES, this volume is being published by Mouton as a part of the *World Anthropology* series. The discussions, which were taped, have been edited and presented as a supplementary but independent volume.

The prevailing feeling among those attending the symposium was akin to having a split personality. The participants looked upon themselves as concerned human beings — concerned with the continued use of war as a means to settle disputes among nation-states and the continuing danger of global nuclear war. But the participants were, for the most part, also research scientists. The role of "concerned human being" had brought about the focus on the problem of war, but it was realized by all that to confuse this role with that of the objective researcher would only multiply the problems involved in analyzing data. War is a complex enough phenomenon to study without its student becoming emotionally involved.

For the activist wanting an immediate answer to the question, "How can wars be prevented?" the present volume will not be very satisfactory. Rather, what was accomplished at the conference and is presented here will serve more as a starting point for future endeavors. The basic research tools for the investigation of aggression, violence, and warfare are available; unfortunately, except for a few pioneering works (Sorokin, Wright, Turney-High, etc.), the sciences of human behavior have only begun to investigate the problems involved. There are many reasons for this, but one of the most significant is the simple fact that far larger research funds have been made available for the development of bigger and better weapons than for peace research. In fact, the student who has attempted research in the latter area has sometimes even suffered some form of "official" censure (see Rapaport, Session 8).

The topics and ideas presented at the symposium and the backgrounds of the participants were too varied to allow a simple summation. Still, a few general comments can be made about the August 1973 conference at Notre Dame.

For one thing, evidence from research conducted during the past decade or more clearly shows a close interrelation between an organism's biochemistry and physiology and that organism's aggressiveness, and this holds for a variety of animals studied to date. To give but one example, if a newborn female is injected with male hormones, she will not grow up to be a normally peaceful adult, but will take on the aggressive characteristics typical of a male of that species.

While this research may not totally explain individual aggressiveness and occasional violence, it does add to our understanding of this behavioral phenomenon. But is individual aggressiveness related to warfare, especially modern warfare? There has been a general assumption, on the part of those studying war and those involved in what has become known as peace research, that such a relationship exists. It may very well be the case since aggression seems to have very deep roots in the evolution of primate behavior. We know that non-human primate societies and even most "primitive" human societies are not able to function without at least some aggressive behavior. Yet there is considerable doubt that the relationship has held since the development of modern military technology, a development that began several centuries ago but which has reached its current heights only since the end of World War II. As Eibl-Eibesfeldt said during the conference, "if war is inborn to man, or if war is in the genes, why do we need so much propaganda to bring people to fight?" (Session 2).

People who participate in modern warfare often show no signs of individual aggression. General S. L. A. Marshall's study of the U.S. soldier during World War II (*Men against fire*) showed that less than 25 percent of the men in COMBAT units ever did any actual fighting; a majority never even fired their rifles. Nor is patriotism or ideology always sufficient to bring about individual aggressiveness. Stoffer's study of *The American soldier* clearly showed that the infantryman who DID fight did so because he did not want to let down the other members of his squad, not because of some ideal.

It is a popular and romantic myth that, except for man, members of the same species do not fight to the death. Actually, the male killing of another male is quite a normal phenomenon among all mammals, although rare among birds. This applies to ungulates, carnivores, and primates. Kortlandt points out that, if anything, it is probably rarest among hominids, not more prevalent among them as is generally thought. "It is just a fairy tale that male-male killing occurs frequently in man, particularly in wars, and is rare among mammals" (Kortlandt, Session 4). In fact, Cancro indicates that the male-male variety of killing found among mammals is not typical within the human species, where killing (murder) tends to be cross-gender (Session 4). That is, men tend to kill women; women to kill men.

The fact is, aggression seems to be related mostly to the individual and cannot be used to explain modern warfare. The latter involves a multitude of factors, including economic, political, religious, ideological, and psychological, and is therefore a very complex phenomenon.

A number of definitions were presented and discussed at the symposium. For one thing, an effort was made to distinguish between war, raiding, and feuding; for another, various types of conflict and cooperation were considered. For example, Tefft suggested that "warfare is armed conflict between political communities" (Session 2), while M. Nettleship felt that war, as we know it today, ". . . only occurs in civilized societies and is first observed at the time of the formation of the state" (Session 2). This was supported by Roper's archeological evidence (Session 1) of war first occurring about 7500 B.C. (at Jericho). Unfortunately, however, there was no consensus on the various definitions offered.

As the conference proceeded, a number of weaknesses in past research became apparent. For one thing, while we have relatively sound information on the micro-level of human behavior, there is little carry-over to the more complex macro-level. We also use the word "war" to refer to what is actually more than one kind of phenomenon. "War is not one thing. War is a great many things, and some of them I suspect are totally unrelated to others" (Rapaport, Session 8). Further, the study of harmful aggression, both on the individual level and the level of organized warfare, has been dominated by disease theory, i.e. the notion that it is atypical or pathologic behavior in man.

With regard to the latter point, we must recognize that war has many positive benefits, especially to some segments of a society such as the military-industrial complex. It also helps to unify the members of a society when faced by a common threat, either real or propagandized. The U.S. military helps maintain itself by offering training in special skills to many who do not go on to college. War may be bad, but for whom?

In World War II, the war was bad for the Japanese military élite; it was bad for the war dead and their families. But the Japanese factory worker of 1973 may very well be better off than the worker of 1933 and he is probably better off than if World War II had not happened.... As scientists searching for understanding, we should not view war as BAD any more than we should view automobiles as bad because they have also resulted in the deaths of a multitude of individuals (Sipes, Session 1).

We had better know what the consequences are likely to be — ALL the consequences — before we try to bring about changes in our current institutions or offer solutions to complex phenomena.

But while the symposium raised as many problems as it found answers, most of the participants left with a feeling that much had been gained from the papers and the discussions. In fact, there was a strong desire to see a follow-up symposium in the future, and one was planned for 1975. Dr. Cara Richards expressed a common sentiment when she said, "I feel, personally, that I can see a very faint light at the end of the tunnel, and feel that research problems, after this conference, for me, are a bit more obvious, a bit more specific, a bit more concrete" (Session 7).

The editors would like to express their appreciation to the University of Notre Dame and its President, Father Theodore M. Hesburgh, C.S.C., for extending to us the privilege of using the University's excellent facilities in the Center for Continuing Education. We would also like to thank the University and Father Hesburgh for the accommodations provided at the Morris Inn next to the campus and the technical staff made available for the recording of the discussions, and Dr. Irwin Press for shouldering the responsibilities for local arrangements.

We would also like to thank the secretarial staff of the Antaeus Institute of Fayetteville, Arkansas, and especially Ms. Darla Clayton for transcribing the taped recordings to a typed manuscript that could be edited. Our thanks also go to Ms. Karen Tkach, who has served as Mouton's editor for *World Anthropology*, and to Peter de Ridder, former Director of Mouton Publishers, who did much to make this project possible through cooperation with Dr. Sol Tax, ICAES President.

On a more personal level, we would like to acknowledge the support provided by Dr. Givens' wife, Mona, throughout the "days of the symposium" and to thank her especially for the help she graciously gave in the final editing.

R. DALE GIVENS   MARTIN A. NETTLESHIP
California State College   *Antaeus Lineal Research Associates*
Dominguez Hills, California   *Fayetteville, Arkansas*

Table of Contents

Introduction, Definitions

Chaired by M. A. NETTLESHIP and A. H. ESSER

Discussion of papers by R. JACOBS, C. E. RICHARDS, M. K. ROPER, S. I. GHABBOUR, P. A. CORNING, B. A. CARROLL and C. F. FINK, G. ANSARI

PRESS: I wish to welcome you most cordially to Notre Dame. We are very delighted that you could all make it and are especially pleased that this most interesting conference on war should be held here on the campus of Notre Dame. This is a Catholic university. It is catholic in two senses. Firstly, it was founded and is run by a Catholic religious brotherhood, the Holy Cross Congregation, and most of its teachers and students are Catholic. But secondly and more importantly, I feel, by virtue of its close identification with a religious and moral tradition, Notre Dame attempts to impose an ethic upon its influence over students. This ethic, most correctly, is larger than any particular ritual tradition. It is a focus upon what might be called ultimate concerns, meaning the potential of our acts and of what we teach and of what we learn for good or evil. Such a tradition dares to say "knowledge for the sake of knowledge is insufficient." For if we are not to put knowledge to use in the service of others, whom do we serve but ourselves? To approach the topic of war without the element of ultimate concern is, I believe, to waste both an opportunity and our own capacity as keepers of our brothers. We all make value judgments in our disciplines, at the very least in formulating the questions we ask. However, we try not to judge and label our research foci in moralistic terms because, as proper cultural relativists, we have to ask the question, "whose morals?" In dealing with war we have focused upon functions, leaving the evaluations to others.

Certainly, there are arguments for war on a small scale. Examples from New Guinea and South America, to name but a few, are fodder for good classroom sessions. Organized aggressive behavior, we teach, furthers group identity. It may serve as a test of manhood or a rite of passage. It may form the basis of age grading; segmentary feuding systems with shifting group alliances may actually form solidarity and peace in the long run by preventing large-scale permanent "sides" from coagulating. And we teach what Max Gluckman and others have suggested, that complementary opposition with potential for hostilities may be quite normal and ultimately non-destructive. The Nuer disperse their lineages through several villages, thus making inter-village hostility impractical and undesirable. The non-localized lineages are all too vulnerable in case of inter-lineage feuds and this ominous threat serves to keep the peace. On a larger scale, we look to other functions of war. The periodic revolutionary upheavals of dynastic cycles in China left literally millions dead and did serve to lower the population pressure and to redistribute land. Every social act, we are told, has a function. Our job is simply to find it and describe it, not evaluate it. And once an anthropologist has assigned something a function, it becomes holy, above value judgment. By function, of course, we mean that it is useful. Undoubtedly we could find some respectable function for the Crusades, the Thirty Years' War, the Conquest of Mexico, the First and Second World Wars, and Vietnam.

I suggest that while we may indeed find functions, we are under no obligation to end our concern at that point. Physicians do not end their concern with the disease when they have identified a pathological microorganism. They try to eradicate it. Physicists do not end their concern with sources of energy when they have worked out a new one. Somehow, only we, the social scientists, must not meddle with our subject matter. If we keep our hands off, our charming primitives and lusty peasants will remain unchanged, our acculturating immigrants or proletariats will experience minimal trauma. We must use the term "applied anthropology" to distinguish our more involved meddling from pure anthropology, which assumes our emotional detachment from the world around us. Even here, it is most interesting to note that when we actively help to drill new wells, to introduce weaving techniques or new agricultural techniques to peasants, or buy their land for them, or introduce a health clinic into their midst, we are doing laudable applied anthropology. But when we try to meddle in their politics of war, we are loudly labelled insurgents or counter-insurgents and are denounced at national meetings.

This brings us to the point of our mission here at Notre Dame. We must ask about the nature of our inquiries. If we must use the term function, what is the function of our expertise, our training, and our control of so much specific data? Without meaning to make a pun of our topic of discussion, are we above the battle or are we in it? War is different from most other topics we study. It is hard to picture the world in peril if the couvade or the Omaha kinship system gets out of control. If war gets out of control, however, we will soon enough be involved beyond our value-free scruples. Unfortunately, our Yąnamamö and our New Guinea Dani are not the only ones who know about war. The hydrogen bomb forces us into the role of evaluators and judges. Therefore, for the next three and a half days we must ask not only why and how, but whence. Our goal must not only be an understanding of the etiology and the form of aggressive behavior but of its necessity in the widest sense, a sense beyond the individual or local function. Let us not forget our ultimate concern. Perhaps we will have succeeded if we leave here with the words of Pogo Possum gnawing at our conscience, "We have met the enemy and he is us."

M. NETTLESHIP: May we begin with Professor Jacobs' summary?

JACOBS: I point out that sociology is beginning to take some responsibility for participating in this multi-disciplinary effort to study, and hopefully to do something about, war. At the last meeting of the ASA a mandate was pushed, principally by the graduate students. A committee for this has been set up with Elise Boulding as chairman, and I am a member. We are preparing the usual materials, distributing syllabi, and so on, and hope to do something, mostly nagging our colleagues, because sociology, in this country particularly, has been very remiss for many reasons which I discuss in my paper. The emphasis on gaining respectability for the science through a lot of microstudies, and also the trauma of the McCarthy era, and even before that, the fear of going against American civil religion, which legitimates war, made us reluctant. You also don't get grants for studying war—you all know that—you get them for making better war. At any rate, sociology has made a minimal contribution recently. Also, interestingly enough, the seminal sociologists back in the late nineteenth and early twentieth century, who did study war and did develop macrotheories, served to paralyze a great deal of sociological effort toward war because their theories, many of them evolutionary theories and some of them Marxist theories, tended to see war as somewhat inevitable. It would be eliminated eventually in the process of evolution and one needn't do much about it: a kind of teleological approach. There were two major sociological studies of war in this country in the middle of this century, or somewhat before, Sorokin's and Quincy Wright's, both of which also engendered a kind of paralyzing pessimism because of the statistical evidence that

led them to conclude that war would always be with us. The work of
another sociologist of this era was greatly neglected. George Herbert
Mead was also a social evolutionist, but he thought that people could
control social evolution and that men could change the kind of social
organization they had. He was a symbolic interactionist and felt that
war was a social institution and that institutions were simply the solid-
ification of habits and that habits could be changed. War is not rooted
in the strivings of man as a kind of fundamental aggression.

I make the points in my paper, which you may all dispute: that
conflict is inevitable; that conflict need not necessarily take the form of
war; that men may hate their mothers-in-law, but they don't necessarily
kill them because a murder is not legitimated in our society; and that
there is a possibility for developing alternative institutions if we have
the will. I went into this in my paper in a rather polemical way because
I feel rather deeply that we should begin now, as social scientists, to
study the Vietnam War as a case study in why people were unwilling
to stop a war that seemed totally useless and non-productive.

The sociological question, and I suppose the question for the rest of
you political scientists and anthropologists, is why, although we do
know that it is possible to develop alternate institutions, we fail to support them? Back in October, I was at a conference at Manhattan College, not quite as plush a conference as this one, but an interesting
conference, where a political scientist named Steven Rosen, from
Brandeis, suggested that since in the end the final function of war is to
make the final solution — it is the final arbiter — that the technology
of peace should be simply to find out which nation would win, or
which group would win (including the ability for endurance of suffering,
which is part of the ability to win) and to award the prize, whatever it
might be, to the victor. All the peace activists and the academics at that
meeting were horrified, because that would not ensure justice; it would
simply ensure less bloodshed. But there are better ways, I'm sure, and
we know about some of them already, for developing alternate institutions. The interesting question is why the same people who would
protest the war will now completely withdraw from activity in doing
anything to develop alternate institutions. Part of it, I think, is because
of the myth that war is inevitable. Is war really inevitable, or do we
have the ability to control our social evolution and to develop alternate
institutions?

M. NETTLESHIP: Now would Professor Ansari like to tell us about
the role of anthropology and the world crises?

ANSARI: Before going on to larger problems, I would like to remind the audience about the growth and emergence of anthropology itself. It emerged in its present form, or rather in its present stature, in the second half of the nineteenth century when a new world structure was developing in which one section of the world was trying to consolidate the other part of the world, and so we find that European and American educational institutions tried to organize the studies of the then newly discovered cultures on the basis of an evolutionary scheme. That particular trend remained dominant in anthropology throughout the second half of the nineteenth century. Evolutionary schools subsided, other schools developed, but one trend remained dominant in anthropology until the beginning of the Second World War, and that was to isolate human communities for a specific anthropological study and to create a distinction between the so-called developed or civilized societies and the underdeveloped or primitive communities.

The Second World War itself was the result of a crisis, a crisis which was not developing in the so-called primitive communities, but rather in European countries. It was a crisis mostly derived from industrial competition, such as markets and so on, which of course created the Second World War. What I have considered most in our present world structure is: What are the basic problems which mankind is facing? According to my analysis, mankind, whether it is in a small community or in a larger society, is facing almost identical phenomena. These problems are mostly derived from cultural and economic and political problems. What the anthropologist has been trying to do, until now, is to concentrate his study on a community basis. To my mind, in our modern world, communities are not isolated from the world situation. If we are able to pinpoint the specific situations in the world and try to analyze specific communities within the world situation, then perhaps we will be able to eliminate, to a very great extent, the conflicts which are functioning in human societies: the conflicts which are originating from political causes, conflicts which are emerging from economic causes, and conflicts which are emerging from cultural causes.

M. NETTLESHIP: I couldn't agree more with the preceding speakers. As an applied anthropologist, I feel that anthropologists have done far too little and that we here in our related disciplines have the tools and the knowledge all ready to begin to do things. I wonder if anyone here would like to disagree with the idea that we should try to be a little more activist in our approach to the problems of war? Dr. Richards?

RICHARDS: I won't exactly disagree, but would like to point out that we need to continue to make a distinction between research and diagnosis and action. For instance, a medical doctor does not misdiagnose your disease because he dislikes you. Nor does he fail to note that you have a disagreeable disease or a humiliating disease because he does like you. In other words, his emotional involvement, his values, do not enter into the process of diagnosis and analysis. We are all of us two individuals, if not more; we are citizens, we are concerned human beings, but we are also researchers and I think that when you start confusing the two, in the sense of allowing your emotional involvement to affect what you see and describe, you create a great many problems in analyzing what is actually going on. Unless you get as close to reality painting as you can, it is very difficult to make any progress in the direction of a sensible solution. For instance, one perfect example is a Latin American country with which I am familiar where they didn't like the census figures. It showed them as not progressing rapidly enough in terms of increasing food and increasing population, so they changed them. If the population outruns the food supply, their people are going to starve. Changing the figures to make the country look better isn't going to help anything. And that's where we have to be very careful and not let our emotional involvement and desire for peace (or something else) blind us to certain factual interactions.

AMSBURY: I agree with Dr. Nettleship that we already have the knowledge. I don't agree with him that we have the tools. You remember that the American Anthropological Association and at least some of the anthropologists here started on this peace business early in the 60's and then in the late 60's came the clinch: a specific situation. And that's where the argument begins. Everyone was for peace until there was a specific situation and the letters in the then *Fellow News-letter* specifically pointed out the reasons why they were objecting to any specific activity. One, from the president or the president-elect, objected that there would be a cutoff of grants from government sources if we condemned the activities going on in Vietnam. Dr. Press said we should ask not only how and why, but whence, and this was a slight sidestep because whence in this area is who and why and it is a different why than the why that goes with how.

M. NETTLESHIP: You wouldn't like to say that last sentence in about two sentences would you?

AMSBURY: Well, when we ask whence what we really need to say is, WHO is saying this and what are his purposes, and this is not the same as asking HOW is it being done and what are the means by which people are motivated to go along with the purposes of the people who are doing the manipulation.

SIPES: I believe that I agree with the two previous speakers, insofar as they object to an immediate judgment. They place immediate judgment on war as bad. I am constantly pulled short in my own tendency toward absolutistic moral judgments by the Kapuoku Papuans as they are recorded by Pospisil. They do not have the concept of absolute badness or goodness. An act is bad: well, who is it bad for? I have an enemy; I will kill the enemy. Obviously that is bad for the enemy; it may be very good for me. War is certainly bad for many people. In World War II, the war was bad for the Japanese military élite; it was bad for the war dead and their families. But the Japanese factory worker of 1973 may very well be better off than the worker of 1933 and he is probably better off than if World War II had not happened. We can't say that World War II was bad for him. I say that, as scientists searching for understanding, we should not view war as BAD any more than we should view automobiles as bad because they have also resulted in the deaths of a multitude of individuals. If we desire to try to eliminate war, we should try only after we understand the totality of those real world events that we refer to as war. I'll go further, I think we should even DESIRE to do so only after we understand all of the ramifications of war and of its elimination. But I do believe that some of my work suggests to me that the required cure may be worse than the disease.

M. NETTLESHIP: Since morality is something we are supposed to remain very relativistic about, and I believe that is the tenor of your argument, I wonder if it is not possible to take action to eliminate war — to find something to take its place — without making any moral judgment as to its goodness or badness.

SIPES: Let me clarify that a bit. I am forever making moral judgments. I think rather absolutistically and, offhandedly, as an individual, will make a moralistic judgment on anything. When it comes to science and research I am an instrumentalist. I think that science is good only insofar as it permits you to control or predict, preferably control. If the phenomena are too massive, such as in astronomy, we can only predict. Now, if you are going to control, obviously you are going to have to have end states that you desire. Well, any desire of such a nature is in essence a moral judgment. You are saying that, "Well, this is desirable, therefore I am going to try to bring it about." Before we do that, and I don't think there is anything wrong with it, we better know what the devil it is we are doing and the consequences of it. To learn that, we had better set aside all our desires except the desire to find out what is going on and what will happen if we do A, B, or C.

YOUNG: The discussion that has been going on has been the sort of thing I've been working on for about two years, and I believe that the points of view that have been presented can be resolved this way: The scientific movement is only half complete. What those who are trying to establish a science of irenology — that is, a science of peace — are trying to do is to establish a new kind of science. It isn't entirely new. It is simply a policy science. We do not feel that we have to know all about everything before we advise a client what he should do about a given problem. What we do is find out everything that is relevant to his problem and advise him on this. But, you see, what has resulted from this in science is that the applications of science are made for the purpose of whoever can pay the most money for policy advice and the result is, of course, that the most money has been paid for the thermonuclear bomb. What we are trying to do is to establish a policy science for the human race, and when you do that, I think you are bound to accept an objective view of ethics. Ethical philosophers argue about this. If we want to establish that kind of science, that is what we have to do. The philosophy that has summed it up best for me is simply this: Ethical rules should be made for the good of everyone alike. That is the simple solution. Policies should be made for the good of everyone alike. If we take everyone alike as our client, then our problem is to give this client the best advice we can. If in our opinion it is going to be to the advantage of the client to end war then we must advise him how to do it, but as good policy scientists, we must be absolutely objective in our judgment of truth. This is not a business of bringing your emotions into the thing; what you are trying to do is make the best practical judgment you can. War has its functions and you have to figure out for the client not only how to end war, but how to replace its functions. That is part of the problem. And let me say that I don't think this is something that we can do by tomorrow. That is, we have to develop a systematic science, a set of systematic world policy sciences, that takes the human race as its client. I may talk later on how you can go about this rationally because you have to introduce rationality into it. But what I am saying is that this is the flowering of science, if we can do this. This is what science is for, and if we aim to do it, well, in due course of time, I think it can be achieved.

CARROLL: One thing that seems to be coming out is that there is relatively little feeling about war *per se*. We're saying that there is something there that is inefficient or in most cases not desirable, and let's try to find some substitute. From having read all the papers we are talking about this morning, it's not so much war as such that we are objecting to, but the associated destruction and suffering. If we could have decisions made over a chess board, I don't think people would object to "There's going to be a war next year" in the same way. Certainly wars in which we are inundated with news about military loss of life do not affect us so much as information about wars in which there is loss of non-combatant life. The thing that I'm trying to get at is: are we really talking about war, or are we talking about something more gut-level — just destruction of lives?

We can have cold war politics, we can have secret trade agreements in which negotiations have a zero sum result. The results of these can lead to a hell of a lot of suffering for the people who lose out in those situations. But we don't get the same kind of hullabaloo, of public uproar, about this kind of non-physical destruction. This is what I seem to be missing. We have been talking only about a kind of war with destruction and suffering. Somehow we have to broaden what we're talking about or narrow what we're talking about.

M. NETTLESHIP: We would like now to get into the more substantial papers dealing with definitions and trying to agree on some terms. I don't want to get bogged down in words, but I think we need to know what terms we are using and what they mean to us, if we are going to make it work.

Dr. Eibl-Eibesfeldt would like to make a few remarks bearing on this morning's session and carrying us on into the definitions.

EIBL-EIBESFELDT: I would like to refer to Professor Jacobs' paper. If I understood rightly she referred to the biologist's point of view, which is evolutionary. In a way, that made me feel that she assumes that if we accept her position, i.e. that phylogenetic adaptations pre-program man for behaving aggressively in certain ways, and that therefore even war has its biological phases, this would lead us to the acceptance of a fatalistic attitude. It is as if we were saying that war is inevitable. I want to make clear that no ethologist ever accepted this view. Lorenz made it very clear in his book on aggression. For example, he is concerned about war and he says explicitly we don't have to accept it as something inevitable. There is nothing mythical about it. But we have to study the phenomenon, its physiology, and its causes in order to control it. My comment is just to make that clear, otherwise we are hampered by etiology in our discussions.

M. NETTLESHIP: There are four papers that I would like to have summaries on and then we'll discuss them. First, would Dr. Richards like to give us a summary of her paper?

RICHARDS: I am glad to have an opportunity to do so because there was a revised version which is pointed a little more to this particular topic. What I was concerned with was the definition of competition. I basically used the dictionary definition: the act of seeking or endeavoring to gain something for which another is also striving. I divided it into two types, basically: a predatory competition that attempts to destroy or to eliminate the rival (actually many of the socialistic writers explicitly limit the term competition to what I define as this type, that is, predatory competition which will destroy or eliminate the rival) and a second type of competition in which there is an attempt to outdo the rival, to beat him at his own game. Again, socialistic writers tend to call this type socialist emulation, and so emulative competition appears to be a useful term.

The second point that I tried to make is that competition and co-operation are not mutually exclusive behaviors but instead are inter-related. In the paper I refer to several examples to bolster this point, but basically the same incident or the same example of behavior can be labelled as either competitive or cooperative depending upon the unit that is being studied or the level of analysis. For example, a team of fishermen cooperates to get the fish, but may at the same time, with the same act of fishing, be in competition with other fishermen, other boat crews. Are you going to label it competition or label it coopera-tion? It depends on whether you are studying the entire village or whether you are studying the single boat crew. (I have used two terms here. I hate to keep adding labels, but sometimes they seem useful.) When there is the latter kind of behavior, I have called it team com-petition. It is where you have a group of people cooperating but in competition with another group of people. When a group of girls or women work together to get the dowry for the chief's daughter, I regard this as competitive cooperation. It would include such things as husking bees, anything in which there is a single group goal, such as raising a house or barn, or harvesting a crop, where individuals work to ac-complish this goal, but at the same time may compete with one another to see who can advance this goal most rapidly.

In the revised version of the paper, I pointed out that war can be considered as an extreme form of competition but it has elements of cooperation depending on the level of analysis and also the definition of war. Between nations you've got prizes, such as territory, markets, and sovereignty over particular groups of people. These are of limited good, and I feel that predatory competition is related to Foster's con-cept of the image of limited good. When one wins and another loses, competition tends to be predatory, but even here the predatory com-petition is at the intergroup level. You are trying to destroy or eliminate the enemy, but within the group people are cooperating. An army squad, for example, while busily trying to kill the enemy, will be co-operating with each other, so again you get the question of the difference in levels.

Where you've got warfare between groups, such as headhunters in New Guinea or American Indians on the Plains, the subjugation or destruction of the enemy is not a significant factor. It is not even important, in some cases; for instance, when counting coup was given more prestige than killing the enemy. In these cases, the violence between groups simply seems to be a vehicle for expressing emulative competition within the group. Here, you don't have the concept of limited good, because when a team goes out and raids for horses there is no decrease in the herd of anybody within the group. It just adds to the horses of the total group. Each person tries to have more horses than the others, but they are not taking them from each other. Similarly in headhunting, you are not taking your neighbor's heads, you're taking your enemies' heads, so you simply add to the number of skulls or heads that the whole group has. Death in this kind of situation seems almost incidental, practically an occupational hazard, and not the central purpose. So, basically, I think these concepts that were developed in competition can be applied to the general picture of war and conflict between groups.

KRAKAUER: A war situation probably involves the most cooperation of any situation in which a large nation may be engaged. If you look back to World War II, for example, you find an enormous amount of sacrifice, people moving from jobs and placing their whole concentration on winning. We have to realize that cooperation is an enormous factor in the war situation.

RICHARDS: One of the points that I make in the paper is that the threat of war and war itself has been used frequently in nations to bolster their own position, relying precisely on this factor — that the attack of an opponent will frequently cause the group itself to pull together and to increase either emulative competition or just working together.

A. NETTLESHIP: Dr. Richards, I can never understand in reading the stories and accounts of counting coup if this was a feedback mechanism. After you hit the guy, did you quit and run away or did you stay and fight? Does this make the tribe fight harder? Once you strike coup, do you get a credit for it?

RICHARDS: Yes, once you strike coup you get a credit for it. It is not necessary to kill the individual and frequently one of the things, showing their magnificent horsemanship, was for one Indian to ride rapidly by and reach out and touch his living enemy and ride rapidly off before his living enemy could kill him. This was especially regarded, as, "That man has really done something to be proud of: counting coup on a living enemy."

A. NETTLESHIP: Then it's really feedback for more power. Does it make you stronger to do it again, or do you run away?

RICHARDS: Well, you may do it again. You run away at the time because if you are unarmed this makes it even better: you are unarmed, touching a living, armed enemy. That is really flying in the face of everything and you run away at that time or you WOULDN'T repeat it.

M. NETTLESHIP: I'd like to ask Dr. Fink if he has some remarks about competition and conflict as they may reflect on all this.

FINK: The question I was going to ask bears on a problem in the whole analysis of forms of antagonistic relations. Really there are two questions. For one, I am curious about why you chose the term competition for the inclusive concept. From the classification that you have given, this is a concept that is often called conflict and of which competition is a special case. Some people with biological and anthropological backgrounds tend to use competition as the inclusive concept and conflict is the special case. I am just curious about this terminological choice. The second question I have is whether it makes sense to emphasize the cooperative element in intergroup antagonism when the cooperation you are talking about is within each of the groups. The question about the link between cooperation and conflict, or between cooperation and competition, is whether there are cooperative elements between the ANTAGONISTS. This is a theme that Georg Simmel tried to play with in some of his discussions of conflict. The important question is whether the implication of this is that war between nations is something in which both sides have a vested interest. It's the cooperation between the antagonists that I think is the really crucial element.

RICHARDS: I'd like to get rid of the simpler one first: I chose competition because I was concerned about what seemed to me to be conceptual static in the use of the term competition. I was very tired of hearing people emotionally say "competition is great," and on the other hand say "competition is terrible." I figured something had to be done about it and I wanted to do it. I was not thinking in terms of larger and smaller. I wasn't going from conflict to competition; I was going from competition and ended up in conflict, which was not my original intent. It was a historical accident, if you wish to put it that way, that led me to choose competition.

Second, I do feel it is important to note that competition and co-operation are not mutually exclusive. Although what I gave as an example in this brief summary section was the cooperation within and the competition between the people who are cooperating in order to compete, I would also agree that what you said is quite correct. There is cooperation between nations fighting a war. We see it not just because of their vested interest but in hundreds of other things. The party that doesn't play the game, for instance, one who starves war prisoners or does something "naughty," is not doing what they are supposed to. There are rules for this kind of conflict, for everybody gets annoyed with people who don't abide by the rules, even in warfare. So, in a sense, they are cooperating. They are in conflict but they stop conflict in order to exchange prisoners, or to allow the wounded to be taken off the battlefield. The American Indians who shot from behind trees instead of standing up in battle created all sorts of havoc because they weren't playing by the rules. So I think there is a great deal of cooperation even between the antagonists.

FINK: May I respond to that? I laid out that question in order to follow it up with one possible practical implication, and also a scientific implication about research priorities. Isn't it conceivable that most of the work which has been done to try to prevent conflict, or to find ways of preventing conflicts between nations in order to prevent war, might be misguided in that really one should want to find ways of preventing cooperation.

RICHARDS: Cooperation for disruptive ends.

FINK: Cooperation in the war system.

ESSER: These definitions have been extremely useful for me personally but I would have liked to have seen a development of the relationship not only of competition to cooperation but of both of these to synergy (which can be defined as a cooperation of which the end results cannot be foreseen or predicted). Much that we have discussed really relates to such a synergic action that happens in a war. All nations go to war and think that they have predictable outcomes. We know too well that there is no predictable outcome. That is an example of negative synergy. (There is also an example of positive synergy in the paper by Corning, in a reference to the synergic process in altruism.)

MIDLARSKY: Dr. Richards, if we use the term emulate, that, at least to me, brings to mind certain aspects of social learning theory as expressed by Bandura and Walters in terms of imitative or contagious effects. Whereby, not only can we have "a keeping up with the Jones's effect," as Dr. Richards defined in her term "emulative competition," but also the predatory effects. That is, the same process may apply to both the learning of predatory violence and the learning of peaceful competition which Dr. Richards talks about in emulative competition.

RICHARDS: I agree that imitation is an important factor in the learning of behavior. "Emulative" may not be the best term to use, but in attempting to distinguish the essentially destructive approach from attempting to do what HE is doing, only better, it seemed that emulative was a useful term. Now, it is possible to imitate, and in fact the Indians in Chile did this very well, learning Spanish warfare techniques the hard way. That is, the Spanish used them against the Indians, who promptly adopted them and effectively fought off the Spanish. But I would prefer to use imitation for this. I would be happy to choose another term, but for my purposes I felt emulative was useful.

M. NETTLESHIP: I wonder if Professor Eibl-Eibesfeldt would like to comment about aggression and violence and how we might go about defining them.

EIBL-EIBESFELDT: I would only speak about aggression, since it is a term widely used by ethologists, and I would say we work operationally. That means we classify behavior patterns as aggressive when they lead to either a spacing or a dominance-subordination relationship. We exclude, for example, the intent to hurt, which is often used in psychological literature, because if we included intent then we couldn't speak about the marine iguana's aggressive behavior. They are fighting in a highly ritualized way. They are not hurting each other, and after all, we couldn't speak of any intent in animals.

M. NETTLESHIP: I wonder if we, as a group, can accept this kind of definition which is so different from the popular one and the popular misunderstanding of the use of the term by ethologists and others who have written on it recently. It sounds good to me. Would anyone like to speak on that point?

SCOTT: The term aggression is too widely used and has such a variety of definitions that it has become almost useless for scientific analysis. Consequently, in working with animal behavior and human behavior I prefer the term agonistic behavior, which is a new term and is defined as behavior which is adaptive in situations of conflict between members of the same species. As such, it would include not only fighting, but also running away, escape behavior, defensive behavior, subordination, submission, and the like. This becomes a kind of concept one can work with scientifically. Then, with respect to violence, one can simply extend this and say that violent behavior is agonistic behavior which results in serious injury or death to the participants.

And, there again, you have a clear and fairly limited definition of a term which is almost as badly misused as the word aggression.

M. NETTLESHIP: I, too, would like to use something such as you have described. But I wonder, since this applies to interaction between members of the same species, if it can be used in man where so much of our aggression is between members of different ethnospecies?

SCOTT: From a biologist's viewpoint (I'm sure Eibl-Eibesfeldt would agree with me) human beings are all of one species, so of course, agonistic behavior would apply to all conflicts between human beings.

CORNING: One of the things left out by Dr. Eibl-Eibesfeldt is maternal aggression in defense of the young. He also left out predation: some other people do and some don't include it.

EIBL-EIBESFELDT: Intra-specific aggression.

CORNING: Intra-specific aggression? You are saying that your definition applies only to intra-specific aggression? Well, how about cannibalism then?

EIBL-EIBESFELDT: What do you mean, "How about cannibalism?"

CORNING: Well, that's a form of predatory behavior. Is that aggression? It's predation. It's intra-specific. Is it aggression?

EIBL-EIBESFELDT: Cannibalism is certainly a special form, but it is certainly intra-specific aggression and I think that as a phenomenon we need to ask anthropologists whether the prime motivation is indeed to eat a member of another species, of another tribe, or is that a side effect of warfare.

CORNING: I think this bears out what Dr. Scott was saying because now, you see, we get into problems of intention, and when we begin to think of other things besides very narrow definitions of dominance hierarchy or mating privileges, then it gets kind of messy because there are all sorts of other situations that are involved. So that with something like "agonistic behavior" in which intra- or inter-specific conflicts are involved, some of which include violence and some don't, you have a term that is a little bit cleaner which I would definitely support.

SCOTT: I would like to say one word about cannibalism, at least from my reading of the anthropological literature. There have been very few, if any, human societies which have deliberately tried to obtain a living by eating other people, and for the most part cannibalism is very much a ritualistic kind of behavior. And so, in a sense you can call it predation but it is actually not comparable to the kind of predation which a wolf demonstrates when he is killing a deer.

CORNING: Of course there are known instances where cannibalism was practiced specifically for food, in situations of desperation.

BISHOP: Cannibalism can exist without aggression. For example, there was a case in northern Canada about a year ago where an individual wound up eating a nurse who had died. This created quite a furor in the news media for a while.

RICHARDS: I like eliminating intent for a couple of reasons. First of all, it is not something you can observe directly — you have to infer it — whereas you can observe behavior. And secondly, motivation can be both conscious and unconscious and these kinds of motivation may even be in conflict with one another. You get into a real mare's nest when you try to predict or interpret on the basis of simple behavior what the intent of the participants was. You are more apt to project what YOUR intent would be in that circumstance than you are to be sure that that's THEIR intent. So I think leaving intent out of it as much as possible helps.

M. NETTLESHIP: An anthropological footnote, though. We HAVE to interpret intent, like everything else, from what we observe: behavior. I don't think it is any more of a problem to investigate intent than it is to investigate any other aspect of human relationships; especially the whole field of value relationships which must be observed in the same way.

RICHARDS: Granted, but it's not easy.

KRAKAUER: I think it is important to define aggression. I feel, however, that we should at least be aware of the very much accepted psychologic and psychoanalytic view of aggression as a continuum. In other words, I am being aggressive this moment in wishing to give you my point of view. When we look at it in that way it does give us complications as well as simplifications. Aggression even includes my kicking a tire that went flat when I was angry at it. We may wish to limit ourselves somewhat, but we must keep in mind the fact that there are so many aspects of aggression that we have to know that perhaps we are only talking about a piece of it. May I make one comment on Dr. Richards' conflict versus cooperation? You have to see that, in terms of fact, every human act involves both of these. The psychological view is that every act involves both libidinal and aggressive attitudes and feelings. It is a part of our problem that as we talk about war we must know that we are dealing with a complicated species that is always working in two directions simultaneously.

CARROLL: On the question of intent perhaps one should use another word such as collaboration for the kind of cooperation that I think Dr. Fink referred to before. When we talk about cooperation, what we are talking about — in general understanding, and what I think maybe we ought to be talking about and investigating — is a mutually supportive and intentionally helpful kind of activity. Collaboration might not have that intent. Collaboration is simply a form of working together in some way, doing something which is perhaps jointly beneficial, but not particularly intentionally so.

RICHARDS: I didn't mean that we should ignore intent, I simply meant that I think it creates problems to include it in the definition of aggression. I think it is extremely important to investigate intent, but it is more useful to investigate it somewhat apart from aggression because one of the things that is the curse of our discipline is that we keep confusing levels of analysis. I find that intent is terribly important but I feel it needs a different methodology than simply the observation of behavior. In terms of getting social change, for example, what do you have to do in order to get millionaires to distribute their wealth in society? Do they have to want to, or can you get them to do it to avoid taxation, or can you get them to do it to avoid having their house burned down, or something else? In other words, do they want to do it through altruistic reasons? Does it matter? I think all these are very important, but if you find that you can bring about the result without having one specific motivation, if you are trying to engage in change, this is a useful thing to know. I don't think you have to try to make everybody have the same motivation, if you can bring about a particular kind of behavior through a variety of different ways.

HUBER: For the human participants in any kind of warfare or violence, the interpretation of intents behind the actions of others, the people that you might potentially be fighting, can be extremely important. I think one of the central issues is how intents arise and are articulated and/or created in others towards violent or aggressive behavior or towards war, depending on whatever social context you are dealing with.

M. NETTLESHIP: Nobody has taken me up on trying to define violence. I think this also must fit into our sphere.

ESSER: I feel that violence is a derailment of legitimate, and if I say legitimate I mean biologically based, aggressive feelings. In other words, if I am legitimately aggressive, but come to a point in which I cannot dominate and bring out my intent, then I can resort to violence. In that resort to violence, all the processes that apply to learning are, of course, functioning. This is no longer the prepotent part of my brain; now the learning process is fully at work. That is why I call it a derailment: it's not part of our original biological makeup.

M. NETTLESHIP: Would anybody like to speak to the point of the definition of violence, either in agreement or disagreement with Dr. Esser. Dr. Cancro, how about a psychological definition of violence from your point of view?

CANCRO: It's probably a question that is better evaded than dealt with, although I offer a definition in the paper that we'll be discussing in Session 4. I think the major distinction that one would want to make between violent behavior and aggressive behavior, which is a broader concept where humans are concerned, is that in violence you are dealing with destructive or life-threatening behaviors which are likely to inflict serious injury or destruction on the individual who is the object of this behavior, or against his symbolic equivalent. Very often, to use Dr. Richards' example, "You can't hang him, you burn his house down, or if you are really angry, you hang Louis XVI AND burn his house down." You get him and the symbol. It's a more thorough approach. I think one must make a distinction between the broader category of aggression which includes, for example, much ritualized behavior (and not only in other species, but the human types, where we set up dominance hierarchies in groups without resorting to violent activity) and violence which would involve physical threat or actual physical injury or destruction.

M. NETTLESHIP: So our problem really is "How much does violence have to do with war and does war have to be violent?" Professor Jacobs?

JACOBS: I've become very unhappy with the discussion of aggression, because I don't think modern warfare has anything at all to do with aggression. It has a great deal more to do with compliance. The studies of the troops in Vietnam show that they are, if anything, less aggressive than the people at home. The people who kill with modern technology and don't even see their enemy are not exhibiting aggression at all. They are exhibiting obedience. We are fighting modern wars with drafted armies. I don't think we should get bogged down at all on the issue of aggression because it is totally irrelevant.

M. NETTLESHIP: Since we are talking about more than just what has gone on in Vietnam, I think we have to have a certain, agreed upon, basic terminology, including definitions of terms like "aggression" and "violence." That's what we have been aiming at. I agree with you that perhaps modern warfare has other aspects to it, but I don't think the discussion so far has been totally lost.

CANCRO: Let me just briefly respond to that point, since I am very much in sympathy with your position. I feel that we can confuse war, which is a far more complex phenomenon, as just a special case of intra-species aggression, when it is not. There is certainly no *a priori* reason to assume that an insight into violence or aggressive behavior would be helpful. On the other hand, there is no reason to assume that there won't be, and I think we are so ignorant in this area that we should keep an open mind and allow the data to dictate our decisions. For example, the data might force us to some other conclusion. That would make me very unhappy, but I would try to live with it. I personally do not think that a study of the biological bases of aggression will give that much insight into war, which I see as a much more complex phenomenon, but it might contribute some small portion of the total picture and, in that sense, turn out to be helpful in the longer run.

EIBL-EIBESFELDT: Yes, I would believe exactly what you said, and would add that we should be careful in making sweeping statements as to what is not relevant for the study of war. We simply do not KNOW. But it is a good hypothesis that there is a continuum and that we may well learn quite a lot about the motivational structure of man's behavior by studying the phenomenon. May I also return to the question of intra- and inter-specific aggression. Animal behavior studies have clearly shown that there are different neural structures underlying predatory behavior and intra-specific aggression. I am in complete accord with Dr. Scott in this regard.

M. NETTLESHIP: Mrs. Roper, will you give us a summary of your paper, please.

ROPER: I define warfare as sanctioned violence, including killing, of one group against another. This is boiled down from Margaret Mead; of all the definitions of warfare that I have read, hers seems to me to make the most sense. I think I'm one of the few archeologists here and my particular interest today is in setting forth for other social scientists the archeological records in the Near East from 10,000 to 4000 B.C. I wish I could do it from more areas, but I can't; my training is in the Near East. I think archeology has been far too much concerned with pretty Greek vases and things like that. In terms of the terribly important issues we seem to have fallen down.

I also want to bring to your attention my paper, "A survey of evidence for inter-human killing in the Pleistocene." What I tried to do there was present the actual physical evidence (the crushed skulls and cave paintings which are really all we have from the Pleistocene, and for the Australopithecines, *Homo erectus*, Neanderthal, and *Homo sapiens*), so that those of you who aren't in the field of archeology will know what the physical evidence is. Now, this doesn't mean that there wasn't rampant warfare in the Pleistocene. What I have tried to do is to simply set down what we have from the archeological records.

In my paper on the evidence of warfare in the Near East from 10,000 to 4000 B.C., I start at 10,000 because that's the beginning of the Holocene, when the Pleistocene ends. The first evidence of warfare that we have is at Jericho, about 7500 B.C., where we have massive fortification walls. From the archeological evidence it seems that trade was the catalyst that caused warfare, or there may have been accumulations of negotiable wealth and people were raiding to get into these cities (they were really towns of about 2,000 population). We know that settled communities happened before the domestication of plants and animals, and it does seem that trade was what brought people into certain concentrations.

It seems to me that there are two important potential outcomes of this conference and I hope that we will have specific outcomes, so that we won't again just be talking. One of these, I think, is to differentiate between the causes of warfare and the functions of warfare. It seems to me that the conditions of warfare, the immediate causes of war, are entirely different from the functions of war in society. One function of war in the United States is training young men on the job for work skills. We just don't have this after high school in our society and the military takes care of this. Until we can get an alternative institution that can replace this function, I don't think we can get rid of warfare. There are good and bad functions of warfare. We need to know which are the obsolete functions that won't have to be replaced and find out what the good functions are and start building alternative institutions so that the functions can be transferred and war will wither away.

Secondly, I was very impressed by Macdonald's suggestion, in his paper, proposing a resolution to the U.N. that they set up an agency for studying the etiology of war. I believe it was last December that the U.N. General Assembly voted to set up a world university and I hope one of the first things this world university could get going on is studying the etiology of war.

M. NETTLESHIP: Thank you very much. The importance of Mrs. Roper's paper is that it can be used to help us pin down the beginning of what looks like real war as opposed to the fighting which takes place among primitive peoples.

We've been asked by the Congress to discuss a paper by Dr. Ghabbour. Unfortunately, he hasn't been able to join us. Some of you have copies of his paper. I think the first part of the paper is probably relevant to this part of the discussion. I would like to read a portion of his summary:

The armed hunting bands of the Paleolithic were at a very loose level of social organization. This was man's first experience with sociology after he became man. Man's innovative powers prevented him from establishing a certain set of social norms and equilibrium with the environment as had happened with his fellow primates. One very important innovation in the field of social organization which was devised in the great river basins of the Middle East, India, and China was the state. It was a very successful device and was adopted by newer civilizations until it now covers the globe. A final spread of this type of social organization took place in the 1960's when former colonies became independent. Now almost the whole of the human species is divided up into these entities which control all exchanges between sections of the species located within their boundaries.

The rest of this paper has more to do with ecology and we'll discuss it a bit more at the session on ecology, but the point that he raises is the importance of the formation of the state. In my reading, this correlates closely with the beginning of what looks like war. I wonder if, before we have discussion on these two papers, we might also hear Dr. Corning, so that we can discuss all this at once.

CORNING: I'm reminded, in trying to summarize my paper, which covered an awful lot of territory, of the old chestnut about the student who was studying for exams and read a volume which he had to learn for the exams, and he boiled it down into five pages, and then boiled that down into one page, and then he boiled it down into one paragraph, and then into one word, and he forgot the word. Well, I haven't forgotten the word — the word is EVOLUTION, but I am not sure in the time available that I can expand on that word far enough to shed any real light on the discussion.

One theme of my paper, perhaps the most important, had to do with the utility of adopting an evolutionary framework for analyzing human aggression and aggression in general (or agonistic behavior, to use Dr. Scott's term) of which human aggression is one dimension. Arguments were that adopting this kind of framework would lead us to different kinds of questions about human aggression, to different ways of organizing data and systematizing data, and to different ways of approaching the relationship between human violence (or agonistic behavior in humans) and the agonistic behavior of other species. One of the cardinal sins of a previous generation of social scientists was that they extrapolated from animal data to man rather readily so that pigeon aggression presumably told us something about human aggression. Only by being sensitive to the differences, the commonalities, and the contrasts between different species, can an evolutionary approach which puts each species in its own niche and deals with it holistically (in terms of its entire behavior system and its problems of survival ... the total problem of survival and reproduction) help us to organize the way in which we look at aggressive behaviors. I think this sort of reorientation of our way of thinking is the most important thing that we could gain from an evolutionary approach to aggressive behavior.

A corollary of this was the topology of violent aggression which has been developed by Kenneth Moyer, a physiological psychologist at Carnegie Mellon. His work is a very useful first step in elaborating on what has heretofore all too often been a unitary concept. It suggests that, in fact, there are many different kinds of violent aggression or agonistic behavior. In this light Dr. Eibl-Eibesfeldt pointed out that there were physiological differences between predatory aggression and intra-specific aggression. It may not necessarily be a valid distinction in terms of definitions because, in fact, there are neurophysiological differences between various kinds of intra-specific aggression, maternal aggression versus intermale aggression, for example. Adopting an evolutionary approach helps us to clarify these problems of definition. Apropos of the Moyer topology, what he has suggested is that, in fact, there are several different kinds of aggression, each of which has a distinct physiological basis, each of which may have different functions for the species, but all those functions come together and can be understood under the rubric of the overall problems of survival and reproduction for that species. It's a way of dealing with one or another aspect of the total problem, and that is what provides the common thread for these behaviors in terms of functionality. What the Moyer topology has done is to suggest ways in which we can link the evolutionary behavior with the genetic basis for the behavior, with biochemical and physiological aspects of the behavior, and also with the functions of the behavior. You can establish systematic linkages in all of these dimensions.

Perhaps I should touch briefly on one of the other aspects of my paper (which was not so much addressed to the implications of an evolutionary paradigm as it was addressed to the question of an evolutionary approach to human violence, collective violence in human societies), that is, how such behaviors evolved. I considered in detail some of the theories that have been put forward to explain collective violence in human societies and suggested that they are not necessarily incompatible, but that in fact they may complement one another. The explanation of collective violence in terms of the "hunting pack" is not necessarily in contradiction to explanations involving competition between two groups of humans. These behaviors overlap in topography. The two possible "functions" of the behavior may have reinforced a trend toward the fixing of genes that make such behaviors possible in the human species. It is not necessary to choose between the thesis, currently most closely associated with Dr. Bigelow, that warfare between human groups was the principal engine of the morphological evolution of man, and the alternative hypothesis, associated with people like Washburn and Pfeiffer, that the development of hunting was the most important set of selection pressures. That, I think, gives you an idea of the framework within which I wrote my paper.

A. NETTLESHIP: One of the things that has constantly disturbed me is the occurrence of simultaneous events which we tend to think of as either cause or effect. This bothers me very much. For example, with due respect to the walls found from the Halafians in the Near East, maybe it was the immobility that caused the problem, maybe it wasn't the walls at all, maybe it wasn't the fact of just being there but the fact that they could no longer move about. They could no longer leave their dead where they died, but they had to put them in a pile. So, the simultaneous occurrence always bothers me very much. As I listen to the papers here, time and time again I say to myself, "Is that just a simultaneous occurrence or is it a cause and effect occurrence?"

CORNING: I'd like to add another of these problems of correlated events which may frustrate you further. One possible explanation for the emergence of warfare in human groups might be found in correlating the archeological data for warfare between human groups, with the data for the extinction of large game animals in the late Pleistocene. We have some reason to believe that one of the steps in the several-million-year sequence of the emergence of man was large-scale hunting of large-herd animals. This necessitated cooperation beyond the level of the individual bands, including communications, organizing the hunt, sharing the spoils after the hunt, and so on. As far as I know, nobody has considered the implications of the large-scale extinction of what may have become the resource base for our Pleistocene ancestors. If large-game hunting did permit an adaptive radiation, did it permit the expansion of human populations in such numbers that at some point we began to overhunt the species? If so, we then began to produce a change in the environment which increased selection pressures, increased pressures on human populations, and increased competition for food. An increase of competition for food when you already had large-scale cooperative hunting behaviors among human groups could then have turned hunting into competition for food using violent behavior toward other groups.

BIGELOW: I would like to try to clarify one point in Dr. Corning's paper. I think it is an excellent paper, but at one point he quotes me as saying, "The Spencerian thesis is that in the case of human evolution, success was dependent primarily upon the ability to learn social co-operation for defense and offense against threats from other groups." Well, there is some justification for linking me with Spencer and the Spencerian thesis but I would like to remind everyone that there is one very important difference between Spencer and me and that is that I was born one hundred years later than he was, and therefore we can't quite be said to have had the same, or that close to the same, hypotheses. The other point is that Corning then calls this a "single factor" explanation which rules out such things as hunting and group agonistic encounters. Again there is justification for Dr. Corning's conclusion that I have taken that point of view because I did emphasize intergroup competition very, very much, and I still think that this was a MAJOR factor, but I will agree with him that this is by no means the ONLY factor.

SCOTT: I would like to make a brief critique of the evolutionary point of view. In fact, evolutionary explanations of behavior are inevitably scientifically weak, for the reason that they cannot be subjected to experimentation. You can't go back to the Jurassic period and run the evolution of mammals over again under different conditions to see how things would have turned out. You are also, particularly in the evolution of behavior, extremely limited in the amount of evidence that is available for study. This means that evolutionary explanations of behavior and contemporary events are at the best unprovable hypotheses and at the worst are poor excuses. The argument that "I did it because my ancestors did it," can be a very poor excuse for behavior which has harmful consequences. I'm not saying that we should discard the evolutionary point of view. What I AM saying is that it cannot by itself serve to explain behavior. I doubt very much, and would like to argue this with Dr. Corning in a friendly sort of way, that one can even develop a general theory of behavior or warfare on the basis of evolution alone. I'd also like to comment in view of Corning's remarks on the evidence concerning warfare that it's very obvious that warfare, in the sense that we know it — combined coordinated agonistic behavior — is something which has occurred very recently and is something which it would be very difficult to explain on the basis of genetic changes.

M. NETTLESHIP: Those of you who are interested in the evolutionary problem will be happy to know that there are several papers in Session 2 which attack it from one angle or another and I think you'll all probably get a chance to get your teeth into it pretty thoroughly then.

I would like to have a few more remarks on Mrs. Roper's paper before we get into the final paper of this session. Would anybody care to comment?

SMITH: With reference to Mrs. Roper's paper — in fact, generally in the papers this morning — there seems to be a concern with the genesis of warfare. Does warfare start as the result of crowding, the beginning of cities, etc. People differentiate between raiding and warfare and I ask this seriously, not polemically: if we are concerned with aggression and conflict, what is it that is so important heuristically about the difference between raiding and warfare? Is there really a difference or is this simply a different kind of aggressive behavior? If there is a difference, what is the heuristic utility, if any, in the study of conflict and aggression?

ROPER: I don't see too much difference between raiding and other types of warfare because, as I define warfare, it is sanctioned violence, including killing, of one group against another. I think a lot of us were stimulated by Ardrey and Lorenz. I got upset because I thought they were pulling facts out of context. Even Lorenz did it, though of course Ardrey did it much more: selected facts from archeological evidence that didn't give the whole picture. They were saying that man biologically is this way because we have evidence from the Pleistocene, when man was developing, that shows that such and such occurred. That's terribly important because if man is biologically innately aggressive and is going to develop warfare, we have got to either get drugs to help us or we have to select genetically very peaceful groups and breed them if we are going to have mankind survive. Those are the alternatives. If it's culture, then it's an entirely different matter. This controversy hasn't really been resolved yet, and that's why some of us have gone back to the evolutionary approach.

EIBL-EIBESFELDT: On an exact biological basis, we have (in publications) repeatedly emphasized that man is a cultural being by nature. We don't NEED drugs. We don't need genetic shaping. What we need is EDUCATION. And we know that man indeed has such power as a cultural being that you can even educate a child to be horrified, let's say, of sex. The question is only "What do we need to impose on men to have them living peacefully together as happy beings." That means knowledge about the nature of man will help us to find the adequate strategy. So I hope that the question of drugs and genetical shaping doesn't come up again in the discussion, nor the insinuation that we use it as an excuse, which again and again pops up individually. Nothing is used as an excuse!

M. NETTLESHIP: Well, now that we have eliminated this afternoon's session. . . . Could I have just one more remark, then we'll go on to the last paper.

ESSER: Although I fully agree with Dr. Eibl-Eibesfeldt's exhortation, I do think that it is good for us that there are still people who feel that if there is a biological background to aggression (aggressive behavior), then maybe one of the solutions could be drugs. I mean, that's just a thought, and put forward by Moyer it is completely legitimate. In addition, education put forward as the solution to the problem of keeping our aggression in rails (so to speak — in my language if violence is the derailment of aggression, we should keep aggression in its rails) is only part of the solution, although I feel that it is a very important one.

We must consider the solution of design. Education is part of design, design of what we want to do with this world, with what I want to do with myself, the way I design things for myself. (I believe that THERE is really where the shoe may pinch and we might actually have had some designers at this conference.) How can we design (socially and physically) a world that can contain aggression? This is really the overall problem and education is a big aspect of it. But, let's not forget that education rests on conscious knowledge and on reason — at least in our culture today. Perhaps one of the aspects that we have to design into education is education in emotional, non-rational behavior. Dr. Eibl-Eibesfeldt observes this with his pictures of primitive people and the way they ritualize with each other. This kind of education is just as important as the rational type of education that we go to school for.

M. NETTLESHIP: Already we have begun to talk about different theories of violence, aggression, and war. We have a paper which will perhaps help us to keep these in order. Would you like to give us a summary of your paper, Dr. Carroll?

CARROLL: My paper was an attempt to deal with the proliferation of theories which consist of attempts to explain the occurrence of war and most often take the form of theories of war causation, although some of the attempts to explain the occurrence of war are not causal explanations and therefore, in a sense, the title is not all-encompassing. We refer to various attempts to bring order out of the chaos of theories, such as the efforts of Pitirim Sorokin and Quincy Wright. These generally are classifications either of the causes of war or classifications of theories according to the main factors or causes which the theories emphasize. Most of the previous classifications focus on causes as the central criterion or object of classification. The paper suggests several defects in this approach, one of which is that it's very often inadequate as an explanation. One of the inadequacies has been mentioned here: the problem of simultaneity and how you determine what is cause and what is effect, or whether they just happen to be simultaneous occurrences caused by some other factor. Another of the problems is that there is a tendency for prior classifications to be catalogues. Sometimes several catalogues parallel each other but are not really synthesized in such a way as to make any sense or to help us choose between the theories in terms of validity or clarification. Finally there is an underlying problem when you classify explanations of war according to causes: the theories do not deal with the underlying question of causality itself. Most of the theories of war causation, and attempts to classify such theories, seem to ignore the whole problem of causality. We therefore suggest an effort to analyze theories of war causation, perhaps choose between them or find a way to choose between them, along two different dimensions other than the causes. One dimension is related to that problem of causality. One might say that the problem of causality is part of a more general problem of deterministic versus non-deterministic social theories; that is, the spectrum of social analysis from highly deterministic theories of social behavior to non-deterministic or free-will theories of social behavior. One of the dimensions of the matrix on our chart (Table 1) is the dimension of determinism and free will. There are six main positions indicated on that chart (of course there are more intermediate positions):

1. Strict determinism; that is, not admitting any possibility of individual free will having significant influence or even perhaps not admitting the existence of any such thing as individual free will.

2. Causality; that is, a limited form of determinism in which the weight of emphasis is heavily on deterministic factors but where some leeway is allowed for the play of free will in some form.

3. Gross predictability, in which the focus is upon statistical analysis and an attempt to predict behavior on a mass scale with no definite conclusion as to whether behavior on an individual scale is determined or non-determined. That is, presumably it might be possible to predict behavior on a mass scale even if individuals have choice. Similarly, it is possible, obviously, to predict on a mass scale if individuals have no choice. The gross predictability position is one which allows for either determinism or indeterminacy on the individual level.

4. Indeterminacy postulates contend that individual behavior is unpredictable, which might be either because it is undetermined or because we are unable somehow to predict it. But, in any case, the difference between gross predictability and indeterminacy is primarily on the

Table 1.   A two-dimensional matrix for analyzing theories of war causation

Ontological assumptions / Level of analysis	Determinism (strict)	Causality (limited)	Gross predictability	Indeterminacy	Free Will (limited)	Absurd Universe
System international supra-national nation-state	*On all levels* God Fate "laws of history," "necessity," teleology cycles	Balance of Power Historical Materialism Systems theory and Equilibrium Theory (Kaplan, Liska) Richardson Processes	Generalizations and theories based on *correlations of data*, e.g. in Wright, Deutsch, Singer, Janowitz, Richardson, Kelman	← Either →	Historical sociology (Aron, Hoffman) Some strategy games and simulations Normative theory (Balance-of-power)	*On all levels* There is no external order; order is a creation of the mind, or an artifact. Nothing is determined (Existentialist and some anarchist pacifist theories)
Subsystem collective "actor," or T, e.g. coalition, nation-state, or group	Complete predestination, destination, *unless* "God plays dice with the universe" e.g. Calvin, Hegel, Comte, Marx, Toynbee, Spengler	"Factor" theories: biological environmental psychological sexual structural social-psychological economic	Short-term, limited predictability of behavior *en masse*		Decision-making and bargaining theories (Snyder, Boulding) Strategy games (Schelling, Kahn) Historical uniqueness Normative theory	
Individual actor "center" or T, "periphery" or U		Behavior Predictable (both long- and short-term, if theory is correct)	←Either→	Behavior Unpredictable: insufficient knowledge or free will	Complexity and liberty of the personality, role of imagination, vision, creativity, ethical judgment, calculation and miscalculation	
Policy implications of ontological assumptions	Fatalism, OR "mission," OR nirvana *Alternatives* closed, in theory...	Assuming correct theories known, policy is shaped accordingly, "to win" *Alternatives* very limited or closed	Policy may be shaped with limited reliance on predictions *Alternatives* open, but limited	← Either →	Though behavior is unpredictable on all levels, it may be classifiable and allow rational choice *Alternatives* open. Utopian possibilities,	Individual choice between submission to illusory external order and rebellion, choice of own order. *Alternatives* fully open.

individual level.

5.   Limited free will; that is, a stance which places emphasis upon individual choices such as game theory and rational decision-making analyses. These place emphasis on individual choice and how people go about making their choices and therefore seem to presume a substantial importance of free will, but they are generally limited-free-will doctrines or theories; they basically assume that there is some determinacy at least, say, in the natural world out there, within which people are operating.

6.   Finally, there is a position which one can call the absurd universe; that is, that nothing is determined, that we make the universe ourselves, and that we have unrestricted free will to operate in the social and physical world, or at least in the social world.

The other dimension on which we have tried to classify is the levels of analysis. Here we are referring to the units or the actors that are involved and are seen as important, ranging in three categories from the system level to that of the individual actor. Individual acts can be broken down in many ways. If you are talking about international warfare, then the system is the international community or the international system. If you are talking about civil war, then the system really is the nation or the unit within which civil war takes place.

We also suggest a third dimension on which one ought to extend this chart or matrix and that is the question of whether a theory gives central importance to élite or mass behavior: to top dogs or to underdogs, to some central leaders (or powers) or to all the actors in the system. Imagine this chart extended so that at each level of analysis you would have a box for élite and one for mass emphasis. One could devise various other ways of extending out this matrix in other dimensions. As it was we could only portray two of them on a two-dimensional sheet of paper and didn't go further in the analysis.

We would like to suggest that some virtues of this matrix are, first of all, that it gives an overview, in a very confined and readily visualized space, of a very great range of theories and thereby helps us to keep in mind some of the theories which are on the outer peripheries. This is especially true for those in the strict determinist and the totally free-will categories, which are normally on the peripheries of our consciousness, since most people in the world of social analysis tend to be somewhere on the spectrum of limited free will to limited causality. We thought that this gave a breadth or comprehensiveness that would be useful and we thought that analyzing on these dimensions might provide some help towards determining the criteria one would need to evaluate theories against each other. In other words, perhaps one doesn't need to use, or it would not be appropriate to use, the same kinds of tests or evidence to determine the validity of, or to choose between, theories in one position on the scale of determinism as one would use in choosing between theories in another position on the scale of determinism.

MIDLARSKY: I like the comment, "God plays dice with the universe." Apparently Pauli and Einstein made comments like that upon hearing Eisenberg's Uncertainty Principle and THEY couldn't quite believe that God played dice with the universe. But I would like to possibly add a frustration-aggression theory which, in my limited reading of the table here, I don't think appears. Frustration-aggression theory in Dollard, et al.'s statement of it might actually fit somewhere in Carroll and Fink's matrix. Dollard's position is, at the very least, in the causality-limited range, but very possibly in the strict determinism section.

I would like to comment that the only place where the idea of probabilistic interpretations or probabilistic calculations (that is finding out how much order there is — in direct calculations of uncertainty which I've been involved in) appears is in the absurd universe section. I think, rather than postulating that the idea that there is no external order is absurd, we can say something like "how much order is there in any given particular system at any given point of time?" and then talk about a probabilistic approach that explicitly states what probability we can assign to a given event or given process taking place.

CARROLL: Well, I don't know whether Dr. Fink would want to comment, but I would put probabilistic theories of all kinds in either the indeterminacy category or the gross predictability category rather than in the absurd universe (the totally free-will category). If you're talking about different degrees of probability then it does seem to me that you are talking about different degrees of predictability.

MIDLARSKY: With an adequate data basis you can make the calculations of how much order there is in a given system so that you can answer the question of either how absurd it is (i.e. identifying absurdity with lack of order) or you can ask the question of how much order there is directly, and talk about questions of that type. That's what I mean by probabilistic.

CARROLL: Are you suggesting to us another column?

MIDLARSKY: Yes.

SIPES: The list is quite well done; I like it very much. I wonder, however, if it is becoming more slowly or more rapidly historical. You talk about the philosophical arguments on causality. I am reminded of the way that we solved the old, very important question of how many angels can dance on the head of a pin. We answered that question ultimately by not asking it any more. The position I am in is strange. My work would fall into the columns of gross predictability or causality-limited. Yet, frankly, I used to know what causality was; I don't know what it is any more. I think it's sort of an invention of some people's minds. I can see sequencing in time; I can see patterning; but insofar as one thing causing another, I don't know what you mean when you say that. I used to, but I don't any more and I wonder if this might be a good historical document in a few years. Maybe we will stop asking the question of causality.

FINK: I wanted to point out that the general categorization in six categories really does not do justice to the great variety of opinions that people have about determination or the degree of explicitness or specificity in those assumptions. I think, in a sense, you may be right: the question will be solved by ignoring it. On the other hand, something about the whole effort at scientific analysis, something about the idea of the science of peace or science of the causes of war which has under-lying practical implications (that is, which is aiming at finding out what it is necessary to do in order to prevent the things we want to prevent) automatically forces people into making some assumptions, either ex-plicit or implicit, about the nature of the causal connections between the things that they are studying as the sources of war. Otherwise, why bother?

On the other hand, what about the position that you take on what degree of determination you can in fact test? Can you really test causal hypotheses about war or can you do nothing more than test a prob-abilistic hypothesis? What kinds of hypotheses are testable? What kinds of theories are acceptable or rejectable? The main thing is that the assumption you make may color your opinions about what you can do practically. What are the practical steps that can be taken? If you take a very strong deterministic position, that implies you can't do anything to change or prevent wars. It implies a whole different course of action. If you take a position that there is a lot of freedom in the system, there's a lot of indeterminacy, then the problem is to find ways of shifting the probabilities in the direction you want them to go. Even if, on a philosophical level, this problem is finessed, somehow or other we have to be able to scrutinize theories in terms of their practical impli-cations. I think that some understanding of where they fit, of what kind of assumptions they are making about determinism, may be useful. Now I don't say that's the only important dimension. There are several others which are equally important for the same practical purposes.

Bio-Medical Aspects of the Etiology of War

Chaired by M. A. NETTLESHIP and R. BIGELOW

Discussion of papers by N. MACDONALD, C. W. YOUNG, R. BIGELOW, R.D. GIVENS, I. EIBL-EIBESFELDT

Discussion of films by A. KORTLANDT, I. EIBL-EIBESFELDT

M. NETTLESHIP: The following is a brief description of a film by A. Kortlandt, J. van Orshoven, R. Pfeijffers, and J. C. J. van Zon: *Chimpanzees Using Clubs in Fighting an Animated Stuffed Leopard* (Part II of: *Testing Chimpanzees in the Wild*. University of Amsterdam and VARA, Hilversum). Dr. Kortlandt will show the film.

KORTLANDT: During the second, third, sixth and seventh Chimpanzee Expeditions of the University of Amsterdam, the use of (rudimentary) weapons by wild-living chimpanzees was investigated by suddenly exposing a group of these apes to an animated stuffed leopard. Sixteen tests with three different populations were conducted. The responses included, among other things:

1. The "marital dish-smashing type" of breaking off and flinging down branches or other objects with an overarm movement from HIGH over the shoulder downwards, palm forward. In its typical and fully-developed form this is a forest canopy adapted anti-predator defense technique.

2. The "girlish types" of underarm and more or less sideways throwing, thumb forward, aimed at an enemy in a horizontal direction, and taking into account the curved trajectory of the missile. This is essentially a savanna-adapted fighting technique (throwing sand into the opponent's eyes; throwing branches, rocks, etc.).

3. The "police clubbing technique" of overarm clubbing, holding the end of a large stick in one hand, thumb forward. This, again, is a savanna-adapted technique to fight natural enemies.

The film illustrates that the forest-adapted patterns do occur also in savanna-dwelling chimpanzees, but only in a rudimentary form. Conversely, the savanna-adapted types remain underdeveloped in forest-dwelling apes.

In man, the forest-adapted patterns have phylogenetically acquired new (and partly non-agonistic) biological functions. On the other hand, the essentially non-agonistic, exploratory poking and stabbing techniques (both overhand and underhand) which occur in the African apes have phylogenetically acquired new agonistic functions in man, though in different degrees. Furthermore, man has evolved the "boyish" over-arm throwing technique LOW over the shoulder, little finger forward, accompanied by a twisting motion of the spine, hips, and legs, which does not occur in the apes (long-distance throwing and killing by means of rocks and javelins).

A more detailed analysis of the various motor patterns and of the inhibitory mechanisms involved in social intercourse results in a tentative scheme of their evolutionary history.

CORNING: Were the chimpanzees that were engaged in the charges against the leopard in the savanna experiments primarily males? I refer to the early frames where they charged as a group and were acting in a coordinated fashion, rather than the later, more diffuse attacks. Did the females and young hang back and let the males do the attacking?

KORTLANDT: No, it's the opposite. The general rule with all three populations where we did the tests was that the fiercest were the mothers. Next came the males, then the childless females. So this clearly suggests that leopards predate occasionally on young chimps.

CARROLL: I was wondering how much effect there might be, in dealing with the chimpanzees, of projection of contemporary behavior and terminology and interpretations on their behavior. One thing I was wondering about was the differentiation you made between exploratory and attacking motions and behaviors. It seems to me that most of the actions which were designated as attacking (I assume they were so designated because they seem similar to the motions we would make when we hit things or when we are trying to attack something) were in that situation really quite ineffectual as attacking behavior. They seemed to be more like either exploratory or ritualistic behaviors. A lot of the hitting or poking sticks in the direction of the object would certainly never be effectual for a real leopard, and even granting that after a very short time they realize that that is not a real leopard, still in terms of really injuring or attacking — if what we mean by attacking is violence in the sense of an attempt to injure the object — those behaviors look to me as though they could well be interpreted as either exploratory or ritualistic.

KORTLANDT: You are right. This depends on the state of motivation. In the film, there are two full hits with branches as thick as 2 to 3 inches with hitting speeds measured at up to 60 miles per hour. Now if you just imagine that a leopard were driving a car at a speed of 60 miles per hour and hit a tree as thick as that, there is a fair chance that he would break his back. Of course, an objection which you can make is that a living, healthy leopard would be able to defend itself quite adequately, and the theory which is still to be tested is that these methods work mainly against diseased or three-quarters-grown leopards. If a leopard has caught a chimp baby, he is forced to release the victim by these attacks. This will be tested out if I get the chance in the future. We will use a live leopard in a rolling cage in order to suggest that it is the real thing, but not quite able to move freely around and not able to run away. But you are right. This applies to some of what you have seen but there are two hits which are sufficiently hard to break the back of a leopard.

RICHARDS: The purpose of some of this behavior might not necessarily be to disable the leopard. Yet you both seem to be assuming that a leopard would persist in its actions in the face of these things and I suspect that most leopards would tend to run away if they got a big leafy branch thrown directly at their heads. It's not quite the same thing since the stuffed leopard wasn't able to attack, but he also wasn't able to run away. To say that maybe the chimp attack would have been ineffectual is assuming that the chimps wanted to kill the leopard, whereas it would be just as effective (from a survival point of view) to drive him off. The other question I want to ask is: Did the females use weapons more or less than the males, or was there any difference?

KORTLANDT: There is a correlation with motivation, and the females actually did better. To be precise, mothers fought more than just males or females.

RICHARDS: You said they attacked more, but did they use weapons?

KORTLANDT: Attacked more?

RICHARDS: There has been a question, raised several times, that women don't do these things, and I was just curious. . . .

KORTLANDT: Among chimps they do. The implication is that the effective way would be to kill the leopard. That is not the case. I think the effective way from a biological point of view is to hurt the female leopards so that they will always run away when chimpanzees vocalize. In this way, in lots of populations a tradition is built up to flee when chimps are heard. At the same time this would explain why chimpanzees always go Oooooooooooo! You find that, in the wild, animals are silent except for chimpanzees and man.

YOUNG: Do you have any opinion as to whether the difference between the forest and the savanna chimpanzee is genetic or phylogenetic?

KORTLANDT: It is very definitely cultural because forest-captured chimpanzees that we have kept in zoos in a large open enclosure have been discovered, in the course of a number of years, to develop simultaneously the same type of behavior. Yet when newly captured, they do not show this. It developed spontaneously when they were given sufficient space to make such behavior effective. Another argument is that there is no difference between the eastern and the western species. It is definitely cultural.

M. NETTLESHIP: Since he is not with us I will read Dr. Macdonald's abstract to give us a brief review. The paper is entitled "The biological factor in the etiology of war — a medical view."

War has five main etiological factors: biological, psychological, social, economical, and political. The biological is the most basic, the least understood, and the most seriously underestimated. Biologically man is a killer, the greatest predator the world has ever known — the only mammal to slay other members of his own species in vast numbers. Throughout his evolution, the weapon has played an outstanding role; it has always, and for sound reasons, been a tool he valued most. Man's affinity with the weapon is biological. Without it his ancestors could not have survived, and his evolutionary progress has largely been determined by it. He owes the rapid enlargement and improved performance of his brain and his present dominant position in the world mainly to it. The fundamental role of the weapon finds expression by influencing basic human relationships. Its influence also permeates the other factors listed above in the causation of war. Power, status, and (paradoxically) the capacity for joint creative endeavor arise ultimately from the ability to make and use weapons. We must recognize our affinity with the weapons as the first step on the way to ensuring control over it and our own survival. This view provides grounds for hope.

M. NETTLESHIP: Could we hear a résumé of Professor Young's paper?

YOUNG: I was a psychologist for forty-two years. When I retired, I became an irenologist, a cross-disciplinarian irenologist. I studied biology, sociology, anthropology, and philosophy as well as psychology. Now, that is a really risky occupation for anyone to undertake, although it is quite exciting. I'm trying to reduce the risks of it somewhat by bringing to you an idea that occurred to me as a means for clarifying this unnecessary hassle between the effects of the genes and the effects of the environment, as far as war is concerned. I would like very much to have people who know a great deal more biology and ethology than I do give me the results of their superior knowledge because I'm sure I'm quite naive in this field.

If we use the concepts that are used by geneticists in dealing with evolution, we can probably state the problem more precisely than it is ordinarily stated. The geneticists, of course, say that the phenotype (that is, the functioning and structure of the individual) develops as a result of the interaction between the genotype and the environment. One of the adaptive features of the development of the phenotype is known as phenotypic flexibility. That is to say that in different environments different phenotypes will grow as a result of the interaction between the environment and the genotype. I think we saw that in the case of the forest and the savanna chimpanzees. This is a good example of phenotypic flexibility. Phenotypic flexibility goes only so far, however, among the non-human animals. What apparently can happen is that any phenotypic trait may develop which has been selected through natural selection in the various environments in which the animals live.

The possibility of phenotypic development is much greater than that. That is, experimentally, you can produce all kinds of phenotypes, but only the phenotypes that have developed through a natural selection of the genes for those phenotypes appear in nature. This is known as phenotypic canalization. There is very little difference between one set of chimpanzees and another. Even though they are very intelligent animals and capable of learning, there is very little difference between them. The kinds of traits that can be produced in the laboratory are known as morphoses. That is, they are not phenotypic adaptations and, if they were to occur in nature, they would be non-adaptive. The thought I have is this, that somehow the human race evolved a capacity to escape phenotypic canalization, to produce adaptive morphoses. Now, in order to do this, it would be necessary to perceive that this kind of behavior might adapt the individual, might get the individual to its goal more effectively, than some type of phenotypic adaptation. So, I hypothesize that the change that produced this was not necessarily very much of a change in the ability to learn or a reduction in the instinctive learning patterns but the addition to those of an inventiveness. That is, an ability to imagine what might happen, to consider things outside the realm of the immediate environment, and so on. Obviously, language would contribute a good deal to this and I think we can hypothesize that the hunting life, quite possibly the life of competition between human groups, also spurred that on beyond the level of the animals. Consequently, you have the possibility of developing adaptive morphoses which would be non-random. And consequently, they would have a tendency to build up and be shaped into highly adaptive forms of behavior over a relatively short time, a much shorter time than is needed for genetic adaptation. I would suggest agriculture, technology, the state, and so forth as being obvious things of that type.

M. NETTLESHIP: Dr. Bigelow, would you like to tell us about your paper please?

BIGELOW: We have to account for the fact that the size of the emergent human brain doubles in a relatively short period of geological time. Now this means that somehow or another, for some reason, the smaller-brained hominids produced fewer offspring than the larger-brained ones all the way through. Now, some factor was acting against the smaller-brained ones and favoring the larger-brained ones. I'm not trying to imply that you can judge someone's intelligence by the size of the brain, but the implication here is rather clear. The essence of my thesis is one of these unprovable hypotheses that Dr. Scott has referred to earlier. I don't think it should be ignored for that reason. In some ways Darwin's hypothesis was unprovable insofar as no one has ever tried to form a fish into a reptile or a man. The thesis is that cooperation within a group was very important in order for that group to be able to deal with threats from the outside. Earlier on, most of the threats were from leopards, lions, etc.: non-human predators. But I believe that at some period in human evolution the ability to counter these non-human threats reached a point where man could do this reasonably effectively and, at that point, the major threat gradually came from other human or hominid groups. If this did take place as I see it, the whole picture falls neatly into place. You can see how the ability to communicate and cooperate within a group would have a very high selective value in terms of survival against threats from other groups. I do not mean to imply that war is in any way innate in the sense that we are inevitably doomed. I do feel that there is a great deal of hope in looking at the problem or approaching it from this point of view. Because of the intimate interaction between cooperation and competition that was mentioned earlier, the two evolve parallel to each other, and not as two quite separate things. We have now reached the point where we are capable of cooperating on such a vast level that there is hope that we can master our tendency to resort to war.

M. NETTLESHIP: Professor Givens, would you like to give us a rundown on yours?

GIVENS: My paper was aimed at summarizing our present knowledge of aggression in non-human primates. In doing this, I looked not only at field studies but laboratory experiments as well and, fortunately, I have a summary which I think can put together the basic ideas of the paper.

First of all, I should point out that aggressive behavior is no more common or related to primates than it is to other animals. In the past, it was thought that primates were particularly aggressive animals, but this does not seem to be the case. Second, there is a tremendous amount of variation from one species to the next species as to the amount of aggressiveness we find. Some of the most aggressive, such as the baboon, for example, contrast remarkably with unaggressive animals such as the chimpanzee. Another common feature is the fact that aggressiveness — the level of aggressiveness — varies tremendously with the breeding season. This, of course, is related to hormone levels and laboratory experiments have found this to be true also. You get the same kind of reactions. The fourth characteristic which involves aggressiveness is the density of the population. The more dense, the greater the aggression. This is true of almost all species looked at. We find that when you put animals in a zoo, aggressiveness builds up. We also find that rhesus monkeys living in temple areas in India, where there is the tendency for one troop to suddenly encounter another troop, show a great deal more aggressiveness than do rhesus monkeys out along the roadside, where they are not surprised suddenly by rounding the corner and finding another troop of monkeys. Finally, we might look at the kinds of things that bring about aggression. What causes aggression among various primate groups? These seem to boil down to the following: (1) protection of the troop against predators, (2) protection of infants from being harmed, (3) maintenance of order by establishing a relatively stable troop hierarchy (incidentally, we found that hierarchies are really quite stable in most of these groups and do not change except over long periods of time), (4) enabling the troop to reach necessary food, (5) maintaining adequate intratroop spacing, again related to the food supply, and (6) bringing the more dominant members together for mating purposes.

We study primates because we are interested in them. We also study them to see what light they can throw upon human behavior. What does this tell us about human behavior? Well, if we are looking at aggression on an individual level, I think we can learn a great deal about human aggression from studying primates, but if we are concerned with warfare we're at something of a loss because we don't have any organized warfare among non-human primates. Only human primates indulge in this. For studying warfare we have to turn to the human being himself, to ethnographic studies.

M. NETTLESHIP: May we have your summary, Professor Eibl-Eibes-feldt?

EIBL-EIBESFELDT: The question whether man is by nature aggressive or whether his aggressive behavior is merely a result of education is still a matter of controversy. To prove their point, environmentalistically oriented anthropologists and psychologists have repeatedly emphasized that societies without aggression are to be found. Among such sup-posedly peaceful groups are the Bushmen of the Kalahari in southwest Africa. It has been reported that they live in flexible open groups with-out territoriality. The examination of the older literature already casts doubt on these recent statements. Bushmen have indeed been reported to defend territories against members of other bands. The direct obser-vation of such people reveals fully the saga of the peaceful hunter and gatherer as being a neo-Rousseauan myth.

The author had the opportunity to study social interactions in the !Ko Bushmen of the Kalahari. As aggressive actions I defined those that lead to spacing or submission; whether the person is physically hurt or not does not matter in this context. Numerous aggressive acts were counted and filmed. Children proved to be particularly aggressive towards their playmates. During a play session of 191 minutes I counted, in a play group of two boys and seven girls, 166 aggressive acts, e.g. slapping, kicking, throwing sand, spitting, biting, etc.

The patterns themselves were interesting since some highly specific actions seem to be universal. The children used to "threat stare" at each other. The loser, in giving up, lowered his head, usually in a slightly tilted fashion and pouted with strongly protruded lips. This be-havior stopped aggression and even invited bonding. It is a behavior of submission which can be found in other cultures as well. Likewise this also applies to a number of other patterns, demonstrating that quite a number of motor patterns of aggression have evolved in the service of spacing. They are inborn in man. In studying the ontogeny it was found that babies in interacting with other babies demonstrate curiosity with sudden shifts to aggression. Boys, particularly, try to push other babies over and scratch and kick them.

The often depicted portrait of the peaceful Bushmen is, however, not completely wrong. Their cultural ideal indeed seems to be a peaceful one and they achieve a fairly peaceful life by socialization of aggression. The children fight it out among themselves. Whenever fights break out, elder playmates intervene, comfort and soothe, and often take sides, punishing the aggressor. Children experience the negative effect of ag gression on group harmony and try to overcome it by emphasizing the bonding and sharing rituals that are so typical for the Bushmen band. Bushmen do not live in an aggression-free society, but they know how to cope with aggressive impulses effectively. In this, they take advantage of certain bonding patterns which — as their universal distribution demonstrates — are inborn in man. In the final discussion I want to clarify the concept of phylogenetic adaptations as far as aggression is concerned.

M. NETTLESHIP: During the coffee break, there has been a little discussion that perhaps we haven't clarified some of the points that we were setting about this morning. Dr. Bishop and Dr. Sipes have some very pertinent things to say about this. We will start with Dr. Bishop.

BISHOP: So far I don't think we have really made adequate distinctions between aggressiveness and warfare. I see aggressiveness as being the result of some kind of psychological motivation, that is caused, for instance, by astronomical phenomena such as cycles of the moon which we haven't brought up and which certainly affect animal behavior. (The moon affects the behavior of fish, birds, and other non-human creatures, and we might suspect that it would affect human behavior as well.) Aggressiveness, as I see it, is something that is at least partially biologically determined, whereas warfare, on the other hand, is usually the result of planning. People deliberately set out to capture territory, make conquests, etc. These are deliberately done in a rational fashion and have nothing necessarily to do with aggressiveness. In fact, the people who very often determine wars are not themselves involved and make a point of not being involved.

SIPES: We were bringing out the fact that, at certain phases of the moon, there is a higher frequency of violent crimes on police blotters, admissions to mental hospitals are higher, etc. It has been found (someone has done an informal study in Buffalo, New York) that March appears to be suicide month, at least in Buffalo. Not only do suicides rise sharply at that time, but also attacks on family members, etc. And it is said that during the summer, riots start as certain temperatures are reached. Below certain temperatures you very seldom get riots and above 95 degrees you hardly ever get riots starting. So there is a response to temperature. But we find that if we look at organized warfare and the history of war, most wars start in early spring right after the planting or in fall, right after the harvest. This is a rationally determined time. Once you have your food planted, you hope to go out and whup the other fellow and get back before your harvest, or you harvest and then go out and whup the other fellow because you don't have anything else to do.

Clausewitz said that war is an instrument of policy and most political scientists will agree with him. It is another way of getting what you want as a country. You attempt to outfox the other fellow politically, in alliances, in trading of territories or privileges and prerogatives, and if that doesn't work, if you feel that you have a good chance, you will take to the field against him to try to get what you want militarily. But these are rational actions; these have nothing to do with an emotional response. An analogy has been brought up: If Dr. Bishop stands over me with teeth bared, snarling, with clenched fists, and calling me names, I am likely to try at least to poke him in the mouth or perhaps even strangle him. Fine, that's one situation. But what if he has a business; he is a business competitor of mine. I hire a hit man. Now is that the same sort of aggression against him? No, THAT's rational. I may not have anything against him at all. I may even like him, but for heaven's sake I need his territory and so I hire a hit man to get rid of him. It is a rational action. What does it have to do with aggression when he is standing over me and I react to it? Aren't these two different classes of phenomena? What role does aggression play in warfare? Neither of us, I believe, claim that it never has had any role, but how often does it have a role?

ESSER: I would like to take up this point. I fully agree with Dr. Sipes that it appears that warfare is rational, and I should know, because of my orientation on violence and warfare. I said in the preceding session that I believe it is culturally determined and we can learn that type of behavior. However, what must always be remembered is that unless there were an irrational basis for that rational behavior it would not be executed because, rationally speaking, should we continue, once we know that a war is meaningless — let's say, the Vietnam conflict? Yet we do. Also, why should we begin if we know that certain ends are inevitable, like an atomic war?

We damned well know that such considerations in the last instance have nothing to do with aggression. If you are talking about the territorial conflict I would call that irrational. There is no reason at all why man should have a territory, there is no REASON at all. But, there is a biological IMPERATIVE why I like my own property. You see, that's the difference! Rationally, yes, indeed, we could do away with war. Rationally war is something that is planned, carried out at times when it is convenient; done by dummies or smarties, or what have you, that will execute it for us. Yet the ultimate motivational forces are, in my opinion, irrational moving forces and I submit that what we consider rational today, such as that it is "rational" for me to defend my country, is something that we have construed that way. It's NOT rational for me to defend my country. Sometimes it's not at all. Yet we construct it, we have law; we have constructs that make this thing a fully justifiable reasoning sequence. What I'm suggesting is that if you change the perspective, you can come to different reasoning sequences. It is possible to construct a totally different reality.

It was said that the last column of the Fink-Carroll matrix categories is an absurd universe. It is said that it is absurd because order is a creation of the mind or an artifact of it. Well, that is not an absurd universe. I suggest to you that order is an artifact of our mind. I also suggest to you that that is not necessarily a blanket statement, that determination of free will is all that we have. I take issue with this in the paper of Carroll and Fink which is otherwise a good paper. Sartre says, it is a choice of mine if I want to commit myself to war. He doesn't say it is a free-will determination. He says it is a choice. I'm saying that indeed how we want to see things is a choice for us, and that a choice is a choice and no more. It's not rational, it's not necessarily irrational. It is a choice. And that is the way we go about doing things and designing things. Thank you.

PARKER: Thus far we have, I think, somewhat limited our interest in aggression to its relationship as a cause of war or as a stimulus to war. It seems to me that there is another very important area which requires investigation, even if we should at some point in our studies conclude, in fact, that there is no relationship between individual aggression and war; that it is not a stimulus or a cause of war. An area which does require some exploration is its relationship to behavior IN war. I think at this point we should consider things like war crimes, which may be totally unrelated to the individual's perception of either his personal goals or the national goals involved in that war. It may be totally apart from the area of self-defense. The question becomes: Why does he do what he does? Does aggression occur at this point? My suggestion would be, in relating aggression to war, that we not speak simply of its relation as a cause but also as an influence on behavior in war.

CANCRO: I am very much in agreement with Dr. Esser's remarks, but I would like to add one or two points.

There are intentional wars and unintentional wars, so let's look at intentional wars first. There are intentional wars in which there is a large rational component. For example, if Israel can in six days achieve certain territorial and political and economic goals at very little cost to itself that is an enormous rational component in the decision to go to war. On the other hand, if you enter into a thirty-year conflict, or into a multi-year conflict, in which the expenditure in terms of the national wealth, the national product, and lives far exceeds any realistic goals that one can hope to obtain, it is not rational. I think that World War I is a magnificent example of how you can destroy a generation in wealthy, very developed and civilized nations to gain goals which were poorly understood by all parties, and here the irrational component is perhaps greater.

Another point that one can look at is that there's a difference between making the decision at a political level to go to war, and making it happen. For example, if the President of the United States in an earlier administration were to decide to make a commitment to Vietnam HE doesn't go. He gets American individuals to go. How do you make these people willing to go? How do you convince them that this is a worthwhile thing? Why are men at times very ready, willing, eager, and excited to go to war? Why do you usually have a plethora of volunteers, at least early in the game? This readiness to go to war to achieve obscure and not clearly defined goals also seems to have an irrational component, and in this way a study of violent and/or aggressive behavior may give us some insight into the readiness and the state of preparation that men have to accept war as a policy decision.

BISHOP: Perhaps we should make a taxonomy of different types of warfare which run the gamut from culturally patterned warfare on the Plains where an individual would go out with a party he had gathered together, completely willingly, to the extreme type where you have a conscription and people forced into situations.

SIPES: The complexity of the social entity as brought out here is very important. Those who decide that the war is to start are quite rational and very frequently not emotional at all. There might be a very large, irrational or emotional or what have you, component to the behavior of those who do the fighting, but as Andrewsky pointed out in his argument against war being innate in human beings, "if it were so darned innate, why do they have to propagandize so much to get people willing to go to war?" In Germany, in America, and in Japan during the Second World War, in England during and before, a lot of propaganda had to take place to whoop people up to that level. Now those people who employed that propaganda were doing so, I believe, on a rational basis. There was very little real emotion involved, and certainly very little irrationality, except in a view to the rear that allows one to say it was irrational of Hitler because he lost. Well, he didn't think he was going to lose; that was an error of his. We can't identify an error with irrationality. Sometimes you sit down and try to figure out something rationally and you do so. It just so happens you don't figure it out right. With the Thirty Years' War, I dare say that the people who started it didn't expect it to be a thirty-year war. They thought it was going to be a one-season war and it just didn't work out that way. What are you going to do? In a situation like that, I certainly would grant that there would be a degeneration of the rational structure; that is to say, what was going on in people's minds after the first two years of war wasn't what was going on in their heads during the first two months of the war.

M. NETTLESHIP: Can we swing back now a little specifically to the topics for this session? We are talking about bio-medical aspects of the etiology of war and we have a lot of the evolutionary problems left over from Session 1 which fit in very well with this.

BIGELOW: I could anticipate a question that was to be asked as to how I relate my thesis to modern and recent wars. My answer to that can be very brief. I just don't know how it relates to such events as World Wars I and II. What I have referred to in my thesis is intergroup competition during the Pleistocene between relatively small groups and what we would call wars . . . the early historical wars between relatively small groups. What happens from the point of view of natural selection when we get to the stage of World Wars I and II, I just don't know, although some very strange things happen. During, let's say, the last three hundred years there were a great many very bloody wars in Europe which killed off some of the most healthy young men and a lot of other people, but yet during that time Europeans, it is said, increased twelve-fold in number (and they spread all over the world), whereas Asians increased only five-fold. Now I'm not saying I understand this, but something was happening during this time which may have had evolutionary effects. I just don't think that what I am saying really applies to big modern wars or to a nuclear war at the present time.

A. NETTLESHIP: I would like to enlarge a little bit upon what Bigelow has said. During this era of tremendous expansion and extension from the European mainland, which is an extraordinary phenomenon in itself, we almost have to talk about some of the colonies as conquests indigenous to Europe but extending across many oceans and many seas. Some of the bio-medical people have talked about what happens when enormous epidemics almost wipe out a population. For example, there was the Black Plague and the White Plague. In Europe, in a two-year span, some eighteen-and-one-half to twenty-five million people died, and if you look at the birth records (as far as they go) after that, within ten years you not only could not see that this had happened, you couldn't even see the effect of the fact that it had slowed up the actual population increase for a short while. So, I think there are many phenomena that we are not dealing with yet, simply because we can't see them or understand them. I am struck again, as I was earlier by our talk about irrational occurrences; they are merely irrational because we don't yet have the data to understand them. I suspect that many of these occurrences are what you might call biological or bio-medical. We need a great deal more data as to what is happening between wars to explain why a war suddenly occurs. What sent a group of men aboard a ship to this continent [America]? Why did they do this? Well, we say they went to explore for new routes for spices. That isn't a rational explanation at all. They stayed here; they didn't even get to India.

BIGELOW: They were looking for spices but they were also engaged in piracy or warfare.

CLAESSEN: I think it is a necessity to differentiate the kinds of war. For instance, the Thirty Years' War was a rather complicated affair because it was fought out in Germany without many Germans. Armies from Sweden and from France and Czechoslovakia came to Germany to fight it out. So to accuse the Germans of a thirty-year war is not quite correct. It's quite another thing from the Yąnamamö wars where EVERY man is fighting. You could perhaps differentiate between tribal war, small-scale war, and civilized war, and perhaps Professor Young thinks of civilized war in his paper when he combines war with the growth of the state. I don't know if he thinks that no war takes place without the state, but I can't imagine the Yąnamamö having a state. So perhaps we had better make a differentiation in the use of the word "war."

M. NETTLESHIP: I think that is an excellent idea, though it doesn't have a great deal to do with a particular bio-medical aspect. Why don't I toss out a definition of war: War only occurs in civilized societies and is first observed at the time of the formation of the state. Would anybody like to argue with that? War takes place only with civilization. War occurs first with the origin of the state. What happens among primitive groups is NOT war but one kind of fighting or another.

CARBY-SAMUELS: I have been listening to the conferees and I have a question which relates to what you just said. My question can be phrased as this: Making an objective study of the group behavior known as war must be based on one of two things: (a) extra-rational curiosity, or (b) perception that the behavior called war is counter-productive to some preferred ideas. Now, if one eliminates the first, can we intelligently talk about war externally to the context of appreciating the validity, if not the universality, of the preferred idea? Therefore, is there not some arrogance in presuming to delineate ideas for the variety that is man, or does the conference dispute the fact that man is a variety?

M. NETTLESHIP: I think man by nature is rather arrogant and I think scientists are perhaps the most arrogant of all men. But we have gone rather a long way pursuing our arrogance. I don't know if that answers your question. Would anyone else like to answer the point?

CANCRO: Let me respond in the following way because I actually share many of your concerns. I hate to label any activity, including killing, as always bad, because I can always conceive of circumstances or situations where my sympathies would be with the person perpetuating that act. But I think we're really trying to address ourselves to the activities of highly developed, technologically developed nations, where, if they were to enter into a war between or amongst themselves, it would represent a universal threat to the continuation of life on the planet. I would say that is one goal that we can all agree upon as transcending human differences: we must have a viable planet Earth in order to maintain those differences so that we can go each on our own separate ways. When there is a real and not an imaginary danger to the continued existence of the planet Earth it is something that I think we can join in unison and say, "Well, we must avoid this danger at all costs."

CARBY-SAMUELS: Mr. Chairman, in regard to the statements that were made about aggression and cooperation and all these behaviors, would it be proper to say that what the Conference is actually looking at is attacks on the environment or survival of man?

M. NETTLESHIP: That sounds good, though I'm not sure I would want to call that WAR. You see, the trouble is that man faces a number of different varieties of environment, including his own kind and different varieties of his own kind, and a lot of war is focused on that. It is true that we may aggress against other parts of the environment as well.

TEFFT: I noticed that Bigelow's paper responds to the criticism or alternative suggestion that hunting, big-game hunting, might have accounted for the gradual increase in brain size. That is, those with larger brains were able to cooperate more readily in hunting activities to a greater extent than their smaller-brained predecessors. I wonder, however, whether or not the larger-brained prehistoric man may have had certain linguistic capabilities that his ancestors did not have and this enabled him, gradually, to coordinate and cooperate in hunting activities to a greater extent than his ancestors and thus to depend more and more on big game. My cursory reading of some of the materials on the early Pleistocene seems to indicate that men at that time, or hominids of that time, tended to rely on small game, game that was weak; they tended to hunt younger animals, and so on.

BIGELOW: I don't by any means exclude hunting as a factor in human evolution. Certainly, the more successful hunters tended to survive in greater numbers than less successful hunters. But then, I don't look upon hunting as an alternative explanation or as an alternative factor of intergroup competition which is what I'm stressing the theoretical importance of. I think this has, if not deliberately, been brushed aside and avoided more than it should have been. What I'm trying to explain is how our ancestors got to the point where they did have the mental capacity for linguistic communications so that they could be, for those reasons, better hunters than certain other people. I have tried to explain how I think intergroup competition can account for the gradual acquisition of these capacities for communication — which would naturally lead to superior capacities for big-game hunting. I can't see how big-game hunting can account for the acquisition of the capacity for big-game hunting, nor can it account for the actual elimination, if you like to use a rather blunt term, of the people who were less successful. The people who were less successful at big-game hunting apparently would have had to starve in large numbers, if big-game hunting was the major selective force which accounts for the trebling in size of the human brain, but I can't see how this would happen. People are very omnivorous and if they couldn't eat big game they would eat something else. Whereas intergroup competition can, in rather unpleasant ways, account for the actual removal of the less successful or, if you like, the favoring of the ones who are more successful.

KRAKAUER: I think that we have to go back a little bit further. It was hominid intellectual development in general that led to the increased ability of man to survive. I think this is pretty well accepted. That included a gradual improvement in many conscious capacities: perception, memory, thinking, imagination, control of the voluntary muscles, and even contact with emotions. These are the areas that are psychologically and psychoanalytically observed as being related to the development of the intellect. Now the intellect was used for all kinds of purposes, among which was hunting — and even figuring out what to do when you no longer had any animals to kill. But basically we have to think of the human brain developing primarily in terms of a whole range of capacities and adaptability which we were then able to apply in many directions, but were applying in many directions as we went along.

BIGELOW: The capacities for cooperation and communication within the group are what I say was favored. This covers a very, very wide range of capacities and is a very broad generalization.

ROPER: If warfare was very important in the Pleistocene (which we don't know yet) why is it that not until about 3000 B.C., just before the rise of Sumer and Egypt, do we have weapons differentiated between the hunting of animals and killing of *Homo sapiens*? Before that we only have archeological evidence of things which can be used for either. Why isn't there a specialized tool for hitting humans or killing them more efficiently? Are there, in many primitive societies, weapons that are specially used against human beings as opposed to animals? (They could be wood and then they wouldn't be in the archeological records from the Pleistocene.)

BIGELOW: I would like to just comment here that weapons that could be used for either one were probably the sort of weapons that were mainly used in the Pleistocene. When you start to get clearly distinct weapons for war as opposed to hunting, warfare then is becoming much more important. I would even say that prior to that it wasn't warfare; it was intergroup competition or something, but you don't have to have mass killings in order for the thesis that I'm putting forward to be valid. I mean they could just drive each other out of fertile areas and so on.

SCOTT: I think there are two ways you can look at this problem. One is the effect of evolution on warfare: Has war evolved? There, of course, I think the answer would be that there is no evidence that war has evolved AS SUCH, but rather that man obviously has the capacity for doing this. If you want to look at human capacities in general, in comparison with other species, what we see is that there are two very obvious peculiarities about the human species: one is that man is above all, a talking animal. This is something which no other species does to this extent. Other species communicate, it is true. (They signal and so forth, but they do not talk and communicate to the extent that man does.) The other obvious thing about man is that he is characteristically a tool-using species. Dr. Kortlandt has pointed out that chimpanzees use tools also, but no other species uses them to the extent that man does. These two things, these two capacities, probably go very much together. In other words, for the effective use of tools, the skill in making these tools and using them has to be communicated from one individual to another, and this brings up the relationships of tools and communications to warfare. One is that warfare depends upon tools, upon killing instruments. It also must have been quite obvious to the early hunters that tools which were used to kill other species could also be used to kill human beings. But it seems to me, entirely apart from the use of tools as killing instruments, that man as a tool-using species has the possibility of using WARFARE as a tool to get various things. War has been used in a great variety of ways to obtain certain kinds of goals. This is one of the most important general ways of looking at warfare.

Looking at the converse side of the picture, which Dr. Bigelow has brought up, what is the effect of war on evolution? He has postulated that prehistoric man made extensive use of warfare and that this resulted in the elimination and selective survival of certain populations with respect to others. I would submit an alternative hypothesis, which is simply that any early group at the time when the capacity for language was being evolved, any group which had a superior language capacity and communicated skills from one generation to the next which would be useful for survival would automatically have had a tremendous advantage over any other group. Furthermore, language itself tends to create the ideal system, the ideal situation, for rapid evolution in small groups which are separate from each other with respect to breeding and with only occasional crossovers from one group to another. So I think it is possible to postulate a mechanism which would produce rapid human evolution which, from the most general point of view, is an intellectual one, without postulating that this involved primitive warfare.

There has been an assumption here that evolutionary change can only be produced by natural selection. In fact, if natural selection were the only thing that had anything to do with change, very little change would actually occur for two reasons. One is that selection can only act on a variation which is already present: there must be a pre-existing kind of variation before selection can act. Another is that if one has populations which are divided up into small, breeding populations (which, as I understand from the anthropological literature, is a size which most people postulate for small primate troops and primitive human populations), that is, populations of fifty or less than a hundred people, this is almost an ideal size for rapid evolutionary change. While I think it's quite true, as Dr. Bigelow has suggested, that warfare could have produced changes, these would not necessarily be adaptive changes, and they would not necessarily be very far-reaching or continuing changes. In other words, if all you do is eliminate the other competing groups, this preserves the genes in your own particular group, but it doesn't provide the materials for further change.

BIGELOW: I agree with nearly everything you've said. I don't feel that what you've just said is all that different from what I'm saying, except perhaps that I am emphasizing the importance of, not warfare, but intergroup competition more than you are. But as far as the genetic varieties that arise from populations separated into small groups, I agree entirely.

CORNING: The term Dr. Bigelow has been using is competition. There are all kinds of competition, but the competition that counts in terms of evolution is that which gives a reproductive advantage. It is differential fertility; that is the effective form of competition. In that sense intergroup competition may well have been going on among our proto-hominid ancestors. It was undoubtedly going on for a very long time back through the phylogenetic ladder. But I think Dr. Bigelow's thesis is addressed to direct intergroup competition for some valued object in the environment, whether it is a piece of territory or game or whatever; competition which may or may not have involved direct fighting. If that is correct, all that one can say at this juncture is that there seems to be very little direct evidence of this, whereas there is significant direct archeological evidence of large-scale interband hunting as far back as 500,000 years ago in the Upper Pleistocene Levant. (Sally Binford's work on this is quite detailed and quite meticulous.) The one thing for which we do have evidence is that large-scale hunting did emerge quite a long time ago.

Some of the most recent work by Louis Leakey and his son in East Africa (the East Rudolf finds) suggests that fairly large-brained hominids go very much further back into our evolutionary past than we thought only very recently. Perhaps as far back as two million years. If this is the case, then we don't have a problem to explain. We do not have to try to account for some miraculous explosion in human cranial capacity in a very short period of time. In fact, it may have happened a very much longer time ago, coincident with a very gradual, long-term evolution of hunting capacities initially, presumably, of small game. Then one could postulate a sequence in which larger game came to be hunted, perhaps in situations where drought occurred and there was a shortage of small game, or in situations where the human population outran the game and some of the smaller species were hunted to extinction, and then human groups in that environment turned, under pressure (selection pressures which they themselves created, or environmental pressures which they themselves created), to the hunting of larger game. There is a very plausible sequence of events involving hunting and the evolution of human mental capacities that goes back a very long way, so that it obviates the need for a hypothesis of warfare as a principal engine of human evolution.

BIGELOW: I agree with what you said, but I don't think it eliminates the possibilities to the point where we should ignore them as a possibility.

CORNING: No, no, no, well . . .

BIGELOW: This is really all I've been saying all the time, that it is a possible hypothesis and should be considered.

CORNING: It's a difference of emphasis as we said earlier, as I said in my paper. One can also postulate quite plausibly that intergroup competition among evolving hominids at various points in our recent past — that is, the last two million years — could have reinforced selection pressures for the emergence of the same kinds of mental capacities, the same kinds of skills associated with large-scale interband hunting. But the two don't necessarily have to be opposing one another; in fact, they may have reinforced one another.

SIVERTS: Not entering the real hot topic here, but we're jumping back and forth and Dr. Roper raised the question of ethnographic information; for South American Indians and also for New Guinea, there are different sets of weapons intended for hunting, big-game hunting, and (for the biggest of all) the human being. I know that for sure from the Jívaro Indians and I also know it is a fact in New Zealand. Special weapons were designed precisely for warfare or bitter feuding.

RICHARDS: Bigelow talked primarily about the effect of intergroup competition on the persuading group — that is, the group that drove the others out — but I think that it would be equally effective for the persuaded — the group that was driven out — which might provided a steady source of challengers. It is quite possible that the group driven out of its customary home territory was forced to use ingenious and new methods to exploit the new environment that they were in. And they could subsequently come back, so that you get a back and forth dynamic which would tend to increase the effect. I am not disagreeing with you, but I am simply pointing out how the very act of pushing these people out could provide stimulus for their adaptation to the environment culturally, which could then feed back on the original group and thus build it up. And this relates to the question that was raised in Dr. Corning's paper about group evolution versus individual evolution which is perhaps a straw man, because there aren't any groups, there are only collections of individuals who are organized in a particular way. That is, the group doesn't exist without individuals: group survival and individual survival are closely intertwined. Furthermore in primate and other social animals, it is the group that assists individual survival: the lone individual tends not to survive among baboons and various monkey bands and so on. I see these two as closely intertwined. Fewer members die of starvation in the groups than alone. Consequently, the survival potential of this behavior means that you get a hundred percent survival versus maybe zero percent and it seems to me that this would be a good reason for establishing a certain kind of genetic characteristic. This would, of course, provide a tremendous survival potential for that particular genetic characteristic.

BIGELOW: I agree with everything that you've said. We are uncertain, although we can be quite confident that there are usually some genetic factors involved in it, but we need to know a lot more about it. But what you said about the group that is driven out . . . I agree there, too. This places a demand on these groups: those who can improvise, who can adapt to whatever difficulties they might run into as a result of it, are favored by selection and this is another way in which, as I see it, intergroup competition can tend to promote human evolution.

BISHOP: Mrs. Roper made a point in Session 1 which nobody followed through on. That was the fact that warfare, as we know it, arose with trade and you have to ask yourself, "Why was this the case?" Trade came about primarily as a result of the emergence of settled populations with a surplus and warfare came about, not so much as a result of trade, but as a result of a breakdown in trade relations and the actual need of one group for a certain product that they obtained from another. In fact, among most hunters, warfare only came about with the introduction of European products. As far as we know, there were no military societies on the Plains. They were totally non-existent. Big-game hunters shared their products. It was only among the settled horticulturalists that you actually had any kind of warfare.

M. NETTLESHIP: I understand the last part of what you said, but I don't quite understand what you mean about war beginning to take place only when there is a breakdown in trade. Surely, if you see your neighbor has some very successful trade, you might like to make war on him to get what he's got.

BISHOP: You might, but if you establish trade relations with him, then you don't need to fight him. It's only when he decides that he wants to make a profit from you that you become aggressive.

M. NETTLESHIP: Maybe he's in a different group from yours, and you can't trade with him for that reason. That's not a breakdown in trade; it's non-existence of trade. You're still only aggressing against him or fighting with him because of his success in trade.

BISHOP: That's true. Well, all right, warfare, ethnographically at least, did not exist as far as we know among hunters. You have feuding, raiding, but nothing that threatened the survival of the group. Therefore I question whether this type of competition among hunting societies could have eliminated them. I don't think it could have. We have nothing of the type that came about in the historic period where, for example, the Hurons were almost totally annihilated as a result of the introduction of European guns to the Iroquois.

ROPER: I don't think we can conclude nearly as much about warfare as you said, and I didn't mean to say THAT, with regard to trade and some of the conclusions that you drew from it. It could just be accumulation of negotiable wealth. Somebody wants it; it's like in a bank, you know, they want what's in there. Also, I think with other distinct groups you can form trade, so I don't quite agree with Dr. Nettleship, either, on that. Just because there isn't evidence that we can document in the archeological records doesn't necessarily mean that the evidence wasn't there; it may have just disappeared. If there were wooden stockades or something, way, way back we probably wouldn't have it. With archeology, we only find what has remained and I just want to put in that cautionary point.

BISHOP: There might have been a certain amount of feuding going on, but not warfare as we know it or as it occurred among horticultural societies with state organization.

MIDLARSKY: I just want to comment on Mrs. Roper's association of trade and war in earlier times. Lewis F. Richardson, in developing what is probably the most sophisticated mathematical theory on the origins of World War I, found that the arms race was quite a regular phenomenon prior to the assassination in 1914. When he found residual effects in terms of some cooperation, that cooperation is exactly equal to the trade value among the participants that he analyzes, so that there is a direct confluence or complementarity between trade and warfare in more recent situations.

SMITH: I was under the impression that at least a few studies had demonstrated that there was nothing profitable in our wars for trade. That is, for economic purposes we don't have to have war and that certainly in the twentieth century there has been strong evidence that the last thing that corporate heads, the heads of cartels, etc., want is

war. In other words, you can have arms races with just a constant re-
tirement of obsolete war materials that are never used and bring a new
manufacturing in without having war. War is in fact a detriment to
trading . . . most industrialists agree to this.

M. NETTLESHIP: You're talking about a contemporary function or
malfunction of war rather than the problem at hand, which is more on
the origins of war as a result of trade. . . .

SMITH: No, I'm trying to say that, given that we have evidence for
this in the twentieth century, some evidence for it as well in the nineteenth century, and I think the eighteenth too, I see no reason why it
shouldn't hold true in the beginnings of trade.

M. NETTLESHIP: Colonialism and capitalism didn't begin with the
beginnings of trade. They did begin in the eighteenth and nineteenth
centuries, and I think there's your answer.

SMITH: How do you say that is the answer?

M. NETTLESHIP: You're talking about a contemporary function of
war in relationship with the particular economic structure which
arose. . . .

SMITH: I'm saying that the last thing that you want, in trade, is war.
You'll do your best to keep peace. Why wouldn't this have been so,
say, 7,000 years ago?

M. NETTLESHIP: The total economic structure was a completely different one.

CARBY-SAMUELS: I'd like to jump in here because my field is economics and because I'm interested in this debate and conference here
and I would like to get back indirectly to what I raised earlier. The
point is made that war occurs as a result of a breakdown in trade. I'd
like to pursue that a little bit more; it is important to look at the trade,
but also to look at what is traded and why it is traded. Therefore, I am
a little bit uneasy about those individuals who say that war is not important for the survival of man, because this is taking a thing out of
context. If we see that things are traded because they are important to
some perceived survival patterns, and if war causes a breakdown in
trade, then we can say war occurs because there is a perceived threat
to the survival pattern. Therefore, it is important to discuss what is
perceived as necessary for survival, biological survival, and that perception is very important for the decision as to whether to go to war or
not. The artifacts system and biological support system and the relationship to trade are integral parts of the survival of man and therefore
we have wars. We should not dismiss out of hand the proposition that
wars are important to the survival of man, external to the perception

patterns that specify what constitutes survival.

PARKER: An evolutionary approach forces us to focus on a particular kind of question about the phenomenon we are studying and that is, "How does it relate to the problem of survival and reproduction?" That is the essence of the evolutionary view of the life process — that the central problem of all species is survival and reproduction. And it is from that central question that all else flows: about how these particular kinds of behaviors evolve; what biological processes are involved in the manifestation of these behaviors; what the genetic architecture of them is; what the functioning of them may be with respect to that same problem; and how they relate to the same behaviors in other species. What provides a common ground for analysis, between species, is how that same problem is met and how aggression in different species may serve the same or different functions. It also provides the same kind of framework for questions about what are the environmental correlates of aggressive behavior and what cultural factors contribute to aggressive behaviors in the human species. Thus, I would entirely agree with what the gentleman said: that when we look at trade patterns and the relationship between trade patterns and warfare, what we are looking at, under the surface, is some strategy, or set of strategies, by which the human species or some group within the human species, has been attempting to meet its ongoing survival and reproductive needs. Warfare may be an instrumentality by which one or another of these needs may continue to be met or one which is going unmet, may then be met.

YOUNG: In this discussion we need to make a distinction between biological evolution and cultural evolution which has not necessarily been made all the way along. When we're talking about what happened in the Pleistocene, were these adaptations inventions by the groups that carried them out, or were they changes in the pattern of the genes? Certainly, when we come to the historical period, the evolution that we can see going on is cultural evolution. It has meant that men have invented a way of employing agonistic behavior that has been quite adaptive if we consider it first in terms of the population (population growth since that time) or if we consider it in terms of the elimination of those groups that did not develop political warfare. You asked the question whether the only warfare is the warfare associated with the state. It seems to me that there is a particular type of warfare, namely political warfare, which is the warfare we face today. The problem that we face today in warfare is that political warfare has shown itself to be tremendously viable. I think our problem in overcoming war is to find something that can be more viable than political warfare as a means of adjudicating human problems.

RICHARDS: In response to your question about trade and its relationship to warfare, I think that both positions are correct. I think that the archeological evidence, particularly in the New World, in Aztec or in Inca areas and even in the southeastern part of the country, indicates quite clearly that war disrupted trade and was therefore dysfunctional, but I think there are other indications that make it quite clear that war was occasionally a means for defending trade or for establishing it.

In regard to the point just raised by Dr. Young about cultural evolution, we're constantly reinforcing the idea that man is one biological species, and I think we're all agreed with that, but I think this has caused us to overlook the fact pointed out in Dr. Corning's paper, that behavior is species-specific and aggressive behavior is species-specific. Furthermore, it's culture-specific in man. You have certain kinds of aggression that are characteristic of certain cultures, unique to that culture perhaps, or virtually universal in that culture and perhaps not in another culture. It's the same thing with the submissive techniques in aggression. Lorenz points out, for instance, that a turkey that can get along fine with the submissive gesture of literally sticking his neck out will get killed by a peacock because the different bird doesn't understand. A submissive gesture of one culture may be totally misunderstood in another culture. You pointed out, Dr. Nettleship, earlier, that much of our warfare is between cultural ethnic groups. I wonder if our concentration on the biological single species of man has not led us to overlook the cultural speciation of mankind. I think that this whole question is one that might be of some significance in helping us to understand what looks like intraspecific fighting among men, but which is actually more parallel to the interspecific, that is, between species, fighting in other animals.

M. NETTLESHIP: I think this is an excellent approach and I also think this gives us an excellent opportunity to return to our ethologist who has been rather neglected ever since we said aggression didn't have anything to do with war. Would Professor Eibl-Eibesfeldt like to come back? I believe you found aggression to be innate in all men of whatever culture.

EIBL-EIBESFELDT: I would say that it is both. Some patterns of aggressive behavior are certainly universal, others are culture-specific, and therefore we have to define very clearly what we are speaking about. Certain postures of threat are universal. Certain reactions, fear of strangers for example, appear universally and so does the stranger hostility which develops from this pattern. You can even show that this occurs in children born deaf and blind who develop fear of strangers. They discriminate between strangers and familiar persons by smell and they show stranger hostility. Some basic patterns are certainly wired into the system, so to speak, and others are culturally evolved.

M. NETTLESHIP: Can you relate the innate ones more to war than the cultural ones?

EIBL-EIBESFELDT: I would say we need to learn a lot about the motivational structure of man. It was repeatedly mentioned that after all, even if it is a disease and on a high level, you have to stimulate people to fight. That means you are trying to arouse them emotionally, which doesn't mean via cortex but via other older systems and as Lorenz once pointed out, "When banners fly, intelligence is in the trumpet." We are faced certainly with the fact that those individuals who are fighting are quite emotionally aroused. The question which puzzled me was, if war is inborn in man, or if war is in the genes, why do we need so much propaganda to bring people to fight?

Again, nobody says that war is in our genes or that war is innate in man. Now, certain of these motor patterns mature during ontogeny, that's one side. We know that their receptor bias is inbuilt in the species; they are responding to certain stimuli situations at first encounter in an adaptive way. We know that this means they are outfitted with detector devices that bias their perception. We know that there are motivational systems that cause animals and man to be active in certain ways. We know finally that they even cause adaptive modification of behavior. Learning is pre-programmed in such ways that animals learn what contributes to their survival, which is very different from species to species. Animals need to know *a priori* what is rewarding and what is not, otherwise they wouldn't learn. We know from the study of birds that there are critical periods.

We should be careful in saying aggression is inborn. We have to ask the question, "Are there any motor patterns which developed in the service of spacing?" And we can say, "Yes, there are quite a number of motor patterns and signals which are expressions of rage." There are also signals of surrender and that, by the way, is an interesting part, since we have all been looking at aggression as if that was the only thing which is wired into the system. We are very friendly beings. We have a family ethos. We are bonded and we react to submissive signals of a conspecific very strongly. That is why if you have groups going to war you always need to tell them that the others are not people in order to immunize them against the signals of surrender, against the signals that release pity. This process of dehumanization by propaganda, by the way, works even in forest Indians in Brazil, who speak of their neighbors as if they were prey. It's universal, which again shows that there are basic motivational structures which we cannot omit when we speak about war. Certainly we have to deal with individuals that engage in it even though they are misled to do so by certain people who find it convenient.

HUBER: At various points, or almost entirely throughout, we've been talking about violence or warfare as though we were talking about a thing rather than a process, as though violence or war was a definite mode of action or a particular decision or a particular pattern of behavior. Yet I think it was clear in the two movies that we saw that there is a highly tentative and improvisatory element in these violent interactions. So when chimps attack a leopard, at first there is a high element of risk as well as an intention to harm the leopard. There is a high element of looking after yourself at the same time. This is, I would think, built into almost any kind of violent encounter. It is an interaction process as well as a mode of action and this is something that we have to keep very clearly in mind, especially if we want to talk about it in evolutionary terms. The evolutionary paradigm itself tends to reduce violence into a type of thing, rather than a kind of interaction which grows in its own terms in every specific instance.

CANCRO: After a decision has been made to go to war and you want to mobilize the people who will do the fighting you have an enormous tool in man in that he is a symbolic animal to a greater degree than the other living creatures on the planet and because of this, he is capable of the uniquely human act of self-deception. He can believe something that is not true and then respond AS IF it were true. If it is easier to kill someone or something that I see as non-human, all I have to do is convince myself that he is non-human and then the perceptual information will be ignored. I will believe my idea and see you as a non-human or something that is killable even though I have visual, olfactory, tactile input that says "Whoa, stop what you are doing." In other words, my belief system can override my perceptual input, and this creates a unique problem for man in terms of intra-species aggression.

ESSER: I just wanted to underline the importance of what Dr. Richards said about our cultural speciation and the subsequent remarks about how this is facilitated. Man is a typical, group-oriented animal and consequently (regardless of how the position came about of his being in a group) he will always orient himself positively to those whom he is with and against those who are outside and other strangers. In our civilization, we have come to the point that there are more and more strangers. We meet more and more strangers and we need some time to get over the initial shock of strangers such as we experience sitting here. I'm sure, two or three days from now, we will be in much better shape and will not be so hesitant to voice our opinions and put forth what we really mean to say; yet we are still strangers to each other and are holding back. This is a built-in capability, a capacity of man. This is a biological part of man. Cultural evolution has asked us to deal with strangers, whether it is trade or what have you, on an increasingly larger scale. Because of that we really do get different species of cultures and this is the greatest danger I see in this world. We are committed in this country and I believe also in this world, to pluralism, yet we know that the more pluralism there is the more alienation will occur; alienation on a basic biological basis, on a gut-feeling level, unless we can override it by reason (something that we all try to do here). But it is no use only to point to the reason without recognizing that, indeed, alienation will be unavoidable thanks to our continued cultural evolution.

M. NETTLESHIP: I'm not quite clear as to whether you find our reactions to strangers a learned part of our cultural process or an innate part of our biological process. Could you clarify that for me?

ESSER: Well, I'm saying it is a learned process, but it could not happen unless we were biologically wired as mammals to those who smell the same. (Dr. Eibl-Eibesfeldt mentioned it already.) Why does the deaf and blind person who has no contact with the outside world through OUR most important senses still have a fear of strangers? He smells them. Now our learning naturally puts on top of this that to which we start to orient ourselves. Anybody who goes to school has colored clothes on. Anybody who plays in this team has, you know, a different uniform than the other team. The scientist with a white coat is different from the butcher with the red coat, etc. We forget that these are conscious choices of design or at least could be conscious choices of design. The way we lay out our own world, we can design them. We can really go about it in what we call "the right way." We could do that, but we must recognize that our initial reactions are all based on those irrational gut feelings which unfortunately, but maybe not as Lorenz and Eibl-Eibesfeldt and others have shown, are part of our mammalian heritage. Maybe it's fortunate, maybe it's good.

RICHARDS: I'd like to respond to that, because you have mentioned several times the necessity of finding a new way. In relation to this question of pluralism, we must find out what the basic irreducible minimum is that all men have to agree to in order to maintain peace. That's something that you might say the United States has been working on for a good long time. We have by no means succeeded. What, for instance, are the basic values or ideals or concepts that we must accept to continue to function as a viable society, while at the same time allowing as much cultural variation as possible? This, on a world-wide scale, is crucial because there are some behaviors that are incompatible; I mean you simply cannot have them all. You cannot, for instance, practice infanticide and raise all babies. No matter how much you would like to be tolerant you cannot do both. You cannot simultaneously hunt buffalo and run cattle in the same geographical area. Some choices are going to have to be made, but what choices need be made? What is this basic irreducible minimum that we must agree on in order to be able to live in peace regardless of our variation? I don't think we have to have a dead level same culture all over the world. I think you can get a basic minimum within which you can still allow a tremendous amount of cultural variation. This happens to be a personal ideal. Because I like cultural variation, it's a personal value. I don't like the idea of everybody dressing, living, acting, all just alike but I recognize that we must have some common ground for maintaining these.

SCOTT: I want to respond to this idea of xenophobia or built-in fear of strangers and to raise some doubts about it. In the first place there is a well-recognized developmental period in human children, which pediatricians first described as the eighth-month anxiety, where many children do show fear of strangers. However, we should remember that this normally lasts only a few months at the most and that as the child explores his environment, becomes able to walk and interacts with other people, this very largely disappears unless he is trained to be afraid of individuals. One of the problems you have with young children in the city is to keep them from walking up to strangers and taking candy from them and being carried off by them.

We've been exploring a somewhat similar phenomenon with dogs which I think is probably related. Young puppies go through much the same sort of period, and if they are placed out in new environments and have a chance to explore a wider environment at the proper time, they become quite confident in a great variety of situations. Or if you rear them in a very restricted environment, up till the age of six months or so, and then suddenly put them into a new environment, as if for example you take a dog that has been raised in a kennel up to six months of age and then suddenly try to take it out and make it into a pet, it usually develops what we call the kennel-dog syndrome which is a fear of practically anything in the environment; in other words a fear of all strange things. In such a dog you can achieve gradual adjustment to the strange situation. He becomes less and less reactive, but any time a stranger comes in, the animal reverts to his original behavior. This is very, very difficult to eliminate and it is associated with being in a strange environment because you can take animals like this, put them back in their original environment, and they will act perfectly normally.

One of the things this suggests is that rather than there being a wired-in fear of strangers, so to speak, the behavior of the stranger may in fact induce attack. One of the things that invites attack by a strange animal is running away and what an animal placed in a strange environment is most likely to do is to run. If he runs, he thus invites attack by other animals. Another reaction may be to become defensive and aggressive. At the present time we are doing some experiments with well-organized groups of dogs that have been reared together. They are put in with a strange animal and, far from immediately attacking him, they get intensely curious. In fact they get so curious they sort of pile on top of him. This may frighten the strange animal and he may turn around and snap and threaten, and any kind of reaction like this may invite attack. I would suggest that, rather than there being any necessarily inbuilt antagonism toward strangers, the behavior of the stranger himself may have a great deal to do with this. If you look at the behavior of human strangers, one of their first reactions is to get highly critical of the new environment and the new people they see. This is not the way to cultivate friendship.

EIBL-EIBESFELDT: I would say that the dog experiment which you quoted is very relevant to the fear of strangers that we observe developing in children in different cultures. The fact is that, not the behavior of the stranger, but simply the perception of a strange person, either by smell or visually, releases a fear. Later, socialization takes place and children are not so afraid any more. It appears first, and it is well known cross-culturally.

SCOTT: It doesn't necessarily last into adult behavior.

EIBL-EIBESFELDT: Surely that was not implied, but I think that it could well last into adult behavior if it is reinforced and that you have here one biologic root of what we call xenophobia.

ESSER: I would also fully agree with Dr. Scott, that it is learned, and I never said it wouldn't be. It's like flogging a dead horse. It is not a question of xenophobia not being learned and reinforced. The question is, what is easier in this world, given our situation, to get across to children. To trust everybody, or to distrust the stranger? And I submit that in our culture, and practically all the world's cultures, because of our being mammals, and of course because of our being attached to a mother and father, because that's the way we grow up, we cannot survive alone. We can't just be born and then run away and be on our own. Because of that, the father and mother will of course reinforce the child to stay with them and not with others. If you want to design a system, an educational system, that overcomes this, you are quite right that you can design it for dogs and so on. Let us design it for man. That's what I'm saying.

To get back to what Dr. Richards said, the design of what man needs on a world-wide scale is really what should bother us and occupy us. This is only a subjective feeling just like her idealism, but I submit that a design should imply synergism. It should be clear to all of us that only by working together to unknown ends can we design a peaceful world. And the important point is to UNKNOWN ends. Everybody can work together if the end is known. It is much easier for you and me, Dr. Scott, to agree, since we are both Americans and we live in this country and we teach, etc. It's much more difficult for us to agree, let's say with the Chinese when they come in from the People's Republic of China. Unless we learn what to overcome in our biological innards, the barrier will remain between us and the Chinese. The Chinese are now so regimented in the People's Republic of China that they have unisex dress, which is very important to them because that is one way to cut down on the population explosion. If male and female are not too much differentiated, the sexual activities are toned down. So this is a willing and designed effort. But we don't like that; I don't like it. I call that regimentation. Everyone walks in Mao's clothes. The fact of the matter is that I should understand that it is part of the way they build their country. This is one of the designs they have at the moment; they want to construct it that way.

M. NETTLESHIP: I'm not really sure that we understand THE PROBLEM. I like the solution, but could we talk a little more about the problem, before we get on to your solution, please?

ESSER: O.K. Thank you.

M. NETTLESHIP: Dr. Tefft?

TEFFT: Listening to the discussion today, I am thoroughly convinced that *Homo sapiens* has the capacity to act aggressively in various situations. The reason for this apparently varies. I think Alland has suggested that there are hard and soft theories. Today we seem to be dwelling largely on hard theories which may be inevitable when we talk about the human species as a whole and why there is a higher level of intra-specific aggression compared to other species. Alland has suggested that such theories do not necessarily generate the kind of hypotheses that are easily testable in specific situations, such as why does society A have a pattern of continual and frequent warfare while society B doesn't have this pattern.

I think some of our discussion related to warfare is difficult because people have been referring to warfare and then there are other kinds of collective aggression. In my thinking, warfare is armed conflict between political communities. Feud is something else. Often when I am referring to war, somebody else is referring to feuds so some of my confusion may be a semantic one. The point I want to make is that there ARE hunters and gatherers who engage in warfare IF we assume my definition of war. Warfare is not as prevalent among hunters and gatherers, but certainly warfare does take place. I am not disputing that among hunters and gatherers there are other forms of aggression, but I am saying that some hunters and gatherers apparently do not fight wars and others do. Why? And why is there such a great difference in the prevalence of war among hunters and gatherers and advanced agricultural peoples? There are also the basic questions of why war here and not there, or why a peaceful society (a society that has been peaceful for a long period of history) turns to warfare more frequently. I cannot tie in these questions to the general theories that have been discussed so far. For example, the fear of strangers may be a factor, but there are cases where societies fight wars between one another where there has been intermarriage, where people on the other side are relatives to you and they share the same cultural traditions. In other cases, wars are fought, using my concept of war, even as trade goes on. Trade is not disrupted by war. I am unable to find much clarification from the specific ideas which have been advanced so far today.

M. NETTLESHIP: Can anybody help?

HUBER: I'd like to put a couple of things that he said into other words. I think argument as to whether biological factors in human aggression or in warfare are more basic than cultural factors is a straw man. I don't think there are too many people who are pursuing biological factors and who have a biological orientation to behavior who would dispute the importance of environmental factors in the development of almost any behavior in most species, particularly the kinds of species we're talking about: the mammals, higher primates, man particularly. I don't think there are any reputable ethologists today who are arguing that environmental factors are not important in human aggression.

I'd like to make a plea for an open mind on the part of everyone here toward something which we can't explore in detail today, but which is worth our being prepared to explore further on an individual basis. A common ground can be found between those with a biological orientation and those with an environmental or cultural orientation and an interactional view of the development of behavior. That is to say that no behavior is possible in the species without the capacities for those behaviors which can be biologically based. Those biological capacities may shape behaviors in certain ways, may predispose the animal to learn certain kinds of things more readily than other things, and that is the contribution which the biological realm, the biological dimension, may make to a particular kind of behavior. But this does not exclude other variables as being important. What the matter ultimately comes down to is how do we explain the variations in collective aggression in human societies. How do we explain a behavior which does not occur continuously, but is episodic in nature? The question then, is, "What is it that determines those episodes? Are they environmental or biological or both?" Is some of the variance accountable to the fact that there are biological differences between individuals or between whole groups of individuals? Are they due to mean differences between populations and individuals? Are some of the variants explainable by specific sets of environmental correlates which are recurrent? It may be that both are strongly implicated. We don't know; that is a question for empirical research. I don't think we need to necessarily make a decision here today on whether or not biological factors or environmental factors will explain human aggression.

M. NETTLESHIP: I'm glad you said that. I think that makes an excellent summary and a very good place to stop for this session, unless someone is really keen to make another comment. There's a keen man.

MIDLARSKY: Mainly because my light's been eager for a while. We've been going one way, in an undirectional manner, going from the unit of analysis of the individual, either at the animal level or at the human level, and trying to extrapolate from there. I don't quite believe that one can be xenophobic based on some of this evidence — Tonkin Gulf resolution and remember the Maine and remember the Alamo — all designed to develop just the kind of thing people were trying to fight against (the mutinies of the French during World War I, the disintegration of the German army at the end of World War I, the disintegration of the Russians, except for the artillery, who were educated and followed the tradition of Peter the Great to stay and fight even though they were losing).

Even though I have that gut reaction, as indicated, I think one perhaps can go the other direction and say, we have certain bondings in international relations, relating to the incidence of war and if one can find parallels at the lower levels of analysis (by lower I simply mean more individualized) then maybe we can go the other direction. For example, is there any parallel to the following: bipolar systems tend to have more intense conflict with a greater number of deaths and last longer, while multipolar systems have a larger number of conflicts but fewer deaths and a shorter duration for each one of the conflicts? This is rapidly becoming an established, empirically based, finding in international politics. And can one then take that kind of thing, at the level of analysis of international warfare and find some corresponding manifestation at the lower levels of analysis? I am proposing something of the opposite of what we've been trying to do this afternoon.

PARKER: I would like to express a concern while recognizing the topic and the focus of this particular conference. So far we've spoken of societies or groups at war, and we have spoken of aggressive man. My concern is that research that might take place beyond this conference should not limit itself (or those who are engaged in this kind of research should not limit themselves) to the study of man at war, societies or groups at war, and aggressive man, but rather at some point should investigate as vigorously peaceful societies and groups and peaceful men. . . .

M. NETTLESHIP: Peace people get their say a little bit later.

PARKER: Well, I figured that was a possibility, but at the same time I wanted to voice that concern because I think that studies of the causes and conditions of peace are equally as relevant to the whole ball game.

CARBY-SAMUELS: Mr. Chairman, I would like to respond to the unease that this gentleman felt about war. I would like to pivot it on the definition of war in a political group and relate it to what I have been hearing around the conference about biological man and cultural man. We have forgotten a most important thing: that both biological and cultural man have egos and that ego is cultivated as a result of his cognitive understanding of what his survival pattern is. Consequently, the fear of strangers we have been talking about, and the relationship between groups, if we see it in terms of survival patterns and if we see the survival patterns in terms of the conditioning system which allows people to organize experience into what threatens and what does not threaten that survival system, will make us more sensitive to the system that defines man himself. By looking at it in terms of biological man or cultural man, we underestimate the communication system that was talked about that allowed man to perceive himself in functioning reality, and it is a clash of perception that eventually leads to war.

Individual Aggression as a Cause of War

Chaired by J. P. SCOTT

A round-table discussion

SCOTT: I thought that it might be interesting, and perhaps honest, for me to tell you what my biases are and why I am particularly interested in this field. One of my earliest memories, when I was about five and just learning to read, was reading the newspaper headlines concerning World War I, the Germans marching through Belgium and hearing my father say, "They're just too strong for them" or words to that effect. So I was brought up, cut my literary teeth, so to speak, on war atrocities. Later on as I grew up and became a young man I listened to the teachers who had come back from the war, who were tremendously disillusioned with the whole process and the unprofitable end of what some of them, at least, had seen as an idealistic venture. And then I went to Oxford as an undergraduate and observed that all of the professors were either very old or they were young men in their twenties. There was no one in between. What had happened was that the cream of the British intellectuals had volunteered for service in 1914 and had been killed in the trenches. A whole generation of intellectuals died at that point. Thus, what brought me to the topic that we're going to talk about tonight was experiencing in the 1930's the knowledge that World War II was inevitable, and that I, as an individual, could do nothing whatsoever about it. I decided to do what I could through scientific research to understand this phenomenon with the idea that hopefully in the future it might be controlled or eliminated. This is not just a purely academic exercise for me; it arises out of a very strong personal feeling. I am what I shall call a personal pacifist, that is, I would not take part in war, personally. But I can see situations in which, in the present state of the world, it might be a preferable action to some others.

Behind this question of the relationship between individual aggression and war is the question of what an individual can do. Perhaps the best way to start might be simply to present, in a very extreme form, an answer to the proposition that war is a phenomenon which takes place on a different level of organization from individual aggression. It is a different phenomenon and hence has nothing to do with individual aggression. I am just saying this as a way of starting a discussion and I would be very glad to have people differ with it. At the opposite extreme of opinion, I suppose, would be the thought that wars are always started by individuals. I am reminded of listening to Professor North, the political scientist who made a very extensive analysis of the causes of World War I. He wrote down everything that was recorded about the start of World War I and put it into a computer and came out with the answer that the Kaiser started it.

FINK: Let me defend Bob North in psychological terms. One of the principal variables he found was the hostility that the Kaiser was expressing in relation to capability: calculations about the summer crises were primarily centered on the hostility variable, hostility felt towards the British, primarily, and less on the capability dimension. That is, how were the German armies going to cope with this very large land army the Russians had and with the British navy and the French army which were highly rated. North dealt with the crises in terms of the individual decision-makers and that's one way to approach the relationship of the individual to the onset of war in terms of crises. He examined the time when the individual decision-maker, as an individual, has to make certain decisions and carry with him certain preconceptions emotions and feelings that may have some effect on the outcome.

SCOTT: It seems to me that here you have a system which is set up to produce war and what you are saying, I guess, is that the individual in that system does have a great deal of power to determine whether or not war shall take place.

FINK: It's crisis decision-making, yes.

SCOTT: How about President Nixon and the Vietnam War, in that case?

FINK: That would fall into the same category. That is, it is in distinction to other more macro-approaches which would not deal with individual decision-makers, *per se*, but would deal with the aggregate units, aggregate nation-states, and their behavior. But when one is studying crises, one of the most profitable ways to go about it, at least as far as I've seen, is to deal with the decision-maker as an individual in that time-stress situation.

SIVERTS: Since you posed that question and it's also in the title of this session, "individual aggression as a cause of war," and since you took almost mockingly the position, let's say the extreme, of saying that individual aggression is not a cause of war, I will agree that this is not the way of posing questions. This problem has been cropping up over and over again. It's biological, cultural, and social. One way of mapping this out is from the point of view of social anthropology. We need all the help from psychologists and biologists to depict the premises for studying and describing social processes and then, of course, individual aggression as it appears in all mammals, at least in primates. But from there we have to discuss what's going on within society from a comparative point of view. Then I would, as a point of departure, offer the position that individual aggression, as such, is not a cause of war. This has been repeated here from time to time, but this is a more aggressive way in which I do it now: that we could discuss war but not as caused by individual aggression.

SCOTT: Various people have quoted studies on the behavior and physiology of soldiers under modern combat conditions and they report that there is not any great unanimity of emotional response. In some cases it's boredom, in many cases simply fear, and seldom, if ever, anything like genuine anger, the sort of thing that one would think of in a primitive sort of way as being associated with warfare.

AMSBURY: We have to remember that the Kaiser did not have the authority to make war. He had somewhat more authority than the King of England in appointing the Prime Minister, but not much more. He was a ceremonial head. In Session 2 someone asked which biological characteristics are involved in warfare. The fact that this late in the discussion somebody could ask that question suggests that it may be that we are discussing the wrong biological traits. For instance, when we discuss aggression and aggressiveness in connection with war — either some of the kinds of war that anthropologists study, or the kind that apparently most of the people here are anxious to get on to — maybe what we really should be considering is not man's capacity for aggressiveness, but man's capacity for identification, for believing that his dignity and integrity depend upon somebody else's honor and dominance over others. This ties in with the fact that the Kaiser was a ceremonial head of the state, used as we use our flag, to fixate people's attention and their identifications. People will go to war in Vietnam even though they doubt very much whether they should. Once you get over there, and they shove you out in the front lines there is no doubt that you have to preserve yourself. Even if you intend to desert, I assure you it is not easy to do this safely, certainly not comfortably, because it is hard to convince those guys over there that you are trying to desert the army, not them personally — and with these guys back here, if they get any suggestion of it, you are going to have a hard time too.

CARROLL: It's been pointed out a number of times in studies done after World War II and the Korean War by S. L. A. Marshall and others that something like 80 percent of the combat soldiers would not fire rifles in combat even in situations in which it would have been easy for them to do so, that is, in which it would not have been especially dangerous to get out there and fire. Some of them preferred to fire at their own officers. On the other hand very few desert and, in terms of a certain kind of participation and support in the war, they remained at their places and supported war. They choose to make the war exist by continuing to participate, but I do think that there is some significant difference between supporting the war in that way, by staying physically, and, on the other hand, engaging in fighting behavior. I think that the assumption is that their staying means that they are fighting, but that's not the case.

SCOTT: I think there is certainly a field for study here, but it requires war in order to do it.

CARROLL: This relates to what Ruth Jacobs was saying earlier about a need to study compliance behavior. That is, maybe it's not aggression we have to study but compliance, and I think Bill Eckhardt, who works with the Committee and Peace Research Institute, has also lately been saying that what we have to study is conformity rather than aggression if we want to understand modern forms of warfare.

SCOTT: There is another factor there, too, which is made use of by the military probably as a result of centuries of experience, and that is that the business of living together, particularly doing things together in a routine way (a very good example is the old-fashioned, close-order drill), has the result of imparting a feeling of security. This feeling is completely false; nevertheless an individual having been inducted with a group and so on feels safer with the group than he would if he would desert, although the facts would be that he would be a damn sight safer if he would leave at least temporarily.

KRAKAUER: There is another point which many people don't think about so often, and that is that only in the human species is self-preservation not always the top value or the top need. As we grow up, our hierarchy of values sometimes changes. For example, take the common examples of racing drivers or circus performers, who voluntarily risk death. Then let's take another area: suicide. It's a common psychiatric observation that many suicides are performed for spite, to teach some-body a lesson. There are also people who are willing to die for love or religion or for pride or, we have to add, willing to die for their country, because their country becomes some kind of a super symbol that super-sedes the survival needs.

SCOTT: You have to be not only willing to die but willing to kill someone else, which is, perhaps, a different thing.

CARROLL: I suspect you are quite right and that there is, particularly in young males, at least from the kind of behavior that we see in our society, a real reward in risking one's life, not only in warfare, but in other things like mountain-climbing, car-driving, and the like.

KRAKAUER: There are many examples. Another area that we have tended to avoid — I don't mean avoid, really — I simply mean that we keep talking about these basic values of survival and sex, whereas in our species (on Maslow's hierarchy, for example) the need for love and companionship, the need for prestige, self-esteem, become tremendously important values and they are, in the long run, in *Homo sapiens*, biological.

HUBER: If we want to talk about the role of individual aggression in the etiology of things like warfare, we have to be concerned with what we might term objectification. That is to say, how an individually ex-perienced and perceived state of being, an inclination to do violence to someone, can be translated into terms which can be communicated to others to motivate and mobilize them. In other words, the language which each different society provides for mobilizing the group is surely part of the relationship between an individual subjective state of affairs and the other end of the continuum at which you get mobilization of an entire community to do some kind of violence. What kind of lan-guages do different societies provide for individuals to communicate with others and mobilize others and manipulate others in terms of their own subjective feelings?

SCOTT: Are these subjective states necessary for war? Can war take place without them, simply by the presence of an apparatus which can be set in motion by a given individual? For example, the President of the United States could, theoretically at least, order someone to push the button in one of the missile silos.

HUBER: In a sense, then, that would be a peculiarity of the particular American way, or Western way, of language for talking about these things and that would be an institutional form which made it possible for a particular individual, one particular individual, to objectify some kind of sentiment, but in a way that influenced the lives of millions.

SCOTT: Would he have to do that? Would he have to have that sentiment in order to do this?

HUBER: Oh, well, that's another question. But, I mean as far as the question of how an individual sentiment could be related to the onset of a war, the question would be how could an individual influence the course of events. The only means he has available are the ways he has for communicating with the other members of his group.

SCOTT: I think one of the difficulties here with doing something, any practical action, is the fact that we have a system set up, not just a national system, but an international system, such that it is very difficult for an individual to do anything about it. I'm referring, of course, to the phenomenon of the arms race, which results in continued escalation and eventually in the danger of war.

CORNING: I wish to make a comment relating to Dr. Carroll's point and the mention of leader-follower relations. In another aspect, it is perhaps complementary to the desirability of studying conformity or compliance behavior especially where there is not just compliance with the group in a diffuse sense, but compliance with the leader figure whose authority, whose judgment is trusted. (The mass of individuals are willing to follow that person's lead in coordinating their behavior with the behavior of the leader.) A complement to that idea is the discussion of the subjective aspects, subjective states associated with individual participation, and how individuals come to be oriented to feel hostility toward some external sources. This is very interesting from several points of view, one of which is that there does seem to be a capacity for readiness to orient one's emotion, feelings of hostility, toward some external other, which under certain circumstances comes to be programmed in some way by the culture, either in diffuse ways or through cues from leaders. Again, it may be a dimension of leader-follower relations that we're looking at. Followers take cues from leaders not only for their behavior but for attitudes towards external others. The leader exercises an extraordinary ability to orient those emotions, that emotional substrate, which is a contributing factor to participation in group violence toward an enemy, the perception of an enemy.

RICHARDS: Anthropologists study compliance behavior. It's called enculturation, and I think that therein may lie part of the rub: when you are enculturated you are taught the norms, what is acceptable behavior. This is compliance behavior. Anyone who wants not to do what the group expects one to do always finds himself in the bind of saying, "I don't particularly want to do that, but I have been taught to comply with the norms." When you say we should study compliance behavior you have to look at it from this particular perspective of enculturation.

Anthropologists always have a bind about dealing with individuals, because most of us have been conditioned to think about the individual or the great man theory as not permissible anthropological dogma. We get conditioned in undergraduate school and we know damn well we're going to flunk our Ph.D. comps if we say anything to the contrary and so when it comes to dealing with the individual, we have to say, sure Napoleon or Adolf Hitler or Jesus or somebody came along and did certain things, but it was only because the culture was ready to allow him to do it. And that's the way we think about it.

Then, if you look at war, you're caught up in the problem of who starts it. If 90 percent or 70 percent or whatever it was said, "I don't really want to be here, and what the hell am I doing here in the first place," there must have been an awful lot of people who were shooting at their own officers. I just can't accept that as realistic. I have never met anybody who really wanted to be over there in the midst of a shooting war, even the ones who really thought they were saving the world for something.

I would suggest taking it from the anthropological entry point. What we've got is a system, a cultural or sociocultural system, which says that there is some kind of pecking order and there are going to be people who are going to be more aggressive than other individuals. In a social system these individuals are going to be able to find themselves in a position of leadership and they're going to be able to choose from a number of alternatives as to whether they want to make war. We're going to have to deal with the individual from the point of view of alternatives in the sociocultural system. There are choices that people can make and somehow the people who want to be leaders, the entrepreneurs, the cultural manipulators, are the ones that get into leadership positions. Because they are aggressive personalities there is almost a pressure for them to be aggressive once they are in leadership positions and where else can you be more aggressive than to make some kind of war, whatever war be defined as?

SCOTT: One response that I would make is that the idea of the individual is essentially a myth; in other words, there are no human individuals. Any person, even if he's in the desert, is responding to other people whom he has known in the past and so forth. There is almost no situation in which any human being is behaving as if he were an independent entity, not responding to others around him. They are of course a highly social species. This notion might take in the sort of thing that you are talking about. In other words, there are, in any organized system, certain key individuals who do have a certain amount of decision-making power.

RICHARDS: I'm not talking about the power; I'm talking about the fact that they want to be in power. They want to be manipulators. That's why they get into that leadership position. Let's take the anthropology department. Who wants to be the chairman except somebody who likes sitting there at meetings, making decisions?

CARROLL: The source of all the casualties in modern warfare is not primarily from individual rifle fire, but from artillery, bombs and so forth, which are at a distance.

SCOTT: In other words, you don't want to shoot anybody you can see.

CARROLL: People don't. There are 10 percent who will fire repeatedly, that's the other part of that statistic, that 10 percent ... or there's 4 percent of volunteers for the armed forces who will volunteer for combat. But it's only 4 percent. Of course, 4 percent could do a lot of shooting.

FINK: I'd like to respond to Scott's original question in terms of the extreme alternatives that you laid out. It seems to me that there is a position, a logically and empirically almost unassailable position that one can take, and that is that individual aggression is not a sufficient condition for the occurrence of war. That means two things: it means that individual aggression itself will not produce wars; it also means that many instances of individual aggression do not produce wars. Therefore, individual aggression, at least in that sense, cannot be taken as a sufficient condition for war. On the other hand, the question of whether individual aggression is a necessary condition for the occurrence of war is a tougher one to deal with. The question is, what way does it or does it not enter into the causal nexus producing war. In order to answer that, we've got to get more precise about what you mean by individual aggression and in what way you want to conceptualize the beginning of a war or the continuation of a war once it is started. In terms of what individual aggression, how many individuals, in what particular way do these get combined, and what other factors are involved in the process, and can you find an instance of war that did not entail individual aggression in its causal pattern in an effort to move in that direction? That puts one somewhere in between the two extremes that you posed at the beginning.

SCOTT: The viewpoint that you are proposing is that, yes, it has something to do with warfare, but not everything. Would that be a fair way of putting it?

FINK: No, because I'm really leaving that question open as to whether it has anything to do with it. That is, I'm not rejecting that alternative by saying that we really do not have an answer yet as to whether it's a necessary condition for the occurrence of war. If it's not necessary then it doesn't have anything to do with it, or may not.

ROPER: An article in *Fortune* magazine in January has a lot of recent research on the hypothalamus and aggression and the XYY factor, and so on. That article talked about studies that were being done about how infants who were maltreated would more likely be aggressive when they're older than if they were very peacefully treated. This seems to me to be related to what we're talking about in that if you do have a large group of aggressive males and if you don't have warfare to put it outside, you're going to get it inside. But you don't need external aggression if people have grown up in the peaceful way and been treated peacefully as infants.

SCOTT: What happens to the case where you have your peaceful community organized in this way so they do not need to release aggression, but next door there is a community which has been treated in the opposite way? What happens then?

ROPER: Then you would have them on the defensive and of course we do know anthropologically of the various categories of societies. There are some that are really just defensive, they don't seem to seek out warfare, but they do defend themselves.

RICHARDS: Again we're back to the question of individual aggression in the context of warfare. For example, there have been cultures such as the Vikings where there was a great deal of individual motivation, apparently, that led them to engage in raiding. This is individual aggression. But certainly we would have to say that it's culturally channeled, and this gets back to the question about commitment and the conformity aspect and identification because actually that's just begging the question. You are just moving the whole thing back one notch, because if you get people who are conforming to behavior in engaging in warfare, you also get people who are conforming in peace behavior and so then the question simply moves back. Why does this culture enculturate people into warfare, where the other one enculturates them into peacefare, if you want to call it that? So you really haven't answered the question but have simply moved it from one level to another. Whether they're fighting because of aggression which is encouraged by the society, or they are not fighting because of peacefulness which is encouraged by the society, the question remains: Why? You are still left with the same question as to why does one society allow the aggression to take place and this goes back to your comment about the aggressive leader, who gets in charge and is then followed. You might say why does one society let this kind of leader get in, whereas other societies do not. For instance, in Turnbull's discussion of the forest people, he points out that the person who pushes doesn't get anywhere in that society. He is the very person who gets turned off. There are a lot of societies that do this, where you have the one person who really tries to lead and ends up getting no place because he's the one person who can't restrain himself enough to do everything right and thus become the real leader who expresses the group consensus. *A street corner society* points out the leader in many cases as the one who expresses the group consensus, but you've got to wait for it. If you try to force it, what happens is you get ignored. So this means there are societies which don't let an aggressive leader take over in some cases. Whereas, in another society, they may. And again, why? This is where I think you run into some questions.

On the aspect of why soldiers fight, Stoffer's study of *The American soldier* indicated they weren't fighting for our ideals. They weren't fighting for home and mother; they weren't fighting for democracy or anything like that. They were fighting so their squad wouldn't be ashamed of them. In other words, the reason for fighting was the immediate reference group, not all the ideals or anything else that was set up as a reason for war. It was because you didn't want to let those guys down who were depending upon you, and you were depending on them and you didn't want them to let you down. And that, by heck, is why you did your fighting, popular wars or otherwise. So, I think that as anthropologists we should perhaps be looking at this a little bit more and not necessarily just at the aggression of man but the interplay between individual aggression and the social glorification of war or denigration of war or whatever.

SCOTT: How do you explain the fact that though the Vikings were the terror of Western Europe, their descendents culturally (and presumably biologically), the Danes, are now one of the most notoriously peaceful groups in Europe.

RICHARDS: You might say they got Christianized. The religion in the earlier period said that the only way you could go to Valhalla, which was the good place to be, was to die in battle and get carried off by a

Valkyrie. I don't know how much these jokers believed it, but the point is that they could very well have believed that if you died fighting you went to heaven, a good place where there was plenty of food, a good roaring fire, lots of women with liquor coming around to you. So who wants to die in bed? That's when you went down to the cold place where it was eternally misty and rainy and there wasn't anything interesting to do anyhow.

SCOTT: Whenever I get completely discouraged about doing anything about war, I think of the Danes. They at least have been able to change, if no one else has.

CANCRO: One thing I reacted to was the earlier tendency to look upon compliance behavior in a value judgment way, as if compliance behavior is automatically bad, but for society to exist, there must be a fair amount of compliance. We agree that when we drive our automobiles we shall treat a red light one way and a green light another way. You may call that other driver compliant, but I call him colleague when he follows the same conventions that I do. It makes life more livable. I do think it's important for us to be careful to avoid some of the kind of values that are built into these terms.

In 1973, for technologically advanced nations there's a very high probability that it's not sufficient that decisions are made dispassionately. We must be aware that the process and the means of carrying through decisions are established — you have a military force, you have a propaganda machine, etc. Another question is, "Why do we allow this kind of power to remain in the hands of our leaders?" This is a particularly important question in industrialized nations, where activeness and aggressiveness are looked upon in a positive way. Whether individual aggression or the failure to suppress individual aggression in a particular culture may play some role in the compliance of the individuals in that culture in allowing that kind of power to remain in the hands of a few individuals is particularly pertinent when we realize that to most countries war is not a continuous or frequent occurrence. You're talking about an every 20–30–40 year kind of phenomenon. There obviously is a period when people will not allow this power out of their hands, but apparently over time things change. The balance changes and there is a willingness to allow these decisions or at least a passive compliance for these decisions. I think the role of individual aggression might offer some insight there.

SCOTT: One of the dangers here, and one which is possibly an organizational danger, is that of the typical hierarchical military organization, wherein one individual at the top essentially has the power to make decisions and he has relatively little feedback from other individuals lower down. We have that in our society, in the president, and I certainly agree that that kind of power is no longer appropriate and should be limited. I hope that other people see it the same way.

MRS. ESSER: I want to continue the point about the possibility that aggression isn't quite so necessary to warfare. For one thing, there are usually social sanctions in every society against not going to war, if it happens to be a decision of society to declare war or commit war on another society. Secondly, there have been a lot of wars in the history of human populations which stemmed from ideological beliefs, which seem to be far more important than innate aggression in man.

JACOBS: I think that we ought to talk a little bit about social organization because it seems to me that's more important at this stage in history than individual aggression. Quincy Wright and Pitirim Sorokin, in their monumental studies on war, came to the conclusion that stable and democratic countries started or engaged in fewer wars than unstable and autocratic countries. It seems from the evidence that it is the social organization that prompts people within a nation to comply in warfare. And where I think we ought to go in this conference is in looking at our own social organization, since we are the nation which has a pretty bad record.

It has been mentioned a number of times that people have to turn against an out-group in order to vent aggression, whatever that is. I am reminded of a very interesting essay by George Herbert Mead called "International-mindedness and national-mindedness," which was in answer to an essay by William James "On the moral equivalent to war." Mead pointed out that you have to have national-mindedness before you have international-mindedness and by that he meant a sense of community, a sense of integration, a society where people's needs for community, etc., were met. That sounded like exactly the opposite of the kind of society we have and the kind of society that exists in most of Western culture. It seems more appropriate to look at the kind of social structures we have developed and the kinds of ways we might reconstruct our social structures rather than to get into endless arguments on the evolutionary, "basic motivational structure of man," and so forth. In my lifetime I have seen a tremendous reconstruction of personality in the Soviet Union and in China (old China hands who were there before the Revolution and then went back will tell you that the people are entirely different). We have empirical evidence in our own generation that human nature is quite plastic. It changes when there is social reconstruction.

SCOTT: That is a very good point and one that I don't think has been raised too often so far: to try to look at this problem in a positive way rather than a completely negative way. One of my colleagues, Ben Rosenberg, has pointed out to me that in this whole field of harmful aggression, whether it be in war or on the individual level, we've been dominated by disease theories. In disease theory, you find out the cause and you eliminate the cause and everything is perfectly happy after that. Rosenberg also points out that psychologists know all kinds of things about suffering, pain, mental disease, all that sort of thing. But they can't give you any answers as to what makes an individual happy, what makes a good life. They haven't bothered to study this sort of thing, and I suspect this may be true in other disciplines as well. Years ago as a sort of practical step which didn't work out I suggested that as well as the Department of Defense in the government we ought to have a Department of Peace. I was hoping that perhaps President Nixon in his enthusiasm during his first term and coming from a Quaker background and so on, might take this up as a political gesture. As you know, it didn't work.

TEFFT: It seems to me we also ought to study the latitude which various societies give to two things: opting out, giving the individual a chance to opt out of a particular combat situation, and the role which various societies give to the pacifist. Thinking of the Cheyenne, for example, when an enemy killed a Cheyenne, usually the nearest relative, usually a woman, would try to drum up a revenge party and she would berate the warriors for not organizing a party to go out and avenge her son or husband who had been killed. It was not an automatic thing. Individuals had an option to desert revenge parties as well as horse-raiding parties and other raiding parties of this sort. First of all, whether or not they joined would depend on their assessment of the leader himself, whether he had led other war parties and come back with no casualties, or whether he was a poor leader and suffered a lot of casualties. This might determine their decision as to whether or not to go on a raid, and if they decided not to, their decision was acceptable. Likewise, when the raiding party got under way there were various acceptable options open to go back to the village encampment. If their medicines indicated they were in especial danger, they could opt out. If the medicine man who accompanied the war party determined the signs were bad, they might all go back. I don't think there was a negative judgment. So, among the Cheyenne, at least in certain combat situations, they had individual options to refrain from engaging in the various kind of raids and there were no social sanctions brought against them. Compare the situation to ourselves, where apparently many Americans feel that Vietnam is a very horrible war, we shouldn't have gotten into it in the first place, that it's not a war that we should be proud of, but look at those "terrible" people who went to Canada, and so on. We haven't given them absolution yet. Among the Dani it was even worse. There were pacifists there, but unless they had a powerful advocate people would steal their pigs and all sorts of things to make life miserable for them. The reverse side of the coin is what option cultures give to the individuals to refrain from particular forms of combat, to assume a pacifist role, without negative sanctions being brought against them. We too often think that every society metes out the same negative sanctions against the pacifist but I think this is untrue.

SCOTT: What you're saying is that any peaceful society ought to have an institutionalized form of dropping out. In the Middle Ages, if someone wanted to drop out of the conventional rat race of going out and fighting with the neighbors in feudal service, he could always join a monastery, but at the present time, we do not have that kind of institutionalized escape valve.

TEFFT: One of the questions I'm raising is, why don't we? If a president wants to give absolution to draft dodgers, why can't he? Why is there built into the cultural system a feeling that this is a bad, improper thing to do? Not all societies seem to feel this way in certain circumstances.

CLAESSEN: It's possible to demonstrate that people who are seemingly non-aggressive become aggressive under certain circumstances. For instance, before the Second World War in the Netherlands, war and army were certainly not popular. Then the German occupation came and after some weeks and months feelings of unrest started growing and some people, usually simple people — rather religious people — found problems in their concerns with this new situation of occupation. After long deliberation, they started to fight the Germans. This was a very great decision. They wrote about this question in the underground press and then they shot the first German. It was a big problem, but they felt they had to do it. Under other circumstances they would never have shot another human. They were seemingly not aggressive but at this moment they had no choice. Perhaps in most of us there is a possibility for aggression if the circumstances are there.

SCOTT: I agree that at least the potentiality is there in any human being.

ESSER: I was concerned and actually pleased by the accent Dr. Smith laid on the individual as a leader. I do not think that it is possible that individual aggression accounts for war; I fully agree with Dr. Fink. I don't even think that it could be a necessary cause, but I do think that men, and here we go back to the biological basis, all men look to leaders. Since you are sitting there and are leading us tonight, naturally we give you the attention. This is a typical primate characteristic and therefore, also a typical human characteristic. Consequently, we are always watching for a leader, and as Dr. Smith and Dr. Richards indicated, if the leader, for one reason or another, makes the choice for a course of action, we'll follow. Very often this is a religiously or ideologically inspired choice. I mention in my paper ideoeffective magnification, which is the word that Tomkins used to indicate that an idea symbol, a reasonable thing, can be changed and laden with emotional value and all of a sudden assume a life of its own, purely because of that affect that we want to give to it. We come back, therefore, to the fact that if we are leader-oriented as other primates are, it becomes a question of what the individuals who are our leaders choose for us to be oriented toward. Our human nature is indeed so plastic that we will go along with the choice, as long as we believe the leader. This is really the crux of the situation. If we assume this plasticity and we know that we can learn from each other, then what can we find biologically that we learn by? And, as I said before, we learn by the orientation to our own group and, within that, orientation to the one who is the leader (possibly of an idea or a religion). It is for us, therefore, to make the choice, not to refer to anything innate. No, we as leaders determine. I remember and come back always to this, that our determination is based on the fact that we have a central nervous system, a brain that is accustomed, unfortunately or fortunately, to certain ways of reaction and the reaction is one of following and looking toward something that is attractive to us.

SCOTT: I've been interested in the phenomenon of leadership in animals — particularly in sheep — where the leader in a naturally formed flock is the oldest female. It is fairly obvious how this leadership arises. It is simply from the fact that the young lamb follows its mother, and then as the female grows up and has other lambs, her lambs follow her. Eventually you get the situation wherein the oldest female in the flock is the leader. The males do not have this advantage; that is, they can't feed the young, and the only kind of leadership we see in the males is essentially a tendency in a male flock for a younger male to follow older males. Leadership has not been very much studied in animal behavior. People have studied dominance and subordination a great deal and they have confused it with leadership. (I remember one case where somebody was talking about a group of black bucks, another ungulate where the females tend to lead the flock, and he kept talking about male leadership. I couldn't figure out what he was talking about, and it turned out that the individual was describing the action of a male in rounding up and driving the females. To him, this was a leader; in other words there is a good deal of confusion.) In our own society, in our own culture, there is a tendency to assume that the leader is the best fighter and that the best fighter is the leader, irrespective of what actually happens. I think these two things need to be kept separate: control through fighting and force and control through leadership developing a following relationship. I think you'll admit that in order for a person to be a successful leader, his followers have to be trained to follow.

ESSER: No, I don't admit that. I totally disagree with the last sentence.

SCOTT: You mean they will follow, no matter what.

ESSER: No, No. I believe the successful leader in human affairs is that person who can best construct the realities that can be applied right now. He automatically gets the following, not because we have been trained to follow, but because we recognize the truth, we recognize the structure as it stands and as it is useful or efficient or what have you. I agree fully with you that in our society, because we are so success-oriented, the aggressive structure, the competitive structure (the structure that brings in the most "buck" or the most "bang"), is often the one that carries the day, but it doesn't need to be so. I go back to what I said about our central nervous system. We have choices in the system. That doesn't mean we have a free will. The undetermined free will, I think, is a fiction. But we have choice and the choices that we can make from day to day in everything that we do should really start to be used. This is what I look forward to. O.K., let's use the choices. We have them available and we can do it; at the moment I am ready, I speak for myself, TO FOLLOW. See, it's just as simple as that.

M. NETTLESHIP: I think there is a very interesting example just at the end of what Dr. Esser is saying. He is showing us that there are various kinds of leaders and leadership. I don't know much about sheep. I do know about beef and dairy cattle, and there is more than one kind of leadership with those animals. Yes, usually a senior cow will lead the herd to do certain kinds of activities. However, the bull does lead. It's not a matter of rounding up; the bull does lead parts of the herd at times for other kinds of activities, and I don't see any reason why one couldn't describe both of these as leadership and consider them in that way. By extension, there may be more than one kind of leadership in human society too. To say that there is only this one kind of leader, and possibly only one kind of follower, is ignoring a lot of other phenomena that may very well relate to this.

SCOTT: I think that the same individual may, under different circumstances, take both roles; that is, either be a leader or a follower.

COOPER: It might be interesting to bring up the following case now, thinking of the relationship between aggression and war and the role of individuals, and the role of particular individuals in leadership positions — to get very close to home. I don't know how many people have read Halverson's book, *The best and the brightest.* (I happen to have worked under Kennedy for a couple of years, so I tend to think that he was probably right in his analysis.) The following story seems to be relevant here. It is provocative, so we can think about it though it may not necessarliy be true. Kennedy had just become President and of course was extremely young. He was going to a meeting with Khrushchev. Harriman, who had recently asked for a meeting with Khrushchev and had managed to bring it off and had found what kind of a person he was and how to get along with him, wanted to advise Kennedy how to handle his first meeting with the great leader of a great power. Harriman said play it soft, be relaxed, have a sense of humor, don't take anything he says seriously. The best thing to do is establish a relationship with him and later you can get into specifics, but DON'T get into any kind of argument. Don't try to test his strength and his mettle. First of all, he knows your wife is far more beautiful than his, and he has certain kinds of jealousy; you are young and handsome, etc. So Kennedy went over with that advice and did just the opposite because he felt that he had to show that he was NOT a weak, young, inexperienced president. Khrushchev led him by the nose all during the week and Kennedy was simply on the ropes at the end of the meeting and left, coming home completely dejected. He then made the decision, according to Halverson, to change the involvement in Vietnam from merely advisors to combat orientation. He had to find someplace to show, to prove to Khrushchev, that he wasn't what Khrushchev thought he was. There is some feeling that this kind of emotional desire to be aggressive, a conscious desire, might have been a trigger for the rest of our heavier involvement in Vietnam.

YOUNG: I'd like to try to put this discussion together with some of the advances I think we've made so far today. Let's start with a definition of aggressive behavior. It's behavior that produces spacing or submission. Now what is war? It is an extremely highly organized form of aggressive behavior. It's a form organized by a highly organized society that has survived, that has pushed all other forms of society out of the way, because it has organized this extremely aggressive and very effective form of behavior. Turney-High has written a long book bewailing what punk soldiers the Indians and other primitives are. We don't let our soldiers get by with walking out of battle; we train them so they will fight. Now, when a society has become organized in this fashion, then surely it has to somehow stimulate its soldiers to engage in aggressive behavior. We're going to have to engage in behavior that will produce spacing or submission and our soldiers do that and every individual of them does that. But when it comes to organizing the motives of society, it doesn't depend entirely on the aggressive motives of the soldiers. It may depend upon their submissive motives. It may depend upon their pride; it may depend on conformity. As a matter of fact it's likely to depend on all those motives. In other words, everything that's been said tonight, it seems to me, is picking up one facet after another of all the facets that such a society relies on to get the type of aggressive behavior that has enabled it to be so viable. I AGREE WITH EVERY-BODY.

It's more important to find remedies than it is to look at causes, but it is very important to look at causes because that will help you find the remedy. I think that we need to keep this in mind. This is our problem: how do we change a society that is thoroughly organized to put people into war? We probably need to put a lot of attention to re-organization, to new forms of social organization, rather than putting a great deal of attention on people's motivations. What kind of motivation can we rely on to develop new forms of organization that will enable societies to survive and still not fight wars?

SCOTT: That is something that I would certainly strongly agree with; that war is an organized activity and consequently it can be defined as a problem in organization and so the solution, it seems to me, in the long run, is one of developing new forms of organization. It is very obvious that these must be not only organization on a national scale, but on an international scale. The fact that our attempts at international organization have not worked too well in the past did not discourage us from seeing this to be communication not on a national scale, but on an international scale. The fact that our attempts at international organization have not worked too well in the past, should not discourage us from seeing this. The essence of this problem, I think, is essentially what you've stated and since you've said it so well, I think perhaps we'd better stop at this point.

Psychological and Psychiatric Considerations

Chaired by R. D. GIVENS and A. H. ESSER
Discussion of papers by P. CANCRO, M. N. WALSH and B. G. SCANDALIS,
D. KRAKAUER, U. R. VON EHRENFELS, J. P. SCOTT

GIVENS: We shall begin this session with a summary of Dr. Cancro's paper.

CANCRO: The commonly felt revulsion over war has led many people to conceptualize it as a form of madness. This is particularly attractive because man is unique in his awareness of both his mortality and the risk of death inherent in war. I think that as with most temptations it is perhaps best avoided. I think the contribution of the psychological sciences to the reduction of the risk of war has been minimal historically. I also think it will continue to be so. War is a state of armed conflict between political units. This is quite different from individual violence which is a form of intraspecific aggression in which destructive physical behavior is directed at the person of another human or at a symbolic representation, for example, property, and accompanied by intense negative aspects. As we know, many of the activities of war are not accompanied by intense negative aspects and are rather boring.

It is apparent, since the phenomenon of war is far more complex than individual violence, that there are profound limitations to any generalizations that may be drawn from individual violence to group violence, let alone to that particular form of group violence called war. Now, the feud between two families may have some interesting similarities to war and may serve as a major model. Obviously there are major dissimilarities as well: there are social, economic, political, racial, and ethnic factors that contribute to the ease with which states go to war that are quite distinct from those that may operate in family feuds. Perhaps the task that we can give to psychiatry and psychology is to identify more clearly those psychological elements in man that contribute to this wish for and fear of war. There is no *a priori* reason for assuming that the knowledge of these factors will have any practical value in the prevention of war. On the other hand, there is no reason to assume that it will not.

There are two sources of psychiatric theorizing. It would be hard to find two areas which have been more poorly represented to the general public or more misunderstood. Nevertheless, an awareness of the innate or biological contribution to aggressive behavior has led many people to a position which can only be described as biological fatalism. They speak in a resigned way of man's nature as if it were immutable. A study of ethology does help us to understand the existence of an innate or genetic component to aggressive behavior. The real contribution of ethology is not that man has a biological heritage, but that this biological heritage is mobilized and shaped by an environmental experience. Anthropological studies can show us different social organizations that have been effective in influencing human violence in a variety of cultures and thereby extending and amplifying the animal work. There are societies which can be characterized as relatively warlike or unwarlike. Comparative study of their social organizations can be helpful in identifying those structures which inhibit and those which enhance warring behavior. Understanding of those customs, values, and institutions that encourage man to make war, for example, in primitive societies might be helpful in the study of the technologically advanced states as well. Obviously, there are differences between such societies, but it is a well-established strategy in science to study the simplest case first.

The concept of an aggressive drive as posited by Freud has undergone an appalling series of vicissitudes and has itself been aggressed on. It's a theoretical construct, which is helpful in psychologizing about human behavior. It does not determine future behavior in a preordained, fixed manner. It is absurd to explain national differences in frequency of war on the basis of national differences in the strength of aggressive drive. Interestingly, when Freud wrote about war, he did not bring in the "aggressive drive theory" at all. (He did write about war in the famous exchange of letters with Albert Einstein.)

We make the distinction between accidental and deliberate wars, which I take as a useful one. We must also recognize that there are many positive benefits that a society derives from wars. It is an effective way of mobilizing the population and unifying it in the face of some common threat, real or imaginary. When we begin to look at the range and variety of real benefits derived by the power structure of any state through the simple expedient of going to war, we are perhaps less puzzled at its frequency than we were before. War pays for many groups and so long as it does it will remain attractive to them. Needless to add, the territorial and the economic benefits for the victor have historically often been quite real. I think at times we have psychologized as a kind of red herring to obscure the simple reality that war benefits segments of the population which hold a disproportionate share of political power.

In general, I feel the contribution of the psychological sciences to the goal of preventing war is not likely to be major; war is a complex system, only to be solved by means which are equally complex and which reflect insights from multiple disciplines. We as a field do have a certain knowledge about how human beings function in communities. Communities are held together by rational bonds based on the recognition and identification of common needs, purposes, and activities. The more we can intensify an identification with all men rather than with the man of a particular unit, be it political, racial, ethnic, or religious, the more we reduce the likelihood of war. The more we can help people to see others as basically similar to themselves, the more difficult they will find it to perpetrate aggressive acts. Whoever will unite different political units in common purposes will reduce the likelihood of those units warring with each other. In general, the more we force the transcultural identifications and human interdependency in real and visible ways the more we lessen the danger of all forms of human intraspecies aggression — including war.

GIVENS: The paper by Walsh and Scandalis will be summarized by Mrs. Scandalis due to Dr. Walsh's absence.

SCANDALIS: Our paper is "Institutionalized forms of intergenerational male aggression." Our premise is that most of human behavior is motivated by the unconscious portion of the human mind. Thus, to understand institutionalized behavior as well as individual behavior, it is necessary to examine the unconscious portion of the psyche. We cannot explain an institution merely by reference to society or culture. It must also be explained in reference to human motivations, for institutions are basically the result of human psyche, though the form is designed by culture. Unfortunately, however, forbidden and unpleasant psychic content are frequently held out of conscious awareness, and because this material is not considered, gross misinterpretations of reality and the drawing of inadequate conclusions regarding behavior have resulted.

As an outgrowth of the psychoanalytic approach to an understanding of social motivation and behavior, it is our hypothesis that primitive male initiation rites and modern organized warfare are equivalent behavior patterns arising from the same psychic phenomena. We suggest that both have a single unconscious motivating force in common, which is the Oedipal rivalry. In both initiation rites and the modern military experience, young men are placed in physical danger and often treated with degradation by older men of the society, for the ostensible purpose of making men out of them and promoting solidarity in the society. But in fact, the rites are also a means through which adult males direct their own hostility toward the son generation. In both initiation rites and the military experience, there is an attempt to mute the aggressive feelings of fathers toward sons in a controlled situation, but due to the complexity of civilized culture, in which one institution may serve several purposes, the unconscious motivation that is basic to the institution has been highly disguised.

To explicate the expression of symbolic behavior, derived from father-son aggression projected to an enemy in disguised form, reference is made to the early Egyptian custom of taking the foreskin of a defeated enemy as a prize trophy instead of a head. Whether it is the scalp, the head, or the foreskin that is taken as a trophy, it can be stated that all such trophies express the desire to castrate the enemy. But who is the enemy who needs to be castrated? On the unconscious level it is someone closer to the perpetrator of the act than the unrelated enemy encountered in the battlefield, for he is merely the scapegoat. According to Walsh in a previous paper, the basic motivation for the killing or maiming of other *Homo sapiens*, apart from direct defense against unprovoked attack, is the projection outward of some hated image within that personality. This person is then maimed or killed as a scapegoat, with the unconscious assumption that the internal conflict will then be solved, but in fact it is compounded.

It is our assumption that certain culture traits are necessarily traits which would tend to increase the competition between father and son generations, thus necessitating an abreaction of the hostile feelings existing in both directions between fathers and sons. Examples of such cultural traits are patrilineality, patrilocality, and polygamy, all of which increase male competition. Where male competition is stressed, there seems to be a greater incidence of severe initiation rites and frequent warfare. Psychoanalytic research demonstrates that the Oedipal rivalry alone, of all possible causes, furnishes adequate explanation for such murderous aggression between generations, and therefore the existence of institutionalized situations where sons become the victims of murder at the hands of an enemy as the result of manipulation by the father generation. Such manipulation has been illustrated by the Tiwi, the Murngin, and the Yąnamamö, and, one might add, a most recent war.

In conclusion, we find that initiation rites, warfare, and Oedipal myths are all means by which man attempts to reconcile unconscious psychic conflicts basically related to the competition between the father and son for the mother. The configuration this rivalry takes is molded by a social organization of the society; thus the possibility emerges for widely divergent overt behavior related to the same unconscious impulses. That is, initiation rites, raids, headhunting, or warfare as well as other institutionalized behavior patterns expressing Oedipal rivalry and the means to cope with it.

This statement, of course, represents an oversimplification of the problem, but the elaboration and disguises of such basic, instinctual impulses furnish daily proof of the operation of powerful, unconscious forces in the human psyche of vital importance to the continuation of society. Reorganizing our unconscious motivations gives us some measure of control over overt behavior. Some redirection toward cooperation instead of competition might be a goal to reduce this father-son aggression.

RICHARDS: In their paper, Walsh and Scandalis wrote about the love feelings that exists between generations, and I think this might be important in a comparison between initiation rites and war. In initiation, the actual initiation and treatment of the young generation is in the hands of the older generation who can therefore indulge in love feelings that they may have and keep the whole thing from getting out of hand. Thus, the initiates are really very rarely actually destroyed. In the case of war, the initiation process is in the hands of an enemy who has no need or desire to express any love feelings and the danger of actual death to the son generation is, of course, therefore much higher. This raises the question in my mind: "Is it possible to correlate war, therefore, with societies where the hostility between the father and son generation is greater than it is in societies with only initiation?"

The other thing that somewhat bothers me in looking at the Oedipal explanation is that man is by no means the only animal that demonstrates this vicious hostility between the father and son generation. Tomcats will kill young male kittens and spare young female kittens as soon as they reach the age at which they are apparently distinguishable by smell. Male rats or mice will kill young. I don't know whether they discriminate between male and female. Among many other animals the male animal will kill the younger generation coming along and yet I seriously doubt that it's always involved with an Oedipal situation, especially in the case of cats which seem to have no compunction about breeding with their mothers at all. Consequently it may be that hostility between adult generations and young is a fairly widespread, at least mammalian, phenomenon. Is this perhaps a deep-seated factor that we have been ignoring completely?

EIBL-EIBESFELDT: I would agree with the statements just made that it's improbable that aggressiveness is explained by the Oedipal complex. I may mention that Jung and Adler turned away from this explanation. I think it was Jung who made the remark that it's very improbable that the son indeed would be interested to marry the "old fiddle." Now, if you look at it culturally, you will indeed find that no such wishes are expressed. On the contrary, there exists a strong incest inhibition, which as recent studies by Bishop have shown have a biological base. Kibbutz studies reveal that children who grow up together during a certain critical period (in studies of about 5,000 marriages) in not a single case married each other without a period of separation. All of them considered themselves very friendly, bonded, and considered themselves siblings emotionally, and there was a strong inhibition against falling in love. It seems that there is a critical period in which people learn whom not to fall in love with. Bishop made a detailed study on the subject cross-culturally and there are a number of animals in which the same phenomenon is found. So it seems that the Oedipal complex is fiction. What we find is that there exists a certain rivalry between up-growing generations and adult generations. That this could cause a vicious hostility seems too farfetched. If you would examine how fathers who grow up with their sons are bonded to their sons and to their family in general, you will find quite a different picture. I find it highly speculative to call a vicious hostility between father and son the cause of warfare.

ESSER: Could I ask Dr. Eibl-Eibesfeldt to comment on the claims made about the kittens and the killing of the males.

EIBL-EIBESFELDT: Yes, that happens in some animals, but it's not the general pattern.

ESSER: But, is it indeed a differentiation between male and female killing; I mean does the father go out and kill the males?

EIBL-EIBESFELDT: Well, I don't know that in particular, but if that happens in one species, so what?

A. NETTLESHIP: In America, at least, male cats in heat will attack any male cat or even a female cat who isn't in heat or anything that is in the way or a dog or a human. They will even bite your leg. They don't care.

EIBL-EIBESFELDT: Man is an extraordinary species.

KORTLANDT: It's so often said that killing within a species is a rare pattern. This is definitely not true. In most mammal groups you find that male killing is quite a normal phenomenon. I would rather say that man is pretty unique in that male-male killing is so low in our society. The ultra-romantic idea of mammals living in peaceful ways with one another and having inhibitions to prevent them from killing one another — this is just not true. You find a lot of male-male killing among all of the ungulates, both those that have harems and those that don't. You find it among lions and sea elephants. It is just a fairy tale that male-male killing occurs frequently in man, particularly in wars, and is rare among mammals. It is quite rare in birds, that is true. Among mammals it is quite a common phenomenon. Among humans it is quite rare. There is a fundamental misunderstanding about this.

CANCRO: I would like very much to concur with the remarks just made. In the human species, most killing is across genders. Men usually kill women, women usually kill men; usually it's the mate. Perhaps the period in which we learn whom to love should be extended. But more seriously, to comment on the second paper: I do want to make clear that I am not anti-psychoanalytic in my orientation, but I think we should always make a very real distinction between the meaning of an event and the cause of an event. For example, if I were to have a seizure at this moment, the cause of that seizure would have to be distinguished from the conscious and unconscious meaning of that event to me. Now, if you were to question me afterwards as to what it meant to me and perhaps get my free association and find that I associated it to an orgastic experience or to death, then you would fall into the blunder that the analysts fell into forty years ago when they found these were common fantasies in epileptics and said, "Ah, epilepsy is an orgastic equivalent and if they had good orgasms they would not have seizures." Well, the answer is wrong. They will continue to have epileptic seizures that continue to remind them of something. Now, the fact that you have an association is not an explanatory hypothesis and it is a terrible danger in psychoanalysis that we find that because events have MEANING we attempt to attribute CAUSALITY to the psychological meaning. In terms of the Oedipus complex, I think we should make a very real distinction between the sense of closeness and the intense rivalry feelings that a child can have for the relatively exclusive possession of the nurturing figure, the particular phase of this development, and the idea of vaginal intercourse with the mother. I've treated quite a few psychotics and even some not-so-psychotics and that is not really a very common wish, but wanting to be close to mother, wanting to be loved by mother, wanting to be preferred by mother is a very common wish and one need not even go into a psychopathologically labeled situation to find such wishes. So, again I think we have to understand what Freud meant by the Oedipal complex and I think perhaps the most powerful argument in this regard is that he did not use it in the correspondence with Einstein to explain war.

AMSBURY: I want to reinforce the suggestion that role has a lot to do with the question of incest feelings, and I'll go back to cats for it.

If you raise a mother and son together until the son begins to make advances toward the mother, the mother will reject him. But if they are separated a while just before the son's maturity, when he comes around he will be treated as any other male cat. Now, as to the attacks of tomcats on young males, if the young male grows to maturity and you still have the father around the place, you have to be very careful because the father is apt just to pick up and leave, because he is no longer completely the man in charge, and rather than fight for the place he will go and try to fight for another place.

I think that there are many far more serious reasons why parents and children, not just fathers and sons and mothers and daughters, should have serious resentments against each other than any sexual fantasies they might have about each other. Probably the sexual fantasies are the fantasies of the reinterpreters. I know that if I didn't stop and understand the situation I would have serious resentments over what I went through raising my kids and I'm certain they would have very serious resentments against me. I very frequently said I was sure glad kids didn't hold grudges.

OLDFIELD HAYES: I'd like to comment on the practice of circumcision rites of passage. In the first place, these rites of passage are not universal. They are cultural and they vary from society to society. Some are painful and some are non-painful. Some are surrounded by a lot of ceremony and others are surrounded by very little ceremony — in fact are very casual kinds of practices — they are not universal practices and therefore I don't think that you can choose such cultural traits to account for what we want to call universal tendencies in human populations toward warlike behavior. They also vary in context. They are often accompanied by complementary female initiation rites. They have a high statistical correlation with such things as residence after marriage and sex identity conflict arising from sleeping arrangements during childhood.

In many societies, the female initiation rites are much more drastic and severe than the male initiation rites. For instance, in Sudan, which is traditionally patrilineal, patriarchal, and patrilocal, the female initiation rite is extremely severe. It is, in fact, infibulation, and in my research there I found that it has two functions. The manifest function is to contribute maintenance to the modesty norms of the Muslim Arabs in Sudan and the latent function is to redundantly contribute surety of the legitimacy of the patrilineal members. I contend that each form of initiation rite or *rite de passage* must be considered in its cultural context rather than as a universal trait of human populations accounting for universal behavior forms.

SAXE-FERNÁNDEZ: I would like to emphasize the cultural context of the proposal of the second paper. In general I find the metaphorical world of Sigmund Freud rudimentary but very suggestive, particularly if you apply some of his ideas to what is going on in a post-industrial society, where apparently the traditional distinctions between psychosocial and political marginality seem to be rapidly fading away. The conflict seems to be very clear.

Furthermore, IF, as Margaret Mead has suggested, we are indeed entering a totally new phase of cultural evolution in post-industrial society, and it is the youth of post-industrial society who feel and lead the emergence of a world community in which a distinction between outsiders and aliens is disappearing; IF, as most anthropologists have contended, in post-industrial society, in the eyes of the young, the killing of an enemy is not qualitatively different from the killing of a neighbor; IF in this post-industrial society, by studies of young people, we know that they cannot reconcile the efforts of the generation in power, particularly its readiness to destroy the children of others with napalm, with their readiness to protect their own children; IF for these generations the old distinctions between peacetime and wartime, friend and foe, my group and their group, have lost their meaning; IF the generation in control has failed to provide them with a viable present, much less a viable future, even if they have succeeded on a very primary biological level; IF for these people, the generation in power doesn't offer a workable future, because they feel that their past is rotten, their present obnoxious, their future might be the inorganic; and IF, for the young ones, the future seems to be now; THEN I find here psychiatric definitions and labeling of youthful behavior as schizophrenic, or as "persistent compulsive disorders," or disorders with com-

pulsive components as quite irrelevant to understanding their generational split (or crises, or, if you wish, some form of internal warfare
between cultures).

Being young seems almost deviant and, naturally, the establishment
considers adolescence a major social problem. I find in my research
that establishment psychiatrists in general are fast losing any inhibition
to apply their latest techniques of aversion therapy or other electronic
gadgets, for instant neurosurgery, on their own children. One of the
most interesting statements I've found recently came from a British
psychiatrist who proposes diminishing inhibitions on the part of the
psychiatric profession to apply this therapy on children. He said, "This
is the way which they try to diminish ethical problems to solve the
generation gap." The aversive drug and shock therapies are available
for all the perverts and addicts but for children and adolescents are
still regarded with disfavor ethically and esthetically by psychiatrists.
However, the benefits accruing with the removal of symptoms in certain cases would far outweigh the moral and ethical objections, especially if more acceptable aversive techniques could be developed. The
use of aversive imagery was examined from this point of view and in
the case of this particular group of boys was considered "worthy of
exploration." So it seems to me that, certainly in Sigmund Freud's
world, the son showed respect and was protected by the realm of the
unconscious from his desire to kill the father. In our time, there is no
father to love the son, but there are bureaucrats, dressed-up generals,
corporate managers, presidents, and law-enforcement personnel such
as policemen and psychiatrists.

ESSER: That was a most moving statement. I think you have put the
finger on what I would like to see explicated in this session. But most
important in the last paper and in the paper of Dr. Cancro is the fact
that some unconscious factors were brought forward and for once put
into focus. It is not so important which form we have, because when we
deal with people, with sick people and also with normal people, the
transformations of any inner psychic event can be manifold whether
they show themselves with rivalry, Oedipal conflict, or what have you,
and that has been shown before. The Oedipal conflict is something that
might have occurred in Vienna at the turn of the century in specific
patients but not necessarily in the area where Malinowski did his work.

The point is that we can talk about the dynamics of the transformation and right here, in this session, we see the dynamics of the transformation because everybody brings out from our own experience that
which we have seen and felt about this particular conflict, the Oedipal

conflict. Nobody even reacted to what Dr. Cancro said. Everything on the Oedipal conflict that we might have experienced ourselves came out in every single remark here: it was always father-son. No doubt, Walsh and Scandalis have touched a nerve and that is what we should look at.

Let me tell you that I do not agree with a universal Oedipal complex; I am agreeing that there is something going on which is called rivalry or intergenerational conflict which I have called fear of the stranger. That is another transformation of this dynamic. I would like to ask of Mrs. Scandalis, who suggested that cooperation may replace competition, how would you transform, within the Oedipal complex, the energy that is loosened by intergenerational conflict into cooperation? Could you see anything that points in that direction? I would like to take that and use that as a building block with other suggestions that we had yesterday about how to achieve cooperation or synergy.

SCANDALIS: I don't see any signs of how we can direct this into cooperation, but I can think of ways in which we can reduce the competition between the generations and between males in general. Competition in our society is increasing. This increase has shown in the play of children and Little League baseball is one of them. There are also mini-racing cars in which very small children are taught extreme competition and I think this aggravates the problem. In Russia (I was there several years ago) in nursery schools they try to enforce cooperation by having large toys that children can only play with together and this sort of thing. This sort of cooperation doesn't seem to carry through — it's certainly a competitive society in Russia — but I think less competitive perhaps than in the United States and elsewhere. I don't have the answer that you were asking for.

I would like to reply to a previous remark about the paper. We tried to point out that culture does determine the form of the hostility that the aggression will take and so the fact that there are not initiation rites in all societies doesn't mean that the initiation rites are not the result of an Oedipal conflict or a generational conflict. I would like to broaden this idea about Oedipal rivalry because it has been broadened to a general conflict between generations and in competitive societies as the boy grows up and there is economic competition as well. I think this also plays a very large part in the aggression between the father and son generations aside from the Oedipal rivalry. In patrilineal societies, patrilocal societies, and polygynous societies, the initiation rites seemed to be more severe so there seem to be cultural traits that do minimize this aggression toward the father and son generations. In the case of female initiation rites, which are very severe, I think there is a possibility that there is an identification of the women with the men in this society or these societies, though it certainly needs further investigation. In the societies where there are severe female initiation rites, I'm not sure whether these are in patrilineal societies for the most part or not. I think that in the one you mentioned they were.

MIDLARSKY: I just want to comment on two things. One is on the intergenerational idea. I find difficulty in assimilating it to contemporary international warfare, primarily because we have a case in World War II where the sons went marching off to war with the fathers absent. So here we have a fairly controlled case, within a relatively short period of time, where the factor that is presumed to have some effect, that is intergenerational conflict, in one case may be present and in the other case absent, yet the same phenomenon occurs — that is, war.

Two, Dr. Cancro made a point about Freud's letter to Einstein. If I recall it correctly, I don't think he talked about aggression. I do think he talked about the death wish. This was the collective wish of mankind. I think it was a very depressed feeling, a very depressed sense I got from the letter. I don't think I know what we can learn from it in regard to preventing war.

CANCRO: Your memory is accurate, although it was not the death wish, it was the death drive. I think it is an awfully important distinction for Freud; he never spoke of instinct, he spoke of drive. His conceptualization of the death drive was really not a psychological conceptualization — and that was one of the reasons it never caught on in psychoanalysis. You can't use it. It is, as I mentioned in my paper, a concept that is very similar to what we mean by entropy today. All living systems tend toward inert, non-living states and they are really only at peace when they are dust. He saw this as a kind of quality of all biological systems — there was an inert drive towards the low-energy state, which was the non-living state. He used this in a kind of theoretical, philosophical, and, as you say, very depressed way. First of all he had had over twenty-five operations by that point, was dying, and was living a rather miserable existence, but I think it was more than this. He felt a certain kind of hopelessness about man; he saw man going on a kind of destructive rampage and felt the likelihood that this would change was remote. I think he is right in the sense that if we wait for psychological insight or community "mental health" to have some impact on war, I'll put my money on war. On the other hand, that doesn't mean that we cannot design or introduce social institutions or changes or work in that direction and create instrumentalities which can prevent war, if that is a generally accepted and acceptable goal.

Esser: May I make one comment, because you asked it? I have the letter in front of me. Freud does speak at one point of the Russian Communists. He says, "The Russian Communists, too, hope to be able to cause human aggressiveness to disappear by guaranteeing satisfaction of all material needs and by establishing equality in other respects of all the members of the community. That, in my opinion, is an illusion." That is in the paragraph in which he was talking about his feeling that aggressiveness is part of human competition.

Sipes: I would like to make some comments and ask the others here for some information from their own personal experiences regarding the intergenerational gap and the characteristics of young people today that have been discussed. This information that I am about to relate was gathered at the State University of New York at Buffalo. This was considered to be one of the most radical of the educational institutions. It was a leader in riots. SUNY, Buffalo and UCLA were neck and neck for some time. It seems, at this institution and with my contacts with other kids outside of the institution, that the coming generation (the latest crop of 14- to 20-year olds) has "backlashed" to the standards of previous generations. They are much, much less tolerant of minority groups. They are less concerned for people from other countries. They are much more cooperative in general. The generation gap is closing now. It has reversed in the last ten years and it seems that the sixties generation has passed with relatively few lasting effects. It is over and done with. It was a phase. It was not a permanent change. This is my impression from my limited personal experience with the kids that are coming along in and out of college. I would like to know if anyone else has encountered this.

Amsbury: It's been my observation that the changes that were brought about during that period are the reasons for the backlash. There were definite changes, whether or not they are going to be permanent. (I never heard of such a thing as a permanent change. I have heard of changes that didn't go back to what they were before, but they always got changed to something else eventually.)

Cooper: Stanford University in the latter period of the sixties was more active than any other university. We're not sure exactly why, but the kinds of changes that did occur in the university structures were substantial. I think this is partly a cause for the lack of this kind of aggressive concern for change among the students today. Many of the changes that were being asked for did occur prior to the seventies. Stanford was a very conservative, traditional, parochial type of institution where most of the students were "sons of Republican dentists."

This was the usual reference. The faculty was very narrowly focused on preserving its own image within its traditional academic context, had no focus whatsoever on the reality of society around it, and certainly was not problem-oriented. Today 90 percent or more of the new faculty who have been brought in in the last five or six years have a concern for relating the academic world to the real world. There is a dramatic change within the university itself.

CLAESSEN: I would like to return for a moment to the end of Dr. Cancro's paper where he gives the suggestion that the more we can help people to see others as basically similar to themselves, the more difficult they will find it to perpetrate aggressive acts. I think he's quite right in that, but it will be a kind of balance between the feelings of people in that situation. It would be a precarious balance at the moment that some difference between the groups arises. There are instances of peoples who have basically no cultural differences, no other religion or anything like that — still they fought bloody battles. In our eyes they fought for some small political differences. The more we are similar, the more the balance will be precarious.

SMITH: For the last day and a half I've heard a number of examples of non-realities — not any of them as disturbing as the one that I've just heard concerning the generation gap and the difference between the generation of the sixties and the generations of the fifties and seventies. The generation of the sixties is characterized by Margaret Mead in a way that I find so unbelievably unrelated to anything that goes on outside of perhaps a very narrow sample that it has no sub-stance to it. I bring this up, because one of the things that I have been waiting for is a suggestion that if we are going to talk about the kind of things that seem to be of such great concern to us we might be con-cerned with " how do we know?" How do we know about what we are talking about in terms of it having substance and reality? When I hear someone quote Mead and her remarks that arise out of her love affair with the young, and I know that if we work on the basis of that kind of information we are going to get all mucked up along the line of coming up with something useful and concrete, I get unhappy. I don't think there was a more biased sample that ever existed than the kinds of studies about the young people of the sixties. There were a hell of a lot of young people, 16, 19, 20, 24 who never got included in that sample because they weren't called young people; they were called hardhats, or they were called military people, or they were called dropouts and they never got asked anything. People who did get asked were a tre-mendously selective sample. I don't think we can talk about the "greening" of anything on the basis of the kind of data we got from these people. It bothers me that I have been hearing for a day and a half, not everyone (I'm getting overly reactive I know) but a number of people giving data that's wrong. They are using wrong techniques to gather it or they are depending on people who were selective in the way they got it, and I just want to throw this out, but I have been steaming for a day and a half and it's all feedback.

RICHARDS: I'll try not to talk about the generation gap. To tell you how I got the data about cats, it was based on about five years of intensive observation of, not house cats, but barn cats. I started with a sample of one, a female, whom I incautiously befriended and ended up with some fourteen — four generations later — plus peripheral toms, so I feel that I have a certain justification in saying what I did.

However, the comment that I wanted to make was particularly directed toward Dr. Cancro's paper, where he talks about the importance of more people being more alike and the idea of extending the ingroup to include everybody. This raises a very interesting question: how many people can you feel kinship with? How many people can any human being feel kinship with or identification with at one time, or even in the course of one lifetime? This is the difference, and I think it's a terribly important difference, of scale that Wilson and Wilson talked about in the analyses of social change. At some point a quantitative difference becomes a qualitative one. We don't know what this point is, but there is some indication that, for instance, hunting and gathering bands can stay together peacefully without friction when they include around 25, maybe 50 people. The Hutterites, who have a very, very peaceful system (one of the few religious groups that have managed to retain a very, very cooperative, communistic type of society, without leadership and heavy structure and so on), have explicitly stated that they have to divide up when their ingroups get to be larger than 150. Do we have a limit somewhere beyond which we cannot have this fellow feeling?

I want to reply to Dr. Esser's question to Mrs. Scandalis as to how one can transform some of these things. As I said in my paper, cooperation and competition are not different things, necessarily; they are closely interrelated and not mutually exclusive. The hostility between generations can be termed predatory competition, where one tries to cut down the other. If this energy can be changed into emulative competition or into competitive cooperation I think you will have a much less disruptive situation. One of the ways in which this might be transformed is by changing the concept of limited possibilities or the concept, rather, of limited good. The idea is, "I can be a winner; it's possible that if I don't win now, I can later." This might be a technique or an approach by which this transformation might be made.

A. NETTLESHIP: I'm sorry the cat problem came up, I really am. I'm sorry for a lot of reasons, but I would like to use it as an example of where we're getting away from the reality which disturbs our friend. After all, Aristotle said, "All we know is through our own sensoria." Cats are a strange breed and I point to the work of Baird and associates back in the forties in which he showed that the pseudo-rage center is very close to the sexual center. You can rig up a cat in such a way (you just put a little pin in its head) that every time you walk past the cat's cage it flings itself right at you and tries to get you. You can do the same thing with its sexual apparatus if you put the pinprick just a little differently. This is a species which we should use as an example of physical and physiological reactions which are closely interrelated but I think we'd have a hard time carrying argumentation from there to human beings. I am not quite sure of the exact relation of the sex center to man's rage or violence. I am sure that it is very close to other fundamental, vegetative, centers down in the reticulum cells of the brain, so I think we have to be very careful here to transcribe a social conduct which might have a simple physiological or physical basis into what we're seeing.

Let's start with the organic. This is something we can get hold of, something we can look at. Let's make some sections we can put under the microscope or let's examine them physically and then if we can see this, we can go from there. Yet, all the time I am saying this, I'm sitting here realizing that I have heard, both yesterday and today, a great deal of comment about biological fatalism. Unless we use science as a kind of belief system I am not quite sure what we mean by this. Merely because we're biological, are we fated?

CANCRO: Concerning biological fatalism, what I was saying is that a misunderstanding of what biology contributes leads to the absurd position that "it's in your genes and there is nothing you can do about it." You have to be pretty ignorant of biology to say such a thing, but there is no shortage of people who are pretty ignorant of biology. For those who have some biological knowledge it's an aggravation; for the rest it seems logical.

Apparently I agree with Dr. Claessen's position on the precariousness of balance, and the position that Richards took about the problem of how many people can you feel close to. This is the point, basically, that I tried to make in the paper. The psychological science, the psychiatric field, has a very small amount to contribute, but it can contribute certain limiting conditions or boundaries. It can say, here's how far you can depend on kinship and human bonds to carry you: thirty people, maybe forty. After that, baby, you're in trouble. Beyond that it gets too abstract and to see HIM as an earthling is very hard unless you have a lot of Venusians attacking the place or unless something else is bonding you in a common purpose. That means, therefore, you cannot look to these as the means of achieving your goals. You've got to look elsewhere for the solutions to your problem. But in generating these solutions you will have to see what you might call the psychological limitations as important boundary conditions that must be understood so that you don't do what engineers constantly do, which is to design things that human beings can't use effectively (but which engineers love). Now, in that sense I think psychiatry and psychology have something to contribute: to bring in this human psychological awareness and see it as a kind of limiting condition for anything that you design, but not as a substitute for the institutional changes and social changes that are necessary.

To address myself to Dr. Smith's remark, the difference between a scientist and a polemicist is that the scientist will allow data to influence his position, where the polemicist is always data-free. He knows what is right, and doesn't have to be bothered by such trivialities. There is nothing more absurd than taking a large segment of humanity and talking about the central tendency of that group. "Black Americans" — the only thing you can say about Black Americans that is true is trivial. You can talk about the Duffy gene or something of this sort. If it's a non-trivial statement, it's a lie, because you can't take twenty million people, or twenty-five million people, and say anything about them that's going to be true without being trivial. Or when you say "women feel" or "men feel," those are absurd statements. You don't even have to listen to anything that comes after that; you can turn your head off for the rest of what the person is going to say because it can't make any sense. We talk about "the young" and know it's either going to be trivial or wrong, and yet we have continued it for many years because it's been attractive and TV media have got to generate this sort of thing. When you want to find out how young people feel, you go to Berkeley and you get eighteen kids who represent a subset of 0.000 percent of the population and you interview them in depth and you do a one-hour program, have *Time* magazine do a cover, and that's "the young generation." Well, it isn't. If you went to Southern Methodist University, they are praying for the salvation of those kids at Berkeley. That's the same generation, but they don't make news: who wants to see a bunch of kids at S.M.U.? Dull! So we must recognize the role of the media and the need of the communication industry for exciting stuff that misrepresents (deliberately or otherwise) the prevailing trends in a culture at a given time. Should we or do we; are they separate questions? She's very smart, but Margaret Mead has said a number of things that are staggering. But she also likes to say things in print which are extreme. She knows this; it amuses her.

SAXE-FERNÁNDEZ: It would be a good idea for everyone here to read a memorandum by Hudson Institute Director Herman Kahn, on counterculture and insurgency in America. He proposes a massive law enforcement program to deal with this issue, and maintains that counter-cultural elements are a threat to national security. It is my understanding that now the screening of students at Stanford (the criteria for acceptance to Stanford) is changing, and that they are emphasizing more students with a religious interest and religious background. If man defines situations as real, they are real in their consequence. Therefore you should see how bureaucracy, in particular national security bureaucracy or police bureaucracy, defines the situation. There has been an increased repression which is felt on the campuses, mainly, and in the structuring of faculties. For evidence, I invite you to seriously consider the proposals of Mr. Powell (now Chief Justice) which were sponsored by the American Chamber of Commerce in 1971 and published in a memorandum. It seems, on the other hand, if I read correctly that there has been repression, there is some form of internal war going on and therefore the interests or the manifestations of rebelliousness, if you wish, are changed by the mere fact that there is a counterinsurgency situation. I also invite you to read papers on the symposia on internal war in the United States which came out in April in a seminar sponsored by the Department of the Army, particularly by the Army Intelligence of the United States.

The situation has changed; the ethical assault on the system is annoying. It annoys you, for instance, it is troublesome. It's troublesome and annoying to the extent to which this opposition, first of all, cuts across class lines. And information we do have about blue-collar young indicates that that is the case. This type of radicalism is not expressing itself any more through street marches, through glossy posters, through Che Guevara T-shirts, or even through senseless, if not stupid, manifestations of bureaucratic revolutionary movements. It seems to be indicated by some form of what Herbert Marcuse labelled as total rejection, that is to say, some type of repugnance which is transformed into rebelliousness and incompatibility with the system and is embodied in the continued integrated physical presence of that position. That's why I suggested as an hypothesis that the dividing line between political and psychosocial manifestations is rapidly fading in post-industrial society; that basic institutions are being challenged, particularly the family. These young people are more interested in intersubjective and interpersonal affairs now.

It is worth seeing that over 50 percent of all the hospital beds in the United States are in mental hospitals and that more than half of these beds are occupied by diagnosed schizophrenics. We do know that schizophrenics are people between 8 and 25 who have very strong and powerful family problems. On the 23rd of February, according to the *Congressional Record*, a proposal was made by neurosurgeon Olson of Santa Monica, California, to train 200 neurosurgeons to treat, to operate on, schizophrenics which includes between one and two million people. You have to get into the situation with as much documentation as possible. Therefore, it seems to me that the generational problem is a political problem, is a condition of internal war and should be analyzed very carefully.

GIVENS: The next paper is from Mr. Krakauer.

KRAKAUER: My paper is related to the same disciplines as the previous papers, with a liberal admixture of zoology. I was very much taken with Dr. Press' quotation of Pogo Possum (which he didn't bibliograph): "We have met the enemy and he is us," and I think that whatever we can learn in this direction about ourselves should be useful in our project. Basically, my paper is a naturalistic explanation of the evolution and nature of man's psychological structure.

The first part points out that selection for intelligence also necessarily included selection for the loss of patterned instincts, selection for intellectual detachment, and selection for intense but unstructured motivations. Instincts had to go because intelligence is useless without the capacity for plastic behavior. But when instinct went, so did built-in self-control. Instincts were replaced by a mechanism for early enculturation, the superego. However, early learning means learning from parents, thus enculturation usually continues with modest change from generation to generation. The newborn infant is first totally dependent on the mother figure, but by age two develops also a strong, instinctual dependence on the father figure. Herein lies the essence of the followership syndrome that is so significant in organizing a war. The infant's instinctual needs for survival, safety, and belongingness are imperious. Its immature and inexperienced mind is naturally fearful and anxious. Given any kind of early stress, panic responses are more the rule than the exception, and maladaptive or disproportionate patterns of response are frequently set that stay on for life. Disproportionate aggression, like disproportionate motivation, occurs so commonly because here, too, control is not by instinct but by learning, which is often weak or erratic. Overt aggression, therefore, will occur in individuals who have weakly developed superego and ego controls, whose needs are seriously threatened, or who are driven by the moralistic demands of their own harsh superego, or when approval by father figures or peers leads them to bypass their own inner control. It seems to me that any large-scale, quick change in attitudes such as may have occurred in China, may only be achieved by a powerful mystique-laden leader. In our type of culture, we will probably have to continue the present slower route: continuous education which will feed back on the newborn and change enculturation and the choice of leaders over a period of time. In view of the unprecedented changes in public opinion in our democracy on Vietnam over a mere 10 years, we may be considerably nearer improvement and nearer our goals than many people think.

GIVENS: Dr. von Ehrenfels, would you summarize your paper?

VON EHRENFELS: I am trying to draw attention to a widespread, almost universal, happening in the tropical belt: the adoption of European style, cold-country clothing to a typically tropical, moist, hot climate. European aggression began in the sixteenth century in the tropical belt and resulted in an almost complete wholesale adaptation of the leading élite to the European concepts of dignity and the élite in this tropical belt adopted European style, cold-country clothing. This event, which became more prominent in the eighteenth and especially nineteenth centuries, is still going on today. This event changed the entire structure of personal and social organizations within this belt. A person's (whether male or female) outward appearance, agility, ability to do work or to enjoy sports, etc., have been changed into a completely different life-style and self-assertion. The assimilation of European-type clothing and behavior was intensified by the invention of air-conditioning. A kind of split personality, if not split group, developed: those who can imitate, who can afford to imitate the European style of life, and those who cannot. Those who do succeed in adopting European styles of life are driven far away from the ordinary people and the man in the street, the majority of their co-nationals. Now what is happening after this overall process is a split personality not only of the society as such but of the individual. The individual feels his values and his value systems corrupted and no longer acceptable. He or she tries to accommodate to the foreign pattern of life. Clearly, enough aggressiveness and even hatred are not being directed towards these new forms of life, but to their living representatives, foreigners. In consequence, the subconscious and often not quite realized hatred is directed towards foreigners. We feel that the whole integration of modern inventions is directed towards a new European, cold-country style of life in highly air-conditioned offices and rooms. It has disrupted the no longer valid attitude among those who do not belong to the financial and political power élite. This phenomenon of inner split personality is widespread and could be studied if we realized the basic motivations for this growing apart between two groups: those who freely adopt European styles, and those who are in the majority who are unable to follow this newly changed form of life. This is in brief the main content of the paper which tries to direct attention to the visible appearance of humans.

GIVENS: Professor Scott's summary will be next.

SCOTT: My paper is something of a fake because I had intended to be at Mexico City for the Conacyt-AAAS symposium on the behavior of violence and dependency but for personal reasons was not able to go. Therefore my paper represents, not what happened there, but what I thought was going to happen, based on the abstracts and papers I received in advance, and in some cases only the titles which I knew about. Dr. Tamayo y Salmorán was there and when I have briefly given a few ideas, I hope he will make some comments about the most important things that did occur there.

What we tried to do in the Mexico City symposium was to arrange it along the lines of what I have called a multi-factorial theory of agonistic behavior. Yesterday I mentioned three historical approaches which involved different sets of factors of this problem. One being evolution, biological evolution; a second being cultural evolution; and a third being individual development. What we've been hearing in this session is in large part connected with individual development.

Then in addition to this kind of approach to these problems we can divide the study of behavior according to the levels of organization starting with the genetic levels. Dr. Benson-Ginsburg presented the evidence, which is now overwhelming, that there are genetic effects upon agonistic behavior not only between species but within species and, particularly, that there are genetic effects between the two sexes.

There were several papers on the physiological, which is the next level of organization. Among the most important phenomena to come up recently is the effect of hormones upon the organization of the developing brain of young animals. This has not yet been established in human beings but you can (with certain species at any rate), by injecting hormones immediately after birth, change an animal which would normally develop into a reasonable, peaceful female and which would not respond to male hormones with aggressive behavior when adult, into a male-like animal, which will respond in that way.

There was considerable discussion of the techniques of psycho-surgery for controlling violent individuals along with discussion of its possible benefits and abuses. On the genetic and physiological levels these techniques are not going to lead to many practical applications. They are primarily concerned with the very small minority of abnormal individuals and in the vast majority of cases these factors are not particularly important as potential ways of controlling violence.

On the individual level, one of the most powerful factors affecting behavior, agonistic behavior, violent behavior, is that of learning. On the social level, we have what I think is coming into more and more promise in recent years, starting with studies of animal societies, but producing an idea which can be extended to the human. That is the idea of the relationship between violent behavior and social disorganization. An example would be the Hamadryas baboon studied by Zuckerman in the London Zoo where he observed many extreme cases of violent behavior and assumed this was true of the wild population. Actually the violent behavior was due to there being large numbers of animals, caught, thrown together, mostly males, wrong sex ratio, unknown to each other, and without enough space to get away from each other. Under these conditions violence did develop and this seems to be generally true of animal societies. The idea can be extended to human societies as well. Furthermore, it seems to me that this idea, which at first looked like one that could only be applied to the social level, may in fact have other implications on other levels. It was originally applied to disorganized social systems but you can also say that your individuals who become violent because of physiological causes are showing a disorganization of their physiological systems and also that, where you get the extreme cases of violence which are influenced by genetic factors, you are looking at a disorganization of the genetic system. This suggests that in the whole problem of warfare we are dealing on a world-wide scale with disorganization between societies, and that we, as yet, have no really firm or effective organization between different human societies. This is a situation which, on a disorganization principle, one would predict might lead to harmful violence.

It has been said before that our studies of animal societies do not give us any good models of human warfare. There are no cases of organized groups fighting other organized groups. What you can get occasionally in animals is intra-group conflict, and this is rather interesting to look at if it might give us some idea what human beings were like in prehistoric or perhaps precultural times. One case has come about in our laboratory recently. A student of mine, John M. Compton, is doing his dissertation on conflict between groups of the Mongolian gerbil, which ordinarily is apparently a very peaceful sort of animal. He finds that if he raises to adulthood groups of gerbils that have been born together in the same litter and then introduces two separate groups to each other there is almost immediate conflict. The conflict results in violent injury in the kind of situation which he has where the animals can't escape from each other. Also, one group always wins over the other. This is not, as you might suppose, individual combat but rather that one group wins, though gerbils of one group do not combine and attack the gerbils of the other group. What happens is a series of individual combats, but through more or less accidental factors, one animal gets seriously hurt in one group and then the other group has an advantage and will take over. These kinds of things are worth studying, but they don't give us good models of human warfare.

Finally, I would like to quote Richardson: "Quantitatively war is the greatest of all sorts of human destructive violence." Richardson collected the available figures for violent deaths in the world for the 126 years from 1820 to 1946 and he estimated that 59 million people died violently. Of these, 36 million or 61 percent died in the two World Wars and 9.7 million or 16.5 percent were murdered. The other 22.5 percent were killed in wars of smaller magnitude. This means that for a person living in those years, war was approximately five times as dangerous as murder. He also points out that all of these violent deaths form only 1.6 percent of the total deaths in this 126-year period. In other words, you had less than two chances in a hundred of dying by violence as opposed to dying by other means. What this points out is that violent death is not all that common, but of the various causes of violent deaths, war is by far the most important.

GIVENS: We would like to hear from Dr. Tamayo y Salmorán next.

TAMAYO Y SALMORÁN: If aggression occurs in relation with warfare, I think the conference in Mexico helped us to establish that warfare is a human affair, is a human business, and only exists between political and organized groups. If some violent behavior is our reaction to certain biological stimuli or ecological stimuli, there exists a certain kind of violence, organized violence, that is not a response to biological or ecological stimuli. For example, soldiers make war because they are subjects of a system of sanctions endorsed by threats or evils. Then the soldiers obey the rules for avoiding the sanctions, the punishment attached to the non-obedient behavior, that is, to the contrary behavior. Avoiding the sanction that is inflicted on the individual is the terminal motive which obligates the soldier to make war. The proscribing function, the legal system for example, consists in bringing about a certain behavior of the human being subject to this order. The law is, then, a specific technique which consists in motivating individuals to refrain from certain acts which for some reason are considered detrimental to society (in the case of war, for the international community) and to perform certain acts, which for some reason are considered useful to society. By prescribing sanctions such as deprivation of life, health, liberty, or economic values, the legal system strongly induces men to behave in conformity with the will or wish of the lawmaker, including inducing men to make war. In order to behave in conformity with the will or wish of lawmakers in internationally organized violent behavior we do not need an aggressive feeling. The sanction becomes the determining motive for bringing about the behavior of human beings — the sanction, the punishment, becomes the determining motive for making man make war. Aggression, individual aggression, must be clearly separate from the idea of warfare. Warfare is a qualified act, properly, of organized nations. It is the business of political societies. It has nothing to do with aggressive feelings between individuals.

GIVENS: Are there questions? Mr. Parker?

PARKER: My area is peace science, although if we have to throw ourselves into other disciplines you may call me a political scientist. I've had difficulty throughout the Conference in working with dogs and cats, rats, sheep, birds, deer, American Indians, primitive groups and societies. From my own perspective as a layman in anthropology and archeology, we haven't done much bridge-building. That is, when one talks about animal behavior, one of the few people I've heard mentioning the fact that it can be very difficult to apply this to human behavior is Dr. Scott. If in a conference such as this it becomes necessary to discuss dogs, cats, rats, etc., it seems to me that at one point we must talk about its relevance to man if we consider that man is the warmaker. I'm not saying there isn't this relevance, just that very few people have made an effort to indicate WHERE it is relevant. If in fact this whole area of war and peace studies is by its nature an interdisciplinary, multidisciplinary study, then it becomes necessary for those who are in a particular discipline to begin to translate for those who are not, but who need to use that kind of knowledge the value of which you are stressing. Otherwise, I think we are working for ourselves in our own groups. Lorenz has been criticized greatly for trying to relate animal behavior to human behavior, and yet throughout this Conference the implication has been that if we talk about dogs and cats, etc., we can make analogies to men, although very few have come out and said either that we can or can't.

YOUNG: It is fairly clear that Scott has brought to bear a very important generalization from animal behavior that applies to human behavior, that is, that the condition for peace is social organization. What do we mean by worldwide social organization? We make a mistake if we simply mean worldwide government. Government is either absolute tyranny or absolutely impotent if it is not supported by moral order. When we speak of a moral order we have to make a distinction, I think, between conventional morality and what the philosophers call rational morality. There are all kinds of conventional moralities all over the world. Most of them are pretty superstitious, hence we suspect the conventional moralities and we say we shouldn't try to impose our own conventional morality on other people. But there is a rational morality that is found all over the world and a psychologist by the name of Lawrence Hulberg has studied that. He has found that children go through six stages in the development of their perception of moral issues. The highest stage a very large number of adults don't reach, but this is essentially the state of rational morality. Morality is for the good of everyone alike. (That is a brief way of stating that.) It is a morality that has a high respect not only for the rights but for the dignity of other people. This is the kind of morality that must apply to everybody all over the world if we are going to achieve an effective world social organization. It means that psychologically we are identified with the human race more than we are identified with any nation, and it means that our psychological identification with people means that we are eager to cooperate with them in terms of the good of everyone alike. I think it would be dangerous to establish any sort of world government before we have gone a long way toward establishing that kind of morality throughout the world. We don't have enough of that morality within the political states that we have. That's the reason we have revolutions. Remember that civil wars occur fairly frequently. You aren't going to end war until we have ended civil war and civil war itself, as far as I can see, only can be ended by establishing a social organization based on a very widespread acceptance of what I call rational morality, the identification with our neighborhood, with our nation, and with the whole human race.

MRS. ESSER: I'm trying to make order in my mind of some of the things which have been said which are lying about like artifacts that cannot find a home. Yesterday, three comments were made by Dr. Smith asking for context, which were not answered. Today, she asked a question which was not basically answered. Mr. Parker is now asking for bridging of gaps. It seems to me that the psychiatrists here do not address themselves to the one thing that is necessary for instituting or carrying out or even attempting that which is called capacity for change. Capacity for change is the root of that which has to happen inside of anyone who wants to even attempt to think about how to undo some of the things we have done. Capacity for change, to my mind, is equal to endurance. Now, anyone who says (and many people do, whether they are animal behaviorists in this country, or laymen, or whatever) that Lorenz extrapolates from animal to man has not had the endurance to read him. I would like Dr. Cancro, for instance, to proscribe or prescribe just how he would go about defining or making an attempt at teaching the meaning of endurance in terms of something that we can all agree to. For instance, in Mexico City, I attended the session Dr. Scott reported on, and also others. The Latin Americans continually blasted into the Americans' faces as to what kind of bastards we are and how awful we are and what kind of a country this is and so forth, but never had the endurance to have the Americans reply, "We are a lot of things, we are not just this one thing." Such lack of endurance presupposes that there cannot be capacity for change and there cannot be change.

CANCRO: It's difficult to respond to you directly because I want to think about what you mean and don't mean and I'm not sure if I would want to write any prescription, let alone one that is dictated in very specific terms to me. I and some of the other psychiatrists have tried to indicate what we feel to be the potential contribution of a study of psychopathology to an understanding of war. I think it is bloody little.

The next issue: can we, by better understanding of the limits of man's personality, have some grasp of what kind of institutions might or might not work? There I argue we can and made very specific suggestions in the paper as to the use of animal models, the limitations of the use of animal models, the use of primitive societies, etc. I think we see something in operation though, for example, in this session, where I share the concern that we should look to social structures, whatever the hell they might be, as "the answer." But we are showing a kind of disciplinary irritation, saying, "I don't want to hear all this crap from your field; I want to get to my field because that's where the answers are to this problem." Well, that's a lot of bull. There is no anthropologist in this room that has anything to say that makes any more sense than I do, or any sociologist, or what have you, because none of us really knows the answer. War is not a disciplinary problem, and yet we are very eager to get to where our field is, saying all kinds of inane things that impress each other but have no real relevance to the problem of war. I think that if we can have the patience or, if we could use your term, the endurance to hear each other and to understand what each other can contribute, then we may enrich your approach and you may enrich my approach.

For example, if we can understand some of the constraints that the number of people you can relate to may impose, this would be something you would have to take into account in the development of certain institutions that you would hope have certain effects. If you talk about transnational identity, that your first identity is as an earthling or *Homo sapiens* and not as a Kentuckian, that is a goal. But we should not confuse that goal with a realized fact: when you are in Mexico there is an intense nationalism; in Peru, among other South American countries, it is equally intense. They not only dislike North Americans; if you ask the Peruvian what he thinks of a Bolivian or someone from Brazil, he is not too gracious about that either. So there are intense national feelings and I think they are very dangerous, but they are there.

I think psychiatry can raise one other very profound question, and this concerns man's capacity for rationality and the problems that it creates. A rational being is capable of uniquely irrational acts because of his rationality and the higher the I.Q., the crazier he can be. Let me cite a classic example. A dear friend of mine who is a sweet, nice, human-being-type physicist, was involved with the Manhattan Project, with the development of the atom bomb. At the time of the Los Almos test, the first test of the bomb, the consensus among the group of nuclear physicists there was that there was approximately a 10 percent chance that there would be a runaway chain reaction which would mean the destruction of the earth. I said to him, "My God, if I said to you (we were in an airport) that this plane that we were about to board had a 10 percent chance of crashing, would you board it?" He said, "Absolutely not, you couldn't drag me on it." I said, "Then why the hell did you do it?" He said, "We wanted to know what would happen." Now this is a uniquely human characteristic and it has to be taken into account when we try to design institutions.

MRS. ESSER: Yes, but I think that because these kinds of men are so rational, their irrational behavior, which would be common ordinary behavior in someone else, would be highlighted, so I like to be very specific and precise. You mentioned Margaret Mead. Margaret Mead did not speak about intergenerational gap at all, I'm sorry to correct that for you. She talked about "intergeneration cutoff"; those were her words. She said there is absolutely no communication anymore, there's absolutely no gapping, nothing, and there is a total cutoff. This is a power figure in the world who says "that's all, boys," and now let's just go altogether in our uncouth fashion and let's bring grandmothers and grandfathers back as Lorenz does, and let's go together into a future we create rationally.

So what I'm really saying to you is that I would like you as a psychiatrist, not that my husband is exempt from this, to sort out some of these things. When Dr. Richards says, "It's easier for me to love God than it is to love my brother," I would like for the psychiatrist to say, for instance, "Oh, yes, you know why that is, because the love of God is an abstraction that comes from the neocortex and the love of brother comes from whichever other system there is." It is so easy to make this order and therefore, it is so easy to teach on this level some sort of endurance. I didn't ask for patience at all, but endurance, to hold still in the classroom. Endurance!

CANCRO: I did not accuse Margaret Mead of mid-generational gap; it's probably on tape, but I did not. She has said that all the kids born after World War II just can't talk to their parents. Now, I find that a remarkable cutoff phenomenon and therefore I work under the supposition that it's drivel until proven otherwise. I can say that it is more difficult, that there are more problems, but I can't see it in these absolute terms. My point was that she says things in a very sweeping way; then if you talk to her she says, "Oh, God, no, don't take it literally, I was just being dramatic." But you have to talk to her as well as read her, otherwise you get upset and you don't understand what she's trying to say, and that's the point I was trying to address myself to.

Despite being a professional educator, I am very impressed by the limits of education and I think education should not become the panacea of the 1970's any more than faith was the panacea of the 1670's. Possibly muddling through, possibly intention, possibly moralish muddling. I have more confidence in muddling than I do in modeling: incremental change; substituting trial and correction when something fails; checks and balances. I see the necessity of bringing many, many disciplines together to deal with these kinds of real world problems, and I would also suggest to you that not only should we be bringing together scientific disciplines, but that we should be involving the non-scientific community to a much, much greater degree. If there is any-thing in the world that forty intellectuals in a three-day conference will not solve, it is the problem of warfare or any other real problem that ever existed on this planet. You should have decision-makers in any meaningful conference; you should have consumers in any meaningful conference; you should have individuals who are not blinded by their disciplinary constraints; if you want to organize a conference that's going to achieve practical ends. This is not really what I think I'm sup-posed to be talking about. I'm probably being ungracious to my hosts.

GIVENS: Go ahead, you are being very gracious.

CANCRO: No, at least honest. If you really want to deal with these problems, why do we not have people who represent military interests, or industrial interests, or poverty areas, etc.? Instead we have a group of intellectuals with impeccable intellectual credentials most of whom have never lived in the real world. They were born on a college campus, they will die on a college campus, never been off a college campus.

A. NETTLESHIP: Speak for yourself, Charlie Brown.

CANCRO: This IS true of a large percentage of the intellectual com-munity. Very few have ever had to work or scramble; they saw a ghetto on a field trip, that kind of thing. Now this limits their experi-ence sharply and when they then intervene or plan an intervention it is done with ignorance. At breakfast this morning I was talking to some-one about what happened in Harlem in New York at the end of the war. Some very well-intentioned people decided that they had to im-prove this lousy housing. They tore it all down, threw out what was a very stable community, got them all out, put up some high-rise apart-ments, moved in 1,000 families and it wasn't safe to walk the streets anymore. So it went from a poor area that was safe to a poor area that was unsafe and everybody said, "Look at these marvelous improve-ments that we've wrought upon these people." They weren't marvelous, they were a disaster; a well-intentioned disaster, but a disaster never-theless, where again ignorance of the fact that you had a stable com-munity which had positive factors and real resources was lost sight of because it was ugly by our esthetic standards.

A. NETTLESHIP: It's healthy, it's salubrious. Americans are practical people, it's a good and useful thing to consider this. We didn't really want the more strongly motivated people here from the standpoint of feeling that we could not do something practical now. I will not defend our intelligence or our lack thereof. Rather, I would say we feel that it's a problem of such depth and diversity that everyone who can say anything is of help to us. Emotional, unemotional; it doesn't really make that much difference. I feel the problem has not even been defined or looked at, and I am at the begging stage of saying, "For Christ's sake, let's get more data." So let's get the data, let's get at it, let's be practical about it, BUT DON'T LET'S SEEK SOLUTIONS, let's look at these things which have happened. We are in a quasi-historical method, we are in a psychological method, animal models may be useful or not. Human models are better, but who can see a human model when we are at war?

I've been to many conferences through many, many years and I always come away with the feeling that I'd have gotten much more if I had stayed home and read the whole proceedings in, say, thirty minutes, but it has been a wonderful thing here for me to see people contributing as they felt the thing came up and the problem projected itself before us. We will go away ego-shattered, I suppose, feeling we have accomplished so little. On the other hand, the Conference has made a turn. I can feel this. We are interested, we are deeply interested in trying to find out without defying anyone. When I first discussed this with my son, peaceably and without generation gap, we said this is sort of a foolish thing, isn't it? What are our resources? Well, 20 thousand or maybe 30 thousand dollars. How much does the military spend every year? 87 billion, 88 billion, it's an endless sort of spectrum. But then small things begin some place and there has been a turning here. Your own attitudes have shifted from the feeling of a sort of incomprehensibility to something we can get hold of. We can see it and feel it. We're going to have to go on a lot more field trips; preferably not at war. We are going to have to get hold of what I call the biological. We are going to have to comprehend that there are factors which again and again and again are so noticeable as to cause confusion, and yet we cannot understand what they are. I think if we can go on with that as a background we may get a little further with it than where we are.

SCOTT: What I've seen here seems to be very healthy, because we have a number of different disciplines and no one of us has come forth with the idea that "I have from my discipline the one true way, the one true solution to this problem." In fact, what has happened has been quite the contrary; most of us have stated, "Look, my solution can't solve all these problems. It hasn't got all the information." What it means is that we are dealing with an extremely complex problem and it's going to take, as others have expressed it, a great deal of not only cooperation, but also mutual comprehension.

To return to the animal model idea: there is an erroneous idea of evolution that the utmost peak of evolution is man and that all other animals are evolving on the way toward man and therefore a rhesus monkey is just a small human being with a fur coat and a long tail. He's trying to get to be a man and someday he will and therefore we can look at him as a model of what human behavior used to be. This is not true at all. Every animal species is evolving independently and they are not evolving into human beings. Cats are evolving into cats, monkeys are evolving into monkeys. They are all traveling different roads and from the point of view of the geneticist, there is no justification for extrapolating directly or analogizing directly from one species to another. Human beings are a unique species and they must be understood in terms of human beings themselves. What you CAN do with the animal models is this: if you find that a phenomenon exists in dozens or hundreds of different species, then you have some justification for predicting that this same phenomenon may be found in human beings. In other words, you are dealing with a basic, general phenomenon of living beings. There is fairly good evidence on that, and we're on the way toward a generalization which might have some application to man and be of some truly basic importance. It also points to solutions, but not easy solutions by any means. The immediate question is, what kind of organization are you going to foster; and there is no easy answer, as I see it, to this. What you want to be aware of, if you are not an animal behaviorist, is selecting out a particular species, saying "Oh boy, this is just like human beings and I have proved something." This is quite illegitimate.

I would like to respond to Dr. Cancro on the futility of the academic life. This, I think, arises from the fact that we don't always appreciate what we can do and what our function is in a broader society. Our business is to produce ideas; that is the only thing we can do well. We are not equipped to go out and make social changes or to be action figures. In other words, very few of us anyway are Messiahs who can lead the world toward social change. What we hope to do is to produce ideas which can be transmitted to leaders and persons in power, who can then make these changes. Now these may not be individuals now in power; they may be individuals who are lowly students who happen to pick up these ideas from us. For example, William James was a professor at Harvard when, in about 1910, he wrote an article on the moral equivalent of war, and among other students at Harvard was Franklin Delano Roosevelt. Years later, this idea of William James' was actually put into practice in the Civilian Conservation Corps, and another manifestation of this has been the Peace Corps. It hasn't solved the problem of war, as William James hoped it would, but it probably has helped to solve some of the problems of violence. That's one of the kinds of things I think academics can do, but we have not only got to have these ideas, to produce them, but these ideas must be true ideas. In other words a scientist is a man who can be trusted to speak the truth and one of the contributions a scientist, just by being a scientist, can make to world order and organization is simply that scientists from any culture can trust each other, unlike politicians. In other words, a man from the socialist countries who is a scientist, we can say, we can assume, is doing his best to speak the truth and he may react similarly to us. This does make communication possible across national barriers. It is a small thing in its way, from a practical point of view, but if we develop ideas which are true and which are useful when applied these can be transmitted worldwide.

The Ecology of the Etiology of War

Chaired by A. NETTLESHIP and R. CANCRO

Discussion of papers by A. NETTLESHIP, A. H. ESSER, E. H. GRAHAM, C. A. BISHOP, S. I. GHABBOUR, K. COOPER

CANCRO: Since I am co-chairing this session with Dr. Nettleship, whose paper is to be presented, I would like to call on him first. Dr. Nettleship, would you present your summary?

A. NETTLESHIP: We feel that primitive war, and in this sense not prodromal war as we will treat it a little later, started in time and place where man became settled into communities. This is not specifically traceable, as was pointed out in Session 2, because we do not have the physical evidence for it, but I think it was probably when people began to settle down that pre-war began. We thought it would be important to get a group of criteria which would name some of the factors which we thought were important. I have mentioned these in the paper as a specific type of genetic pool, peoples having physical and mental characteristics different from surrounding peoples. This was talked of yesterday by Dr. Richards as a difference in acculturation amongst peoples. I think these peoples are physically different as well. The size and set of indigenous population growth rate increment is an important factor. This is very difficult to prove because war seems to be a fairly local phenomenon where it begins. To me, one of the more difficult parts of explaining war is how it seems to begin locally and yet can spread or be understood amongst a larger population group, and can increase with seeming insight as to how it's going to go by everyone concerned. Bioenergy quantities are another factor including space occupation and sufficient food for growth. It's notable that the physical characteristics of the American population changed between World Wars I and II with approximately two and one-half inches increment in height and some twenty-five pounds increment in weight. Of course, this is happening whether the country goes to war or not. I don't offer that as a key, but if you don't have that, I think a nation would be ill-equipped to go to war. We are speaking of generative war now. Mobility features we'll talk about a little later on.

We divided prodromal war into three general phases without trying to be too specific as to time factors. I think these are recognizable as phase one in which there is a certain resemblance of a bio-mass becoming unified. Loose-knit tribes become knowledgeable and are aware of each other as a unit. I think this takes place very early. These people seem to have a high energy quotient. This you can call a resting place. (This is why I objected to the word peace, because I'm not even sure that BETWEEN wars there is such a thing.) If one is preparing during a prodromal phase to do something then it's not an absence of it, it's actually taking place prior to the onset of "war." There is a second part of the prodromal phase in which people begin to talk about it. There is a certain successful survival of groups of young, healthy, adult males in ordinary circumstances of war. These concentrations of males begin to appear in mobile groups; they tend to establish leadership and social and military hierarchies. One doesn't get past phase two until the military hierarchy begins to be felt, seen, and understood. There is establishment of leadership. There is a confrontation of groups of differing characteristics. Now this is an end stage of the prodromal phase, followed by an actual outbreak of physical activities in which we say the prodromal phase is now past and warfare as such occurs. Now these are simply descriptive elements.

This analysis is directed in examination of some of the structural-functional changes present in human groups, primarily during the prodromal war phase. The facts as considered, we believe, are largely biological ones. The changed characteristics in these groups spring from and produce an operant mechanism which is war. We don't understand many of these at this time. These are just word outlines of what we thought about it. It seems likely, however, that at the time prodromal war enters its terminal phase, there is some breakdown in the normal controlling feedback mechanisms which keep a population stable and which keep it from going too far. This may be an interplay between the genetic pool and ecological factors. It may be that new variables and mechanisms occur which can upset the feedback mechanism and produce war.

CANCRO: Dr. Esser, could we have your presentation?

ESSER: For me the most important area that we should try to apply to the war problem is the question of cognition. The question, "How do we know?" was raised in the preceding session by Dr. Smith and while I have an answer to that, it is not an answer in terms of cause and effect, but context. WE KNOW, because man as a species has a common denominator which is a central nervous system; consequently it is most important for us to know as much as possible about the central nervous system. There are two aspects to our knowledge of the central nervous system. One is the mental or internal aspect; the other is the environmental, that which is around the mental. Between mental and environmental knowledge, we can deduce some of the inevitable consequences.

My main basis is the work by MacLean on the brain, to which I will refer in a second, and the work on environmental organization by John D. Calhoun. Both MacLean and Calhoun are with the National Institute of Mental Health in Washington, D.C. It is essential for us to understand that there is an environmental and an evolutionary hierarchy in our cognition. We know things in a hierarchy of knowledge, and that hierarchy of knowledge is given to us by the evolution we have gone through. For instance, the implication is that reason, since it came later than feeling, always has to give way if the chips are down. If the chips are down for me and I am driven to a corner, I will start to emote rather than to reason. And it doesn't really matter, you know, that it is with the best of intents that we try to be reasonable at all times; at a certain moment that breaks down — which is understandable in the explanation of MacLean's hierarchies in our brain. MacLean tells us the human brain is really a coupling of animal brains integrated into each other. The most basic brain, in MacLean's vision, is what we have in our brain stem, the part which deals with biological life and its vital functions. Secondly, on top of that has evolved what MacLean has called the lower mammalian brain, the limbic system. This limbic system deals with the emotional life, not just the vital biological life, not with us staying alive, but with enjoying and suffering in life; with pain and pleasure. Again, it can be shown by neurology, by experimentation, that in the limbic system of a cat, for instance, you can find next to each other an area for sex and an area for aggression. In man it has been shown that these areas are also available and can be manipulated. Finally, in higher mammalian brains, as MacLean calls them, we have the development of language, reason, logical thinking — the intellectual rather than the emotional functions. These are located in the cortex, which, especially in man, has become enormous, has outgrown all these previous brains and literally contains the projections of these creatures' brains. You can literally show in brain anatomy that fiber tracts go from the previously mentioned centers, the biological brain and the emotional brain, to the cortex. This neo-cortical system has its own function. It is not going to be crying or laughing about something; it is going to be logical about something. As you know, in man, but not in any other animal, there is a difference between the left and the right hemispheres: the left hemisphere, the linguistic one, reasons in language; the right hemisphere knows space, knows music, and has a couple of other functions which are specific to that part of the brain. In man, we know that with these two enormous lobes that are placed on the previous animal brains, we bring forth all the good things in life, the good things that make us human.

My contention is that if we want to educate intellectually we must remember we are only working with the cortex. We can't intellectually educate the limbic system or the brain stem. You can influence them in other ways, such as with bio-feedback techniques, but not by going to school and telling them exactly what you know.

Remember that Dr. Richards said ". . . it's more difficult to love God; you first must learn to love others, then you can love God." This refers back to the emotions since you are always with your brother, you grew up with your brother, you know him, you are familiar with him. It's easier to love him than God who is really an abstraction. Now, as she also indicated the opposite may occur. There can be situations where I hate my brother and it is easier for me to love God than to love my brother. That is a function of our cortex and is purely a decision that we make, maybe rational or irrational, but we make it as a decision, we voice it, we work with it. That is part of what I have called social pollution. Now there is a most difficult conceptual jump to make: How can you, going from these functions in the brain that are of different levels, all of a sudden decide that this applies to the environment; that it applies to large-scale phenomena such as war? I'll try to encapsulate this thought. It goes as follows: Once man has known himself, which I equate with the cortex, he could look upon himself as somebody who was outside. Once the cortex has mastered that function (which I place with the beginning of language and the use of tools, approximately between 500,000 and 50,000 years ago), we could assign to ourselves alien feelings. How can I feel bad? It's such a nice day. All of a sudden, I can speak about "self." I can objectify "self" and all of a sudden I realize that if I can objectify "self" then the "other" can be self. Here is the beginning of alienation. Alienated people who do not know themselves also don't know other people. That's the paradox. You've got to know yourself before you can know somebody else.

If that is true, then what happens during our growing up, phylogenetically as well as developmentally, is that we start to apply the knowledge of the "other" to those that are around us, in our in-group, and after a while, because we know "self," we know the other operating group and we say we feel familiar. The word family, the word familiar, comes from that. We know what that is. But anything that is outside that is not "self," is alien, is "other," automatically therefore becomes different. There is where war can come in. Because if we have an in-group versus an out-group dichotomy in our brain, thanks to our brain, then it's possible all of a sudden to fight an enemy, and to go after the enemy. Now this is a very difficult point to think through. It's a transformation of an earlier feeling and an earlier thought suddenly projected into the environment and to the enemy.

If I speak for myself and somebody asks me how sure are you of this data, I must give my gut feeling. I love this data, I value the data, but I am not sure of it because there is very little real experimentation except for the experiment by Taifel. This shows that regardless of what you do, if you make in-groups and out-groups arbitrarily, people in the in-groups are automatically going to herd together and treat the others as out-groups. It is very strange, but you form groups arbitrarily and immediately the members identify with them. From animal data, we know that animals don't like strangers. On this small amount of data I base this idea which should explain intergroup aggression and war.

Aggression, violence, and war are really quantum jumps: they are derailments. I do not consider them in the same category. I don't consider my aggression in the same category as my violence, and on a larger scale, war. I consider aggressiveness to be a normal biological phenomenon. I try to maintain myself, or my thought; I try to acknowledge, to have you acknowledge, my emerging structure. I am building here something for you, right? You don't know yet, but we're going to build a structure, right? The moment you start attacking that I will become aggressive, because it's my little structure. But I will not become violent, I promise! I would become violent if that structure were ideal, affectively laden. I have realized that you are the other people and I can force you to submit by violent means. That's typically human.

Anything that helps differentiate people in in-groups and out-groups is being used by us, for instance in colonies, to make sure we have power. I would interpret Dr. Ehrenfels' data about colonies (and I grew up in a colony) as a submissive gesture. If people in the colony are going to dress themselves as Europeans do, then really they want to be a part of the in-group. "Please acknowledge me."

If we know the way the brain is put together, the way we react to our outside unwittingly on many levels and wittingly on other levels, then we do have the responsibility at all times to try to construct a reality which is peace-like. Take the word CONSTRUCT literally. We can decide at any one given time to project out what we want to project out and this sentence quoted from Sartre (in Carroll and Fink's paper) is correct. I don't believe that it leads to an absurd universe. I believe it leads to a beautiful universe if you are responsible for what you do. What are the tools to do that? We don't have the tools, obviously. We are faltering, I know just as little as you do about war and we all sit together and say: what tools? I have an idea that the tool will be EMPATHY, the intellectual identification with other people's thoughts, needs, and emotions. Dr. Cancro said at the end of his paper, "How can we generalize the identification with others?" I believe that empathy can lead to an attitude where we can suspend our disbelief, where we can be tolerant of each other, where we can endure each other.

CANCRO: The next presentation will be by Dr. Bishop.

BISHOP: My paper offers no solutions specifically that would help eliminate warfare. However, it discusses conditions under which warfare is ecologically and demographically impossible. These, I argue, come about among Northern Algonquins within the historic period. More specifically, my paper deals with cannibalism. But where most examples of cannibalism are directly associated with warfare, raiding, headhunting, etc., cannibalism among Northern Algonquins grows primarily from food deprivation and starvation and was associated with a mythological giant known as the Windigo. It would appear that such a mythological creature was actually aboriginal and existed in the folklore of the people of the area in pre-contact times, but there is no information, no historic information, on this whatsoever. I went through the seventy-three volumes of the *Jesuit relations* and the word isn't even mentioned, which is rather unusual considering the Jesuits were concerned with Indian religion at the time. Also, there is no evidence that cannibalism existed among the Northern Algonquins prior to about 1730, which is also interesting. And indeed the literature of the very early periods stresses the abundance of food and food resources.

Beginning about 1600 or perhaps a little earlier, European-inaugurated fur trade introduced a variety of European items, such as guns, traps, kettles, etc., to these Indians. With the guns it took only a few generations, or even less in some cases, to totally eliminate the animal population, first along the St. Lawrence valley, later a little further to the west in the central Great Lakes region, and eventually throughout the northern interior between Lake Superior and Hudson Bay. By animal population I mean primarily the large, gregarious animals, such as the moose and caribou. They were totally exterminated, as well as some of the smaller animals such as the beaver, otter, etc. Beginning about 1620 the peoples of this region were faced with endemic food shortages which created a situation which altered their social organization. Up to this point the primary group had been the hunting band numbering perhaps 25–50 individuals. During the middle of the eighteenth century, these bands engaged in intergroup feuding as well as actual warfare with the Dakota of Minnesota. It was not unusual for some of these groups to travel as far as 200–300 miles to take a whack at the Dakota down in Minnesota and North Dakota. But once this annihilation of the game came about, this was no longer feasible and, in fact, the larger hunting groups atomized into extended families and family units. It's also at this time, about 1820 and thereafter, that cannibalism arose and is documented in the historical literature.

The Windigo phenomenon, which is practically trivial up to this point, takes on greater importance, and it became possible for individuals to become transformed into human Windigos if they had engaged in cannibalistic acts. Thus, instead of becoming involved in open hostilities you had the emergence of sorcery and what came to be known as Windigo psychosis, a phenomenon I don't think was aboriginal since it was not adequately documented prior to this time for these groups. For this reason warfare and feuding cease and under these ecological conditions, where you have a population dispersed over a relatively wide area, engaged in trapping, highly individualistic, with no hope of help from other families also so engaged, you could have no basis for collective or communal behavior which could result in actual open feuding.

A. NETTLESHIP: Dr. Cooper, would you give your summary?

COOPER: The focus of my paper as it relates to the discussions here on causes of war is more on the possible and probable causes of war in the future than it is an analysis of how we got to our present state. It tries to get at some of the pressure trends in the world as a whole today that pose problems for tomorrow. At a recent interdisciplinary symposium at Stanford, called "The Earth and Its Limits," we began by viewing the world as a whole, more or less closed system, in which the earth provides a limited life support system, including such basic ingredients as air, water, food, and mineral and fossil fuels. Of course it includes man and woman who have certain needs and desires for their survival that depend on this life support system. For the first time in the history of human life on the planet, we know that the path of development that civilization is taking is leading us unquestionably to disaster in the future. The earth has only so many resources. How we use them, how many of us use them, will determine whether civilization as we know it can continue to exist.

If we take, today, just one example, let's say energy, we can get an idea of where we're heading. Some of the other variables are population, food supply, mineral resources, environmental pollution, but I am just going to refer to energy resources and from a sequence of events will indicate where I think some of the pressures are coming. Eighty-five to 90 percent of the world's energy comes from fossil fuels. Today the rich nations, representing less than 30 percent of the world's population, consume over 75 percent of each year's world energy production. The rate of usage is increasing exponentially. If we stabilize population immediately, and that means at 3.7 billion (which, of course, is impossible since we're going to have 6 to 7 billion by the year 2000), and bring the energy consumption in the world up to the level currently enjoyed by Americans, then coal, and this means unexplored coal, dirty coal, and all kinds of coal in the world, would last less than a century, and oil less than a decade. Furthermore nobody expects new technologies to be perfected, if they in fact ever do become perfected, before the year 2000. So, the short-term rush to guarantee access to the remaining oil and gas supplies on the part of the rich nations is going to be tremendous. The power, wealth, and technologies, and thus access to new energy sources, will be available primarily to the already wealthy nations. This increases the gap between the rich and the poor in the future.

This brings us to a second kind of pressure trend in the world today in addition to the continuing exponential depletion of the earth's resources. This is the desire of the other two-thirds of the earth's people to live as good a life as we are living. In addition to the need to take a new look at how we ourselves can live good lives without our continued rape of the earth, the developing world needs to find new models that do not proceed along the same technological and economic development route that we took. Our successful formula simply will not work very much longer for us, nor for the rest of the world. So we need to find new models, new life-styles. We'll have to evolve new social, economic, and political systems that will allow humankind to bring its desires more in harmony with the planet's resources and that will allow for a more completely equitable sharing of access to these resources. We see that the present world social system simply does not do this and is in a very dangerous disequilibrium. That was the general tone of our symposium.

Let me just refer to a couple of specific kinds of things that we dealt with. Population pressure is something we really can't ignore. As I mentioned we have 3.7 billion now. If you look at the current trends of population development there will be 60 billion people in the world by the end of the next century which, of course, will not occur. And then the question is why it will not occur and what kinds of changes will occur in the future to prevent this. The changes can be classified as either disaster or planned change. And if you think of planned change the statistics seem to go like this: if the developed world reaches zero population growth by the year 2000 and if the developing world reaches zero population growth by the year 2040, then by the end of the next century, you end up with anywhere from 12 to 15 billion people, four to five times as many as we have now. And even with this kind of growth in population with the rich countries trying to hold to their present way of life and with this growth of population being primarily in the poorer countries, the gap that exists today is unavoidably going to increase drastically.

Let me suggest two scenarios I talk about in my paper which might result from these current pressure trends. First of all the United States could continue its privileged access to the world's technology and resources with the kind of cooperation that it has for the moment from the leaders of the Third World, leaders who are looking for short-term benefits for their own survival as leaders. In the United States we find the leaders and the people benefitting from this kind of short-term continuation of U.S. exploration. In 1973 we find Admiral Zumwalt, head of the U.S. Navy, saying on television that with the current energy crisis and the need for access to the diminishing petroleum resources in the world, he is talking Congress into giving him 6 billion dollars for an aircaft carrier because, "We simply must control the seas." Now this means long-term disaster for everybody since the prime materials that are to be the basis for the development of the Third World will have vanished. This is the current state of affairs.

There is another scenario and just a few economists are talking about this; you have Mishan, Boulding, Heilbroner who imply that possibly the rich countries will realize soon enough. We find some of the young people today trying to work for the stabilized kind of economy; an economy based upon services and quality of life rather than quantity of life and consumption and production of material goods. They say if the developed or rich nations move in this direction, there are going to be tremendous short-term difficulties in the Third World, which currently depends upon the wealth from the developed world buying their prime resources. So this will mean a lot of difficulty for those countries in the immediate future, but long-term survival. Our focus at Stanford was on the foreign student and foreign scholar population. We have about 1,500 and our work is getting them to think about some of these major trends in the world so they can relate their work at Stanford more to how they could be effective in the major kinds of changes that should occur in their own country. This was very difficult, because they, like all the rest of us, are looking for short-term benefits and by copying our models, they can make some short-term progress although the long-term effect will be disastrous.

CANCRO: A comment about making predictions beyond this evening, which we are often called upon to do, but which has some inherent dangers: This is an area where I have long had an interest. I share the biases that are implicit in your statements and very much share your concerns, but I think if we had held this conference in 1873 and projected the population of 1973 and the number of horses that would be required to support that population, we would have drawn the conclusion that the planet Earth would now be under six feet of horse manure. That may well be, in a sense, but we could not have foreseen the directions that development went because these were not linear growths. There are new things which come in which simply take you in a totally different and unforeseen direction.

COOPER: The same thing can be said about artichokes. We would actually be swamped if we looked at the trend toward increase in consumption of artichokes. However, if the Incas had had a conference such as this, if Rome had, even England or France, I think maybe their futures might have been a little different. Our focus is not really to be soothsayers or to forecast disaster. We were working very specifically to see what kinds of changes need to be and can be planned in the near future without a tremendous waste of resources or deterioration of the environment. To look at São Paulo in Brazil, you can predict right now that their life is deteriorating badly, whereas new kinds of technology and new kinds of transit systems could have avoided some of this.

ROPER: Back to Dr. Esser's paper: I was wondering if the mix-up between the different parts of the brain is something that could be overcome by this design that you are speaking of, or whether this would continue to mess us up since we are structurally what we are.

MIDLARSKY: I want to ask Dr. Esser about the data (which is essentially social-psychological) on the individuals arbitrarily assigned to various groups and who, even though arbitrarily assigned, still treated the other group as the out-group, and how that relates to the structure of the brain.

CARROLL: To answer what Dr. Esser said about the absurd universe in our outline: that was not a pejorative expression; it was an expression related to existentialist theories of the nature of the universe and the characterization of the universe as absurd simply is intended to imply that there is no God who specifies, or any external force which specifies, an order which human beings cannot control or do not have any freedom to act within. In fact, the implication of that absurd universe, as I tried to indicate in the policy column, is that human beings have enormously open possibilities to design society and the future themselves and also the responsibility for doing so.

ESSER: Well, I thank you very much, Dr. Carroll, that you said that, because I stand fully corrected. I made the remark on the absurd universe because it had something to do with design or the fact that if you believe that man has certain biological characteristics then you are fatalistic. I am not. I am just the opposite. I believe that choice within options that are dictated by our brain is really what should NOT make us fatalistic.

Midlarsky asks how I would explain this difference in intergroup relations once you are oriented to a group even if it's very arbitrarily designed. Well, the explanation is that our bonding mechanisms — which, because of the hierarchical organization of the brain, have preference over intellectual, reasonable bonding mechanisms — are at work. Suppose some of us were put together for an hour and part of us put together in another room for an hour. When we came out we would all be more in agreement with the group that was here than with the group that was there. Why? Because we are familiar. We see the face, we have smelt each other, we have clothes, we have seen how somebody dresses. (That's why I make my curriculum vitae available, so you know I am not so bad, you can read up on me.) This is the only reason; familiarity makes for bonding mechanisms. Bonding mechanisms, because of the fact that we are group-oriented animals because of our mammalian background and we have to stay with mama and daddy and stay together just to survive, have preference. (If you read the book by Lionel Tiger on man in groups you see the argument worked out, but again, as I say, it's soft data. It is insufficient.)

Now, going to Mrs. Roper's question. Where do I stand? Am I an optimist or a pessimist about the future? You are right in both senses. I am an optimist because I believe that with empathy (which is an intellectual function — it is not sympathy) we can overcome some of our built-in polluted structures. However, it is part of our brain that we are continually polluted in this sense, and I believe it's part of our further evolution. I do not think that we stand still today. I think even literally and anatomically we are still moving in the brain, although it is very hard to prove. So I believe you have a continuous evolution and the drive for that evolution is provided by this social pollution principle. If all were harmony we would sit under a banana tree and enjoy ourselves, which you can do in Tahiti. We do not sit under banana trees; we sometimes do not enjoy ourselves and therefore we still have to make primarily environmental moves although there must still be some mental moves going on here. We make primarily environmental moves because man the manipulator will take the environment and shape it. And I believe that the important task is for us to fully realize what that implies.

HUBER: I'm still a bit puzzled over what seems to me a contradiction in this notion about the absurd universe, an absurd view of the universe, and seeing it as an optimistic way of looking at the world. It strikes me that one of the things that the whole idea of the technological manipulation of the world is predicated upon is the idea that things are controlled in a certain way and that you can tap into that control, and if you postulate that there really is no determinism going on, then on the one hand that liberates you, but on the other hand, it doesn't give you any handle over anything else. This is a true contradiction that also comes out in the notion of synergy that you mentioned; the notion of people developing a relationship out of interaction but not knowing what the end of it will be. How do you reconcile that with the idea of design? How can you design a synergy? There's a problem here which I think we have to confront and I think it really is central to the whole idea of engineering and the whole problem of violence in society. It may be that, in fact, violence is precisely that aspect of social life which is the opposite of control and in which there is no way to structure it. It's the antithesis of structure.

KRAKAUER: Although we were talking, essentially, about ways of altering our mental anatomy (in terms of what can WE do to change the internal connections — because obviously there are internal connections changing all the time), once we started mentioning physical anatomy we seemed to look at this in a different light. The odds of changing the physical anatomy are very small. The various techniques, such as even psychotherapy, are ways of changing the structure, but they are limited.

CARROLL: Back to the determinism question which Mr. Huber mentioned something about. When Dr. Fink was discussing this over and over again in the course of developing this paper, we realized that this was a contradictory position, that you cannot be free unless you can count on some elements of determinism in the situation around you, so that what you want to do can be done. Because if everything is undetermined, then you can have no possible control over anything outside yourself and maybe not even over yourself. Therefore, you know it's obviously a contradictory position. What I would say about that and about the relevance of that dimension is that there are serious contradictions, both logical and practical, in every column of that determinism, non-determinism chart. But, for the most part, they are totally unrecognized by the theories or theorists who fall into those categories. There is at least some need to recognize them and explore them and possibly try to resolve them. Whether it's possible to resolve that contradiction between freedom and determinism, I don't know, but there is a need to explore the contradictions in the context of theories of war.

TEFFT: One of my interests has been trying to determine why levels of violence vary in tribal warfare and I was struck by a statement in Dr. Esser's paper where, in referring to the Dani, he suggests that the battles among them miss the characteristic cultural derailments of aggression, that is, the occupation of territory and the destruction of the social order of the other party. Apparently this is a case where social pollution does not take place and one might wonder under what circumstances these alliances broke up and one confederation of the alliance, when it built up enough grievances, secretly raided and killed and destroyed the fellow members' group and eventually took over their territory.

MIDLARSKY: I want to deal with the question of prediction again and go back to the example about population growth. Not being a demographer, I wasn't concerned with those growth curves at all, but I was curious. If somebody had looked at the rate of growth in terms of some overall trends and seen change in growth over time, and then seeing how much of a change was needed to reach zero population growth, even if we allow for a maximum amount of error (meaning a total change, not only in the form, but in what is happening, i.e. a totally new element, a new invention, a new scientific development), then I think some good will have come from the prediction. That is, of course, going off the curve in a technologically entirely new area, but I think the prediction does have value even allowing for a large amount of error.

CANCRO: There are obviously many benefits from an exercise which may turn out to be inaccurate. My concern is that when we make these extrapolations there is a tendency to present them as *de facto* documents. You will hear statements like, "In 1983 (and you know he really knows it's going to be February 19, but he doesn't want to scare you) this is going to happen," and we have, in all of us, enough of the belief in magic that in the face of certainty we become convinced. When some of my patients tell me with total certainty that they are Jesus Christ, I'm not so sure, because they are so sure that they are, and I'm not really sure that they're not. I begin to have some question as to, is he right or is he wrong, or I could be wrong on this, he's certainly more convinced than I am. I am not being facetious.

Part of the problem in this whole area is that you only have a certain number of cracks at the public and when the professional viewers-with-alarm get on television and regularly predict that the world is going to end next Tuesday at high noon and it doesn't, you turn off the public. If we make pollution, if we make the dangers to the planet into one more kind of fad, you're not going to be able to reach the public in an effective way to make the kind of changes I am personally committed to, and personally feel are essential. I think that our efforts to design, even though they will be feeble and idiotic in many ways, are necessary. I don't believe we should make instant massive changes. I don't think we know what we're doing, but to begin to make changes and to study the effect of our changes and see where we've loused up and whether we can improve and do things more effectively is absolutely essential. In a sense we must try to design and choose our destiny.

OLDFIELD HAYES: According to Dr. Bishop's report, I would assume that the model would go something like this: elimination of food resources led to elimination of hunting bands, which in fact were the war groups, which in turn led to an elimination of war. Then perhaps this inner frustration was manifested in another area such as an increase in cannibalism.

I would also like to briefly outline another development in another time and in another place that is similar. During the First Intermediate Period of ancient Egypt there was a widespread drought over a long period which in effect led to the disintegration of the state into nomes, or smaller districts. There was a lack of warfare during that period and an increase in cannibalism. I think this points out the complexity of these issues evolving on the interrelatedness of aggression and violence and warfare. If you get an inverse ratio, that is you get a decrease in one when you get an increase in the other, I don't think you can actually say that the sources, that is violence and aggression, are the causes of both cannibalism and warfare. Warfare seems in both of these instances more dependent upon social organizational factors than on innate aggressive instincts.

BISHOP: Implicit in the discussion so far is the idea that a drying up of the world's resources will somehow automatically lead to warfare. I think that this is false, as witness the case in India where people are dying on the streets constantly and you don't have warfare. Or witness a more simple example, the Ojibwa, which I brought up earlier and which got misinterpreted. I do not say that the deterioration of the environment through overhunting led to cannibalism. Or at least led to Windigo psychosis. What I said was the deterioration of the environment led at the same time to changes in the social organization, which maximized people's efforts under new conditions, but which even then were insufficient and which frequently resulted in cannibalistic acts, merely to stay alive. Overt hostilities outside or beyond could no longer exist under these conditions and I don't believe they can exist in places like India. It's inconceivable that people in Bombay could organize, given their present social organization, to overthrow the contemporary system and create a revolution.

SCOTT: I would like to question the relationship between energy and warfare. From what you said, among primitive social people it would be essentially impossible to carry on warfare without having a certain amount of surplus energy. Therefore it would seem to me that Dr. Cooper, on the basis of his predictions of changes in energy supply, ought to be able to make some predictions about what might conceivably happen to our own capacities to indulge in warfare. A very interesting phenomenon along these lines, going on at the present time, is that the economic growth both in Japan and West Germany seems to be doing a lot better than it is in Russia and the U.S. One of my friends has suggested that perhaps the reason for this is that recently neither Japan nor West Germany has put out a very large proportion of their total energy supply in preparing for war and hence has an enormous economic advantage over the two major nations which are competing with each other. I wish there were an ecologist here who could look at this systematically in terms of energy, but I'd like to ask Dr. Cooper what he thinks about what is going to happen to warfare as an institution as a result of these modifications in energy supply.

RICHARDS: One of the things that got lost earlier was an implication about the rapidity with which people can change. There is a great myth abroad that it is SO HARD to change people. And that is just sheer nonsense. The problem is, it's very hard to change people in the directions YOU want them to go but it is almost impossible to stop them from changing in the directions THEY want to go. The zero population growth achievement that we made so rapidly in this country should sound a note of caution. In the U.S., with people's access to the mass media and the responsiveness of the public to the mass media in unpredictable ways (who would know that people would keep smoking cigarettes and would stop having babies), it seems to me that we have to be extremely cautious. It is all too easy to get the general public to go haring off down some incredible path that may get us into a box that is even harder to get out of than the ones we are in now. Again, the alternatives sometimes may be worse. We're awfully ready to rush in, and too much of this and we'll have what I think Dr. Cancro was talking about — the "cry-wolf syndrome." Well, if that happens, they just won't listen to us at all anymore and then when we really have some kind of an answer that will work and will not create a worse mess than we had in the first place, we won't get anybody's ear. I hate to cry caution, because I'm alarmed like everyone else, but at the same time, this particular response has really given me cause to think that if I suggest "A" and it is picked up by the *New York Times* and it is picked up by God knows who all else, and it suddenly comes on television, who knows? I could be wrong, so could we all, and we could have a greater effect. We have been complaining that we may have no effect. I am worried that we may have a very great effect and we don't know what we're doing, necessarily.

ROPER: I am very pleased with Dr. Cooper's approach and feel that we need more of this type of thing to educate the public. Where is our tax money going in the United States? Not much of it's going to develop solar energy, is it? But a great deal of money is going to develop military ways to get oil and as you probably know, the Marines have been training in our deserts, recently, which I am sure all of you think of as, "Oh, well we're just having games," but they are desert games and some people are very concerned. It is very important for the public to be informed so that they can lobby for more rational activities on the part of our government as to how our money is being spent. Not to make a decision is a decision, or not to make a change is a decision.

HUBER: I have two points actually. One is a clarification of what I think is a misconception: the notion that in primitive societies some kind of surplus energy is required before war can be made. The idea is not so much empirically false, but the concept of surplus itself is extremely difficult if not impossible to define in terms of energy. The energy requirement of primitive society is almost meaningless to talk about in terms of setting some level of what the essential energy requirement is and what is above that. In a sense everybody has surplus energy.

I also wanted to respond to this business about contradictions. When I suggested that there were contradictions in the idea of an absurd universe or absurdity, I didn't mean that in a pejorative sense. I wasn't implying that to uncover contradictions is necessarily proving an idea invalid. In fact I was trying to say just the reverse: we ought to attend very carefully to the contradictions. Because they may not be contradictions merely in theory but contradictions in social life which may be in some way very closely linked with the nature of violence and war.

RICHARDS: With regard to the relationship of energy to war, Hoffer has said that the abject poor don't make a revolution because they are too busy scurrying around making a living. It's the next people up, the people who are a little better off than the abject poor, who start the revolution.

Now, maybe we can actually make a couple of statements about what can cause war, or what are some of the conditions for war. Let's not say "cause," because it makes people uneasy, but what are some of the conditions that encourage or allow war to occur? I think we can say, probably safely, that a group of people the size of the Tassaday, 24–25, are not going to make war. I don't think anybody here is going to contradict that case. The most they may do is a little bit of raiding, but they are not likely to do even that, particularly if their neighbors are stronger than they are, because they will get slaughtered like mosquitoes and they can't afford it. With 11 adults, you cannot afford to throw them away. So a group that small is not likely to make war. Secondly, people who are spending all their energy scrounging for food are not going to make war. But, does this give us much help? Can we say that to stop war we are going to break up all societies into groups of 25 people and keep them without any food? Maybe this is the only answer. It will stop war! Granted, it has a lot of complications but this gives us a base line. How can we modify this?

Concerning the relationship of internal aggression to war: war has specifically been practiced by groups from the size of modern states like Nazi Germany to American Indians. To decrease internal aggression, to maintain internal peace, to increase internal bonding and cohesion, you can develop an outside enemy and channel your aggression in the direction of outside. The other way, apparently, works too. A threat to a group from outside, a real threat let's say, not one made up to distract people and focus their aggression outside, pulls everyone together and it becomes a bad thing in people's values to fight internally. It is possible that there is a relationship between internal aggression and warfare and this is a subject for investigation. In peacetime, does internal aggression increase? In warfare, does internal aggression decrease? If it does, I think we've got to say why and how are we going to change this if we stop war. How are we going to keep peace within the group if we stop the group from fighting outside? I've been trying to answer Dr. Smith's comments by presenting some specific things that we can chew on that indicate an area for research that comes out of some experimental data that we have.

CORNING: It might be useful to try to put Dr. Cooper's discussion more specifically into the context of warfare. This brings us back to a point that I tried to make yesterday about the fact that systematic forms of behavior, such as violent aggression, evolved in accordance with our understanding of how the evolutionary process works, how the behavior systems of different species evolved because of their functions, because of the utility to a species in terms of solving the basic problems of survival and reproduction. That's a fairly safe generalization for all species and, I would argue, for man too. A systematic form of behavior like collective intergroup violence would not have come to be, had it not, on balance, been useful to the species in terms of solving the problems of survival. It's doubtful that it would have become so widespread had it been dysfunctional. This is not to say that it is not dysfunctional today or that the forms of society that we have evolved today make warfare an effective or desirable or functional form of behavior. On the contrary. But the point is that in the past and for other species there is evidence that warfare has been associated with fundamental problems: of territory, of food supply, of threats from other populations or other species. That is why I think that there is a very close relationship between the future of warfare in human society and the kinds of projections that are being made by the *Limits to growth* people. Even if their projections are only half right, they suggest that there is going to be a serious intensifying of competition for scarce resources relating to the problems of survival and reproduction of *Homo sapiens*. It's not reasonable to assume that there will be a simple drying up of resources around the world all at once for everybody and that we will find ourselves in a situation comparable to the Ojibwa or to a population that is close to starvation. In fact, what will happen first, much sooner than that, is more intensive competition for those resources that do exist and warfare will very likely be one of the tools which human populations will use to compete for those resources that do exist. So I would suggest that we, as students of warfare and human populations, pay very close attention to the implications of these limits to growth studies. I don't in any way disagree with the other points that have been made about how we should be skeptical about alarmist projections, how misrepresentation can be dangerous and dysfunctional in terms of dealing with these problems, but I do suggest that there is a very close relationship between warfare in human society and the kinds of problems that these projections suggest for the future of the human species.

COOPER: The only disagreement I would have with Dr. Corning's comments is that individual and group violence and the functions they serve in relation to survival are very different from the kind of pressure that now is exerted on the world and the causes of it by the United States. The U.S. power drive (and you can lump Japan and Europe and the Soviet Union in with us) is to preserve our status quo. The status quo is not survival. It's either having a Cadillac or the potential of having a Cadillac or one TV set or two TV sets; trivial in comparison to survival, which makes it even more to be criticized.

Responding to Dr. Scott's question about the potential of war-making power when energy is depleted: If you look at it as a continuum of having energy or no energy either within a country or in the world, if you have no energy sources, you have no war. But the current situation is that the United States still does have power, still does have energy sources and can use power to gain its goals. Now the end of this kind of ability to use power by countries like the United States is in sight. Whether or not we will be able to use this power to exert or preserve our way of life at the expense of the rest of the world, or whether we will run out of these energy sources soon or whether this will cause conflict with the other countries who are also going to be needing this, I don't know. Third World cooperation at the moment gives us the kind of oil and nickel that we need and since we are more powerful than the other developed countries, the current trend is that we will just deplete the earth and no one will have our kind of war-making power again.

There were a lot of comments about predictions and this really isn't what I was talking about; it's more looking at actual trends and trying to clarify major problems that are existing in the world. If people had looked, just after the Second World War when the United States moved into the void left by England, France, and the rest of the colonial powers, what this trend might lead to could possibly have been foreseen.

To go back to what Dr. Jacobs has been trying to do for a couple of days and think about the focus of the Conference: causes of war. If we do see some undeniable trends that are occurring (I like to think I mentioned a couple) which, if we don't change things will lead to war and disaster and violence, then in this Conference is there (and if not in this Conference a later one perhaps) any vehicle for working on looking at possible specific actions that can be taken to avoid some of the obvious things that are occurring? What kinds of social changes, social organizations will need to be structured, or is this Conference going to be limited to the causes of, rather than solutions to, war?

ESSER: I would like to structure with you some answers to the questions as they have been raised just to indicate how I would be thinking. Where I was talking about mental and environmental, Mr. Krakauer said, apologetically, that psychotherapy should also be part of this design. I would like to firm that up. Psychotherapy (in any internal mental manipulation that psychiatrists, psychologists, or anybody might do) belongs to the ordering of structures—MENTAL—and design (especially environmental design, architecture, etc.) belongs to structuring—ENVIRONMENTAL. The important point here is that as far as mental structuring is concerned, we practically only structure conceptually. We cannot change the way we breathe too much, we cannot change the way we cry too much, but we can change the way we rationally think very much. But the conceptual changes are those that would account for war.

For instance, the Dani were brought up by Dr. Tefft. Why I would not consider them to have war with each other is because I believe they are in harmony with each other. The situation is one of two tribes that fight in a no man's land. They do not invade each other's territory; they do not burn each other down. The concept is lacking in their minds, that you can really obliterate or obfuscate somebody else, totally do away with them. That concept is not there. (If you put it into their minds, no doubt they will go out and try to wipe each other out.) The harmony with the cosmos, therefore, maintains their non-warfare attitude. The only difference between battle (or a legitimate aggression, ritualized aggression) and war is the intent. In war the intent is that, in case we do not get what we want, in case somebody else threatens our structure, we have to destroy the other person.

To suggest, by an analogy, that it's not only some Stone Age people who are sitting there that have none of this intent, I want to refer to China. China has for centuries been self-contained. Why? Because in their concept they were the middle of the world. They had no intent to go out and conquer the rest of the world. That was not necessary. In the harmonious concept of their cosmos, they had everything, they were the Middle Kingdom. Why should they go out and conquer something else? It is not only aggression of scale, it's aggression of concept. Where it is destroyed, as in the most tragic recent example of the Eke, the mountain people that Colin Turnbull describes, or the Ojibwa as Bishop described (and Oldfield Hayes has described something like that for the Egyptians), something has happened. We know that in the case of the Eke, something happened in their ecological environment that then in turn changed the isomorphic mental concept that they were working at. They changed from a good-natured, laughing, hunting people to vicious agricultural people. It's not always possible for an outside observer to find this conceptual change, and, as Dr. Tefft mentioned, some of the Dani tribes later may wipe each other out in raids. We don't know what conceptually changed their minds, but I would bet that you could go out and find it, that it's either missionaries who have given them something or some ideas or acts, or some other influence has interfered and made them catch hold of some ideas and go on and have this type of war.

Finally, what Dr. Cooper asked me, how can you reconcile the paradox between the control that is obviously needed when for instance the violence gets out of hand. How is this not a paradox? Well, first of all I'd rather not say control; I'd rather say the order. We are ordering structures. And indeed, when it derails we go into violence. How are we going to solve this? If the lower part of the brain allows a certain order, you always have this fight between the two parts of our central nervous system. I suggest that this dichotomy which is built into us (irrational versus rational; biosocial man or biological man versus cultural man) can conceptually be looked at not as a dichotomy, but as a complementarity. It's just as in physics where you can fight until eternity about whether it is the wave theory of light or whether it is the particle theory of light. It cannot be resolved. In the last thirty or forty years you come to the conclusion that there must be a complementarity principle, and that it is in other aspects of physics also. I would say that the complementarity principle we have discovered in physics is environmental, naturally (and I say "naturally" very deliberately: naturally it must exist within the head; otherwise we would not have come up with it). Consequently there must be a complementarity principle in my central nervous system also and in my mental structure. It is my personal intent to go after that, because I think only with the discovery of the complementarity of all of us and all our structuring can we come to (and that is the word that I dropped earlier) synergy, which is very strange and maybe I'll make it expressly strange and mysterious, a working-together, a cooperation of systems without being able to predict the end results. That's a jump of faith. Again I'm on weak data, but I am looking for that jump to make and to put that on hard data.

HUBER: One point of fact that I would like to clarify. With respect to the Dani I am not sure which of Heider's publications you are referring to, but I do know, as a result of a personal communication, that on his first trip (he made two field trips with the Dani), he saw the ritualized aspect of war which is presented, for example, in the film *Dead Birds*, but on his second trip he discovered that there were other things going on at the same time which he simply hadn't realized on the first trip into the field. I think it would be misleading to think of the Dani as having at one time lived in the perfect harmony of a well-defined cosmos into which violence does not penetrate and having been changed at some later point by outside intervention. It seems that both the idea of an harmonious cosmos and the possibility of really massive violence (in the standard sense of the word) were parts of the Dani social experience. This was also true of my own field experience and I think would be to some extent true of a large number of New Guinea societies that I am familiar with through the ethnographic record. There is a certain kind of danger in postulating some kind of primeval paradise in which a society lives and sees itself in the center of a very well-ordered and neatly balanced cosmos which later becomes imbalanced by some outside pressure. Both of those possibilities — the possibility for violence, the possibility for order — are part of the same ongoing social system; the potential for both exists at the same point in time.

RICHARDS: I think most of us are familiar with the general Eastern concept of harmony which Dr. Esser mentioned. He says that it's impossible to conceive of war, for when one strives for unity with the cosmos, how can one wage war without violence to himself? I don't know the answer to that question, but the American Indian and an awful lot of the Asiatics have figured it out, because the Iroquois, who have this concept of being one with nature and being in harmony with the universe and the necessity of maintaining this harmony, managed to do a very neat job of exterminating through warfare five or six different Indian groups that were around them. Consider furthermore the Chinese movement into Southeast Asia, long, long before it was South Vietnam or anything else, movements into Korea, into Formosa. There's plenty of historical evidence of what I think would have to be, by any definition we're using, warfare. The Thai have engaged in warfare, the people in India have engaged in warfare, and I think it's a myth to assume that the Eastern philosophy necessarily eliminates the possibility of war. I don't think it has, historically, and I don't think it does today.

I also find it very difficult intellectually to call killing another human being anything but violence. I will say, all right, maybe it's not warfare, but it certainly is violent and if you kill a lot of them, collectively, as collective group action against another group, I'm really not sure how much I want to distinguish this from warfare. Maybe scale again is significant and if you really only kill two people in a conflict between groups it's not warfare, whereas if you kill 200,000 it is. As I say, this is one of the things that we haven't come to grips with because we really haven't decided what we're talking about when we talk about warfare, but I do feel that there is plenty of historical evidence.

KRAKAUER: I'd like to make some reference to a remark by Dr. Corning before the break, in connection with warfare. He said that there is probably a connection between warfare and survival of the human race. In my opinion there is no necessary connection at all. There may be, but it's hardly necessary to postulate that.

CORNING: That's exactly what I said, that there is no necessary connection, but that in order to understand its evolution, how it came to be in the first place, you are dealing with positive selection for a behavioral trait or the biological substrate of a behavior trait. I'm not saying it's functional now, which is again precisely the same as saying that there is no NECESSARY connection between warfare and survival. Quite the opposite, I think that there may be a necessary connection, certainly with respect to the nuclear powers, of non-warfare and survival.

KRAKAUER: How about the warfare in the beginnings of man? Were you making some reference to that?

CORNING: Yes, the evolution of warfare in human society, in proto-hominid or early human societies.

KRAKAUER: Well, this is what I'm making reference to. It has some relation to my paper and the way I described *Homo sapiens*. Warfare may simply be what I would call a hyperemotional activitiy, whereas leadership and followership and pride and dominance and safety needs are all necessary for survival. Warfare is probably one of the many aspects of the exaggerated responses of our species. To make a rough parallel, you talk about the survival of a plant which produces twenty billion pieces of pollen and only a few of them happen to land, and you can say the same about human activities which are not bound in very well by instinctual controls. You find that they go off excessively in many directions and are a throwoff and not necessarily related to the survival of the species.

BISHOP: Getting back to this question of warfare among so-called pre-contact peoples, first of all I doubt very strongly that it really existed on the scale that it did in post-European times. For one thing most tribal groups, including the Dani and some of the others, had a no man's land between themselves and other groups. This was the case for practically all tribal groups throughout North America. There was an area in which you just didn't go. Tribal boundaries are not like lines on maps that you see in textbooks. Instead, they usually involve a space. Warfare as we tend to think of it today among tribal groups came into existence in post-contact times as a result of disease, European conquests, a snowballing effect that ultimately eliminated the Hurons almost totally as well as some other groups on the Plains.

It is a difference of scale more than anything and I doubt that warfare came into existence until you had some subgroup within the larger society whose sole function, or at least one of whose functions, was to engage in military tactics (such as the Iroquois war parties). I don't think there is much evidence that they existed early on. A group of males got together and maybe did a little bit of raiding and that was the extent of it. Plains military societies were, as far as the historical evidence goes, all emerging; they all developed in slightly different ways after about 1700. The same is true for other groups as well and these have been historically documented.

A. NETTLESHIP: May I ask if there is a conference agreement as to whether or not raiding parties as such and small group activities are not warfare? Did we generally agree upon that? Any objection to this idea? We've talked of it as a formal thing.

M. NETTLESHIP: I've tried to suggest a differentiation between fighting which takes place in small, primitive groups and war which is a feature of state organization. I wonder whether what Bishop is talking about, primitive groups exposed to higher cultures, is perhaps a middle ground, or does he feel it's one or the other?

BISHOP: Middle ground warfare only exists where you do have sizable settlements and a surplus that will feed a bunch of people who can take the time off to go out and fight. Most people, given the opportunity, don't care to fight if they can avoid it. At least, I don't think they do.

M. NETTLESHIP: Do you feel then that there might be a continuum or do you think there are three different points?

BISHOP: It could be a continuum but I also think warfare in North

America, for the most part, was set off by European intrusion into the region.

M. NETTLESHIP: I would agree with you in that instance but I wonder if this kind of phenomenon hasn't happened many times in the world where there have been higher culture groups with pretty well-developed technology of warfare and what I would call war, coming into contact with primitive groups and creating the same kinds of situations we had in this country.

YOUNG: I'd like to say something about this question of warfare and survival or adaptation. As I pointed out, the growth of the state and of the military state has resulted in the survival of that type of social organization and enabled it to cover practically the entire earth. This is the kind of survival that biologists talk about. They call it intraspecies competition and quite frequently selection for intraspecies competition may result in the extinction of a species because the types that are selected are not advantageous for other aspects of the life of the species. This may be happening with the human species. The military state, through being selected for survival and developing its great potentialities for technology and so forth, may have set up a situation that will result in the extinction of the human species. Nevertheless, this military organization has had a high survival value of its own. This may also have been advantageous up to the present time, as far as the species is concerned, because the type of social organization that we have under the military state makes possible a much greater economic development and hence a larger population. In biological terms that would certainly be considered a survival advantage.

JACOBS: I wanted to point out something that may have got lost when we were talking about energy levels and war for resources. Richardson, for example, did a study of a hundred years of war and discovered that only 40 percent of wars could be traced to economic causes. That doesn't mean that I subscribe to the aggression theory but what we should accept is the idea that conflicts do occur between nation-states for many reasons and I think that we should begin to think about what kind of alternate institutions we can develop.

One thing that has bothered me in a lot of the discussion earlier today and yesterday was the idea that we have to develop greater fondness for other people and extend the kinship group and that sort of thing. I think this is a blind alley. Maybe we ought to accept that there are going to be conflicts between nation-states over values, over resources, over power, over ideas, and that nations will probably continue to endure. You spoke of breaking up into groups of 25. Certainly you don't plan to do that, but it looks as if it's not ideal to have one homogenized group and that what we ought to think about is developing alternate kinds of institutions for settling the kinds of inevitable conflicts that are going to continue to occur.

CANCRO: In defense of the transcultural identification, I think the point being made is that it is more difficult to use war as a solution if people are less ready to go to war. They demand alternatives from their political parties, from their government. They will support alternative institutions more readily if they are more reluctant to use war as a method of policy.

JACOBS: There have been a great many wars between very similar nations, nations which like each other very much in times when they do not have conflict over something immediate.

MELKO: In the discussion of primitive societies and civilized societies there is some implication of evolution. It strikes me, and I've studied only civilized societies, that over the last 5,000 years there has been no marked change in the amount of war from century to century or area to area. What IS striking among the nation-states that have existed over this time is the amount of peace that has existed. We tend to write about war — war is the stuff of history — but there's no question that most nations are at peace most of the time, that peace is the normal condition ALL through civilized history, for ALL nations, and that war is an exception and therefore it might be well, before we revise the political structure, to look at what exists and see why it has worked so often as well as it has.

SIPES: First of all, on the definition of warfare, or what we are going to classify as warfare. We seem to have now a trichotomy: fighting, raiding, and warfare. Groups composed of about twenty people really can only fight. If you have a hundred people you can raid. It takes over a thousand people to engage in what we've been classifying here as warfare. But for heaven's sake they all do the best they can. The little group may lack the tactics and the manpower and the weapons systems, but they are in there pitching and I think we should give them credit.

CANCRO: This is a point that I would very much share with you, that if society is killing only one at a time, but the best they have is a stone axe, they are at their ultimate and we have to recognize this as a maximal effort.

SIPES: I would like to comment in passing on the institutions for solving conflict which develops between countries. This may reduce war somewhat. However, I would like to see the institution which could have solved the conflict developing between Hitler in Germany and

Czechoslovakia or between the world of Islam and the world of the pagan whenever Islam was spreading. Some conflicts you solve only by war.

There was another comment made about the lack of warfare, or anything really too much resembling it, by Dr. Bishop. I would like to know how he explains the fortifications of Pueblo people if there wasn't warfare in North America and I would also like to clarify what he means by North America. The Aztecs and the Mayas were hard at it. If you consider North America to be only north of the Pedernales River that explains it, but the land mass extends down to the Isthmus of Panama and that is a logical place to divide it.

Warfare relative to the survival of the species, I think, has been something of the past. We no longer talk about warfare or warlike actions as having enhanced the survival of the species too much, but, as was brought out, intraspecies competition does mean that a group which is ready, willing, and able to engage in warlike actions generally will have a better chance of survival as a specific group than a group that is not ready, willing, and able to engage in warfare. At least this has been true up until the atomic bomb. Now that we are capable of the sterilization of the planet we are playing a different ball game. However, we still can have brush wars and in all probability, the survival value of war, relative to a specific group, is still present. This, at least, is my hypothesis.

SIVERTS: You mentioned the Aztecs and the Mayas and I have been surprised that we haven't taken that up before as an interesting sample because, for one thing, the Aztecs were not fighting for economic reasons, at least that was not the primary motive as we know it in ethnohistory. The fighting was very much religious fighting and I associate the Aztec case with the discussion of the Dani and their two phases of fighting (how they were in a balance, and then they were not and so they start fighting). The Aztecs did all their fighting because they wanted the cosmos to be IN BALANCE all of the time. They really had an ideology for keeping the whole earth, themselves included, in balance. This is an interesting ethnographic picture that will give us an example from North American raiding society, that kind of thing, that developed into something in the eighteenth century, and other feuding types of societies such as exist in South America. We have here war in the sense we have been talking about but for quite different reasons. This is a complex society and its war is on the basis of ideology.

War in Complex Societies

Chaire by R. D. GIVENS and M. K. ROPER
Discussion of papers by A. LEEDS, C. AMSBURY, MIDLARSKY and
S. T. THOMAS, M. MELKO, M. E. SMITH, H. CLAESSEN, P. POPE,
J. SAXE-FERNÁNDEZ, R. OLDFIELD HAYES

GIVENS: Unfortunately Dr. Anthony Leeds is not able to be with us but Dr. Nettleship has the abstract of his paper and will present the abstract for us.

M. NETTLESHIP: Dr. Leeds' paper is called, "Capitalism, colonialism, and war — an evolutionary perspective."

In the course of the evolution of human society, one variety of human sociocultural organization, called capitalism, arose. It is a subcategory of a larger set of societies we designate as state societies. All states comprise a type of system concerned with the maintenance of some sort of socioterritorial boundary, in such ways that the exercise of force is intrinsically necessary either against external societal entities or against internal subsocietal segments, or both. Most subcategories of states, other than the capitalistic, involve only limited expansionism in the pursuit of boundary maintenance, usually to the physical limits of some geographically defined ethnosystem. The capitalist state is unique in its organization in that the form of economy of such states is a type of system characterized by continuous increment for its survival; an equilibrium of growth or expansion rather than one of steady state. What keeps the capitalist system going is the constant expansion of sociomaterial, territorial boundaries. The history of the evolution of capitalism is also the history of a sequence of forms generated for expanding the sociomaterial and territorial boundaries.

One of the earlier forms is the direct conquest by war of alien, ecologically differentiated resource areas which are then incorporated under the administrative structure of the capitalist state as a kind of territorial expansion. Internal stratification of the conquered people as regards rights, duties, exchanges, receipts, etc. is a structural parallel to the class stratification inside the colonializing polity, which increasingly externalizes the lower levels of the system of strata into the colonies as the colonizing process matures.

Direct, conquest-achieved control initially reduced the cost of resources and labor, producing a net capital gain over the expenses of warfare and administration in the first stages of the capitalist development process. In time, cost of administration reduced the profitability of the return due to competition with other similarly expanding capitalist states. Occasional warfare with these occurred for the physical administrative control of colonial territories, and there was competition with internally colonized continental scale capitalist societies like the United States and Russia and potentially China and Brazil. The cost of maintenance of the colonies and their populations, the cost of the infrastructural investment in colonies (as a technology of production and the rate of resource use both advanced), the increasing cost of maintaining source production and distribution, the cost of new capital inputs in the colonies altogether, all of these things together outweighed benefits and the colonial form of capitalism collapsed. Colonies and accompanying cultural responsibilities were sloughed off to be replaced by neo-colonial forms of socioterritorial control through, in effect, purchase of the productive capacity of the now "independent" former colonies (i.e. ownership through investment of the needs of production, especially industrial and marketing mechanisms). While this reduced social costs, it also transferred administrative costs, order maintenance, etc. to the new nation. These costs themselves rendered neo-colonial nations less independent and hence more tied with the economic invasion of the large capitalist countries. It is a self-intensifying system.

Essential to the system, from the point of view of the capitalist metropoles, is the need to enforce the operation of this system and with it, the internal orders of the neo-colonial states. That is, it involves ready military organization, military training and supplies to neo-colonial countries, and the military suppression of resource areas which do not choose to conform to the international neo-colonial structure or which threaten it. The extent of military action — warfare — is limited only by the threat of the too costly self-damage to any given system (even though all capitalist systems allow for some toleration of self-damage). See, for example, the deterrent discussions. So long as the state is expansive, productive apparatuses are guaranteed continuity.

In evolutionary and natural historical perspective, warfare is a perfectly natural "normal" and appropriate sociocultural institution, just as capitalism is a system naturally evolved in the course of human development. It seems, like some adaptations of other species, also to be non-adaptive and self-destructive to the species in the long run. This probable fact, however, does not make it, as a part of the overall experiences of mankind, immoral or power-abusive, any more thans Tyrannosaural gigantism and violence were immoral or power-abusive.

Judgments as to ethics, immorality, abusiveness, do not belong in the sphere of analytic science and should be clearly distinguished from it. In the evolutionary perspective of the history of species, there is no reason whatsoever why mankind should not evolve itself out of existence by whatever means it evolves to do so, whether population overproduction, capitalism, or something else. But that we choose to believe that it should not become extinct, that therefore some of us, myself included, consider power abuse or capitalism or overpopulation condemnable, is a value proposition not derivable from scientific thought.

GIVENS: We shall now hear Mr. Amsbury's summary.

AMSBURY: My paper is on patron-client structure in modern world organization. In other words, I am interested in the motivation and organization of the same kind of war that most of you are worried about: what Dr. Young calls political war.

Our problems can be reduced to five. The first is a definition of aggression and I am very dissatisfied with the one presented to this conference. My first reaction to it was simply to add "and for control of resources." Then I realized that resource in this sense is the same as "good" in the image of limited good and that space and dominance fall into that category of resource control and access. That also accords with Dollard and Miller's definition of aggression as a response to frustration of a goal response. A resource is something which you want in order to satisfy a goal response. Furthermore, very many cases which ethologists have interpreted in terms of spacing and dominance have actually had to do with control of access to specific resources. This brings aggression very close to being competitive behavior.

The second problem is the definition of violence. If we include in this definition damage to psychological integrity as well as to physical bodies, then it will fit in much better with the methodological aim of warfare which is to reduce the opponent's organization and morale relative to one's own and thus allow him to be put under control as a resource.

Third is the problem of motivation of allies, which is to say, one's supporters, protectors, and so forth. This includes the processes of identification.

The fourth problem involves the organization of these support and protection activities in groups. Ordinarily, these seem to parallel each society's organization of agents and of work groups.

The fifth is the crucial consideration. This notes that competition against others at the level of organized groups is against, not the leadership's competitors, but against the competitor's fields of influence, fields of action, and levels of morale. Which is to say, against the group's and the leadership's confidence. Now, until very recently all civilized societies were organized in patron-client format and empires still are, though the metropolitan society may no longer be so organized. The patron-client relationship characterizes all civilizations since classical times, probably ever since the proto-urban invasions which immediately preceded the organization of civilized societies in Egypt and Southwest Asia. In these societies, the patron-client or humanist societies, work and resource control are organized through a hierarchy of patron-client sets. We know such channels best in our military components. They also appear rather strongly in the family. The relationships are reciprocal and authoritarian and the symbolism is in terms of parent and child dominance, submission, and identification. Although the organization involves groups, all relationships are seen as, and identified as, diadic, and the leader personifies the group. In such societies there is no cultural limit on the dominance goals, only personal and group limitations. Therefore competition between equals is a principle, and revolt against superiors is a constant dream — or from the point of view of the superior, a constant nightmare. Leaders at higher levels compete with each other through patron-client sets, such as voting cliques and fighting gangs. They also consider patron-client sets of the lower level to be resources to be competed for. There are very definite patron-acquiring behaviors and there are also very definite client-making and client-keeping techniques and behaviors. They involve convincing the client-elect that he needs a protector, and then convincing him that no one else can protect him. Then we get the response of turning to the aggressor for protection and, indeed, only with such a mechanism could you explain successful conquest.

In his introductory paper, Dr. M. Nettleship noted that Carneiro, Park, Taylor, and Diamond imply a connection between military warfare and the state. The connecting data lie in the patron-client social organization and most such societies are not only military in form, but also military at heart. As Shepherd and Blake pointed out, differences of opinion are normally settled by suppression of the weaker party. This may or may not include physical violence.

My paper went on to consider how modern empires build upon the patron-client structures within the client countries by maintaining super-patron agencies within the metropolitan countries. These super-patron agencies may be private organizations, multi-national companies, or government agencies. All such types were involved in the attempted reconquest of Indochina.

Two broader points: first, we not only need to know when people are using the same word with different meanings, but also when they are using different words with the same meaning. Thus, often, ethologists speak of spacing and dominance when those are not the particular resources which are being controlled at the moment. And when I speak of spacing and dominance as resources from the control of which one can derive satisfaction, I am not always speaking of them in the same sense that the ethologists are.

The other point concerns the repeated statement that certain wars had no economic causes. We must remember that there are many rewards that are not clearly economic. In the case of the Jihad, we need to know how that culture and that society reward the preachers of holy wars and the participants in such wars. But because we are flesh and blood and we must eat to live, wear clothing to feel modest, and have shelter to be comfortable, everything has an economic base which must be kept in mind. One example: when the military in Indonesia used the Muslim political parties to slaughter the "communists," the chief victims were the propertied communist village leaders whose economic base had been keeping the party moderate. They were not only very visible, but they had property which could be divided among the local Muslim leadership. The laboring members were not only less visible, but were considered relatively unimportant and certainly there was nothing of immediate gain to be had. But within a very few months there were guerilla areas in the backlands.

GIVENS: We'll take a few comments now before we go on to other papers. Professor Young?

YOUNG: I would like to comment on Dr. Leeds' paper because he makes very clear the point of view of what science is and I agree with him thoroughly. If you say that science is theoretical, empirical, that is, essentially descriptive, that's what science has always been. That has been its ideal, but it is very clear from his paper that although he states this ideal, he feels uncomfortable with it because he has a certain moral and emotional commitment that he can't possibly bring into this scientific frame of reference. I have been talking at this meeting about a different kind of science. It is not absolutely necessary to confine what you call science to a descriptive science. We don't. We talk about applied science, we talk about practical science, we talk about policy science. When we talk about policy science, we decide that we have certain goals that our client wants to achieve. He picks the goals; as long as we don't pick the goals we are scientists. If we let him pay us to help him get his goals then we still remain scientists. Why can't we pick our own goals and work for ourselves? I think that people in this room are interested in working for the welfare of the human race, if I may be so sentimental. Down in our hearts, that's what we want. Why accept a taboo that prevents us from doing that? Ken Boulding has said that science has contributed greatly to our civilization by improving the image. This is one of the great revolutions of all time; improving the image of the world that we are in, the descriptive image. Science has also improved the prescriptive image, and it has given us prescriptions for getting to the moon and prescriptions for blowing ourselves into Kingdom Come. Why shouldn't science go to work to give us prescriptions for achieving Utopia? If we're serious about war, we are calling for a Utopian solution to human problems. Let's face that, but there is no reason why we cannot organize a type of prescriptive science where scientists work for themselves, not for a client they are being paid by, and where in working for themselves they are working for mankind.

ROPER: We also have to change our own attitudes because even we so-called scientists are not in such good shape that we can necessarily do this. I suggest that we start by changing some attitudes. One of the ideas of Dr. Press which I thought was excellent is the term "our brother's keeper." I think we should change that to being that we want to be our brother's brother.

M. NETTLESHIP: There is a branch of social science which has struggled fairly successfully with the sentimental, ethical, and scientific problems of helping people. That is applied anthropology. I would beg Professor Young to have a look at that literature before he despairs quite as much as he seems to. If we could now turn the discussion back toward war in complex societies, though these moral questions are fascinating, I would like to take up one of Mr. Amsbury's points. It seems to me that you are expanding the meaning of "economic" to cover quite a wide range of phenomena which usually, in anthropology, are considered under aspects of value systems. Perhaps you might find that values and value systems would encompass a lot of what you are calling economics and you might save two tools instead of losing both of them. Values, after all, are what help us to choose between alternatives.

OLDFIELD HAYES: The Jihad were begun by the Prophet Mohammed and they were participated in by thousands of peasants who gained nothing economically by adherence to the new ideology. The Jihad went on for centuries and seemed to be based on noticeable religious fervor. They were also marked by a noticeable lack of accumulation of war bounty; the sort of accumulation that normally marks other wars. It's true that territory came under the rule of the Islamic leaders, but the economic situation did not change for the people involved in the wars or involved in the territories that were conquered by those leading the Jihad. It has been shown over and over again that religion is a dynamic, integrative, and functional aspect of culture. I'm not against environmental determinism arguments or economic arguments. I simply think it unsound to try to pinpoint one institution such as economics as a reason for evolution, a reason for the rise of particular forms in cultures, without considering other aspects such as religion.

CLAESSEN: I refer to the remarks of Dr. Siverts and myself about the wars of the Aztecs and the wars of the ancient kingdoms. They were fought without economic arguments, so I think Mr. Amsbury is saying too much in his statement that everything has an economic base.

RICHARDS: I would expand on that a little further to include Dr. Leeds' paper. What does he mean by a capitalistic state? Is he talking only about modern capitalism or would he include Islam, Rome, and a few of the other expansionist empires of the past as capitalistic states? To equate capitalistic states with expansionism and exclude practically everything else or any other kind of state organization as expansionistic or warlike seems unrealistic. War, or at least violent intergroup conflict, has been associated with practically every form of social organization we know anything about and I am disturbed, as others obviously are, at confining it to an economic causation.

KRAKAUER: I think the economic basis theory is something of a flaw in Amsbury's paper. It goes back to trying to prove that survival is the only need of human beings or, if it is not true of every individual, then somehow it is true of the manipulators at the top. (Even if we ourselves may have some other interests, they do not.) The human species has basically the same directions as the other species and these directions include more than survival, more than creature comforts, and more than power expressed only in Cadillacs. The general direction in mammals including human beings (if in a less instinctive way) has been defined neatly and broadly in Maslow's hierarchy of physiological, safety, belonging needs, esteem needs, connative and esthetic needs. It would be hard to demonstrate that the astronauts are personally involved and putting their lives on the line for anything but an incredible amount of curiosity or even the self-esteem that they get when they come down, but I think you can read a newspaper any day of the week and find people sacrificing their lives, committing suicide for simple reasons of pride, prejudice, religion, anger, and a whole assortment of odds and ends like that. I go along with most people who feel that you are grossly oversimplifying when you try to tie everything down to that old devil, money, or an economic base.

M. NETTLESHIP: As I understand Dr. Leeds' paper, he is not trying to explain all of war or even (in spite of his title) "the total evolution of war" in terms of economic causes, but is examining the evolution of ONE form of economic interchange, that is capitalism, as it has had an effect on warfare over the last two or three centuries. That is the key point from his paper for this session. Dr. Richards' question is a very good one. Do the other kinds of developed states expand for similar reasons or different reasons? But I don't think it's fair to criticize Dr. Leeds for not having examined the question.

CORNING: I don't want to put myself in a position of necessarily agreeing with the two papers that have been summarized here, but I do want to make some comments that might help to give some perspective to some of the discussion. Once a particular trait evolves in any species, once the genetic basis is laid down in the genetic architecture of the species, it may come to be an end in itself. It doesn't necessarily have to continue to be functional. In fact this is seen in the way in which the psychological organization of many species, particularly higher primates and man, seems to be organized. There is an elaborate internal reward structure for engaging in certain kinds of behaviors. Thus, the reason for that behavior existing in the first place may no longer be relevant. The animal may continue to engage in that kind of behavior simply because there are internal rewards. It is, therefore, not necessarily an argument against an evolutionary explanation of a particular behavior that is not related TODAY to any specific survival need.

We have to keep in mind that economics is a reification. It's a label that we have attached to a very complex array of behavior, some of which some people call economics, other people call ecology. In fact, it's getting very difficult to tell the two apart. Perhaps it's not useful to talk in terms of such global reifications. It's only when you break that reification down into specific empirical processes in the real world that you get a handle on it for what we are concerned about here, that is, explaining the causes and predicting certain kinds of behavior.

I personally think that Maslow's hierarchy is a very fertile conception and there is much to recommend it. Maslow seems somewhat confused in the way in which he has presented it because he was not thinking in evolutionary terms. He begs the question "How could the higher capacities, at the apex of his hierarchy, have emerged?" How could they have evolved in the human species? We are increasingly coming to learn that they exist in other higher primates which exhibit some precursors of the same kinds of psychological characteristics that we used to think were uniquely human. How could these have evolved in the first place if they were not instrumental to the survival of the species? The way evolution works, they could not have evolved. They could not have been positively selected for, unless they were somehow functional. I am suggesting that the hierarchy may be turned on its head: that the most important needs are the basic ones and that the higher needs are needs that evolved because of their instrumental functions for the survival of the species.

AMSBURY: I'm very happy that so many people agree with me, but I am disgusted with a stereotype response which happens every time someone refers to goods and resources and satisfactions. These are not all that we call economics, and I very clearly said so. I pointed out that there were three absolutely separate factors being discussed by me: (1) economic rewards, (2) non-economic rewards, and (3) the necessary economic basis for every human activity including non-economic rewards. (I would like to point out that scientists must stay alive and comfortable as well as everyone else and this has a very powerful influence on whether we do or do not engage in altruistic behavior which is not keeping us alive and comfortable and feeling satisfied.) The paper that I mentioned in passing by Foster on "The image of limited good" was given this same treatment. I still find in literature people, who didn't read Foster but read his critics, repeatedly trying to criticize him and give examples against him but supporting his arguments instead.

GIVENS: May we now have Dr. Midlarsky's summary?

MIDLARSKY: In my paper I was concerned with the onset of war in international systems and recently a lot of research has been done on war in international systems. A greater frequency of war in multipolar systems has been found along with greater duration and intensity of war in bipolar systems. Characteristics of the system have been shown to bear some relationship to the onset of war. In my own research, again referring to the international system as a system of alliances, effective uncertainty is associated with alliances and borders. We have found some relationships between war and the state to be inconsistent. These are all characteristics pertaining to the system. Thus I began to ask the question: What can we learn from properties of domestic political systems? That is, if the system has certain properties that lead to the onset of war, what effect can we see from the internal societal characteristics of nation-states that may bear some relationship to warfare? I wanted to study this apart from modern conditions of industrialization and all of the confounding elements that have gone on in the contemporary period, because they do bear a relationship to politics. I wanted to control for this, to remove it somehow, so I went to a source that had data on pre-modern, pre-industrial societies: Eisenstadt's treatment of the political systems of empires. He has a large number of coded variables describing internal characteristics and because he had so many large ones, I had to reduce the data to manageable portions by means of cluster analysis. The result of the data reducing method was to yield certain dimensions, certain clusters, one of which fairly clearly reflected societal development in the form of structural differentiation. Others referred to the effect of the gentry, the military, the legal, and religious segments. There were a total of seven dimensions referring to overall societal development and to specific societal sectors. Once having gotten these dimensions by reducing the eighty-eight variables from Eisenstadt to seven, I could get scores on these dimensions for each of the countries involved and relate them to the three characteristics of war suggested by Sorokin: the number of wars, the duration of wars, and the battle casualties.

There are positive effects of the religious dimension on the battle casualties, which one can explain in terms of a sacred authority perhaps being more willing to allow a large number of people to be killed in sacred battles, such as the Jihad. A significant effect of the bureaucracy on battle casualties exists because one might need a fairly complex machinery to gather and serve up large numbers of people to the war machine. There is also a significant effect of the military on the years in war, that is, how long a country is willing to stay at war. Again one can't interpret that in the modern setting of Ludendorff and Hindenburg being quite willing to continue World War I perhaps when a lot was to be lost. But in relation to the principal variable of interest to me — societal development — the data are fairly clear that there is no effect. The effect of development is very weakly negative on the number of wars, nowhere near significance. The effect of development on battle casualties is moderately positive, again nowhere near significance, and development as a variable doesn't even appear in the equation for duration. That is, development wasn't even put into that equation (for years in war) by the stepwise procedure, which puts in the most important variables first. Development wasn't important enough to appear in that equation.

How do we interpret this? The results are consistent with other findings in research on war and also with my own research. Apparently the onset of war is better explained by certain characteristics of the system such as alliance status relationships among nations, certain probabilistic properties of the system, bipolarity, and multipolarity. Structural characteristics of the system itself apparently have a fairly strong effect on the onset of war. But domestic institutions have the weakest effect on the number of wars. That is, that which is explained by the system is least explained by the domestic social institutions, so there is a complementarity there. On the other hand, the characteristics of war, particularly battle casualties, are best explained by domestic social institutions. We should differentiate between origin and characteristics because the origins of war may have to do with the confluence and policy interactions of nation-states, whereas battle casualties are properties of bureaucracies and religious authorities which tend to want to continue a war and particularly to incur numbers of deaths, even when perhaps the war itself might be lost. The results here are complementary to both the findings of other researchers and my own findings in the field of international relations.

GIVENS: Thank you. Dr. Melko had to leave early, but we are going to have a summation of his paper by Dr. M. Nettleship.

Since war has its origins in periods of peace, one way to study the origins of war is to consider how peace periods come to an end. I have studied a number of peace periods throughout history. They seem to be works of man, in themselves, just as wars are, and they require the maintenance of delicate balances. Over a period of time, social and economic change takes place and the balances must be modified. If the political leaders fail to make these modifications, war occurs. One reason they fail is that, over time, institutionalization takes place. Institutionalization is the process by which mechanisms, designed to perform a function, gradually require more attention for their own maintenance than for the function they were designed to perform. In isolated societies, great empires, or insular states, governments become so complex that they lose touch with the problems of their constituencies. Then provincial areas break away or peasants rebel and other kinds of conflicts break out. If institutionalization is recognized, and a powerful leader attempts reform, almost inevitably he will precipitate conflict among the displaced priests, nobles, and bureaucrats. If your aim is to increase efficiency, you may want to attempt reform at the cost of civil war. If you want peace, it may be better to do nothing and allow institutionalization to take its own course. There may be no solution to the problem of institutionalization.

Peace is the work of man. If a peace period is well constructed, it may last a century or more. We can ask of the war that follows, what caused the war, or we can ask how did the peace that preceded it last as long as it did. How can we create another period of peace that will last as long?

GIVENS: Thank you. Let's take Dr. Smith's paper and then we will have some questions.

SMITH: Though little has been done on a comparative analysis of violence, it appears logical to assume that there are cultural forces which pattern the expression of violence, i.e. that the violent behavior is not random in its expression. Northern New Mexico offers a situation wherein three distinct cultures seem to demonstrate cultural variability in a response to the "need" for violent behavior.

(1) The Amerindian communities — with a strong, highly explicit theme emphasizing non-violence — were pressured by external events (the in-migration of pre-contact Indians and the late-arriving Spanish) into offering positive sanctions to violence in order that they survive raids, marauders, and conquerers. (2) The eighteenth-century Spanish frontier settlements had to minimize the potential destructiveness of internal violence in a situation where survival demanded that a premium be placed on violent means of coping. The results may be seen in the florescence of the Penitente cult. (3) In the late 1960's approximately twenty "hippie" communes in the Taos area (with about 2,000 members) were forced to recognize that they must resort to violence (despite their philosophy of love and peace) if they were to survive the vigilante movement which had arisen among the Anglos and Spanish of the area in attempt to oust these "weirdos who threaten our way of life and push dope to our kids!"

The need to change a CULTURAL LEITMOTIF and integrate a new element of violence so as to control the "environment" varied in all three cases and the culturally patterned response will be examined and compared for trait variation.

A. NETTLESHIP: We seem to be circling the conceptual ideas of superstructures. This was a very popular concept during the Second World War. To explain how wars began, a superstructure appears within the society and both Smith and Midlarsky have circled this a little bit. Midlarsky brings it up under the circumstance of what he did analyze. I wonder if during this analysis he saw any properties in domestic political situations that he could recognize, or if he could set up criteria to tell us — was there a special superstructure that came up before a war started?

SIPES: I suppose I could discuss some relatively unimportant points in Dr. Midlarsky's work, but instead I would like to say that in my opinion it is this sort of work that we need more of. We need more empirical testing of hypothesized relationships between elements such as Midlarsky has done. We have enough unsubstantiated theory. We should attempt now to clear the boards of untenable hypothesis and theory through objective testing. This is very unromantic and very plodding work and we can't just sit there and blue-sky over coffee; we've got to get down and get our hands all covered with ink and curse the computer, but this is really what we need and these statements are not limited simply to war discussions, but apply to the whole of the social sciences. We have been blue-skying long enough.

BIGELOW: I would just like to make a comment about Dr. Smith's [unrecorded] mention of evil. I don't know that I go along entirely, but I find it very difficult to condone certain activities that other people are perpetrating on others. I do think she has raised a very important and fundamental point. War, as a psychological state that humans can reach, is due very largely, in my opinion, to getting ourselves into the position where we think THEY are evil, WE are good — consider the raid over cattle Smith mentioned. You might make this raid and think, "Well, we're a little bit evil; we really shouldn't steal these cattle; but we're going to do it anyway." But, when we talk about the holy war, we are "white" — it is for God that we are doing this and our opponents are not even human. That is the kind of psychological state that we must try somehow to prevent ourselves and others from getting into; at least try to reduce the likelihood of this kind of state. One example of this has impressed me. Some students in America, who began for very valid and good reasons to oppose the Vietnam War and all sorts of injustices, became pacifists (or saw themselves as pacifists). Then they became more and more frustrated because the establishment and the military didn't listen to their suggestions. They became more and more worked up and finally began to see policemen as pigs. They threw bags of human excrement at policemen and they made homemade bombs and so on. They had come full cycle and got themselves into the psychological state that they themselves had originally wanted to prevent. We are very susceptible to getting sucked in. Every one of us can do this and it is a major problem that deserves a lot more study than it has been given so far.

CARROLL: There is a difference between wars for religious or patriotic convictions and wars in which there is a reality of oppression and exploitation. There is a difference between the conflict involved in the Franco-Prussian War over status in the European system and over a territorial position such as Alsace-Lorraine and, on the other hand, the war in Vietnam. Those differences are very significant in that one cannot suppose that the same kinds of either solutions or responses are as appropriate in one field as they are in the other. It is much easier for me to think about resolving international conflict in the area of symmetric conflicts in which I can say, "Well now boys, calm down; you're really all the same and you're really all fighting over idiotic power objectives, or chauvinistic objectives. If we're all rational and if we set up an international organization that can resolve these things,

then we'll get along fine." On the other hand, I can't say that about
the war in Vietnam and I can't say that about a whole variety of other
imperialistic or anti-imperialistic wars in which I feel there are genuine
stakes having to do with evil or liberation. Almost all solutions that
have to do with "let's all sit down around the table and talk" place
the advantage in the hands of top dogs because they have a whole array
of resources, skills, customary background, and so forth, which enables
them to prevail in situations like that.

Dr. M. Nettleship, in his summary of different positions on structural
and personal violence, did not present the most essential point about
structural violence. It is not that it incites physical violence, but that it
IS physical violence in a certain sense. That is, if you look at mortality
statistics, for example, far fewer people die in wars or even in homi-
cides, suicides, and in all forms of violence of that kind, than die from
a variety of causes stemming from structural characteristics of a given
system, usually of a given economic system but also of a political
system. These latter deaths are from starvation, from diseases related
to poverty, from infant mortality and maternal mortality. Those are
FATALITIES we're talking about, not just psychological aspects. Structural violence has it all over warfare violence and from that point of
view you also come back to this problem of symmetric versus asymmetric war. When you are dealing with asymmetric war, you are generally dealing with a situation in which structural violence has been a
very important part of the background of the situation, and you already
have very heavy violence coming down from the top to which the
response is physical violence in terms, say, of a war of liberation or
anti-imperialist war. But, when evaluating the violence that breaks
out as a response, one has to bear in mind that there has been an awful
lot of violence, structural violence, in the system already.

RICHARDS: The last comment has somehow just reinforced Dr. Smith's
point about the tolerance of evil. When you say there is a REALITY of
oppression, this expresses a very specific definition of the situation.
I am reasonably sure that if you talked to various other people, they
would see equally a reality of something else. That is precisely where
the problem lies: people who are wrong are as sincerely wrong as we
are sincerely right. Dr. Smith's point is a fairly broad one that comes
down to cases of violence, internal violence, within a society. When
I speak of violence, I'm not talking about people who die from disease.
For that matter, death by old age is also the result of structural factors.
If you are going to define as violence all deaths that occur as a result
of structural situations, I think you get yourself into a conceptual box

where you are defining every death as death by violence. This creates analytical problems that are very difficult to solve.

The thing that Dr. Smith said was that a major factor in Western culture is that it is important not to compromise your principles. It is important to fight for your principles or at least to defend your principles and accept no compromises. How many times have we heard that coming from religious leaders, coming from respected leaders of all sorts, and from sides that we regard as right and on sides that we regard as wrong? When you have two groups in contact, both of which are refusing to compromise on their opposing principles, and neither group will surrender or leave the field, it is almost impossible to avoid violent conflict. Never mind who starts it, it's going to occur.

POPE: I'm indebted to Martin Nettleship for informing me about Galtung and structural violence and I'm becoming more impressed with this, especially as I examine it in terms of the institution of slavery, and would say that, through structural violence, maybe seven to ten million people lost their lives who were never involved in open warfare at all.

GIVENS: Dr. Claessen, could we have the summation of your paper, please?

CLAESSEN: In my paper, I discussed some aspects of civil war. I concentrated on he question: How does civil war come into existence? I took war in a rather general sense, as the armed conflict between groups of people — political groups, of course. In defining war in this way, I am doing it in the same way as Tefft or Cancro. The two previous days have taught me this definition may be too wide. Be that as it may, I used this definition when preparing this paper about ten months ago. Civil war is a special kind of war. The fighting groups or parties belong to the same people or nation. One could wonder if this is a sufficient reason to consider civil war a special kind. I think it might be useful to do this. Professor Cancro, in his paper, stressed that the more similar people see each other as being, the more difficulty they will find in perpetrating aggressive acts toward each other. When people belonging to one group become divided somehow and come to an organized conflict, this is something exceptional, and exceptions have to be explained. I have the impression that many peoples studied by anthropologists — Chinese, Japanese, Indians, Aztecs, Tibetans, Incas, to mention a few — did fight civil war.

I analyzed three cases only, and then tried to find common circumstances under which these civil wars came into eixstence. The cases selected are: (1) civil war in the Trinity Islands in Polynesia between

1790 and 1820, (2) civil wars in Buganda, East Africa, in the years, 1888 and 1889, and (3) civil war in the realm of the Incas between 1527 and 1532. It could be strongly argued that so few cases do not allow one to draw conclusions, therefore the results of my comparisons are better seen as hypothetical.

In looking for the origins of civil war, it might be useful to analyze the balance of power in the state under consideration. (In another paper, which I will present in Chicago, I discussed this concept at some length.) For the moment it seems sufficient to say that, at least in primitive states, rulers tried to create counterweights against influential persons and groups. Naturally, this policy is not always successful and not every counterweight is a fortunate one; however, there were regular periods when the several counterweights were in balance. This continually created new possibilities, or institutions, as Dr. Melko would perhaps call them. In the long run this leads to stress and problems. Therefore, one might distinguish several types of balance of power, namely stable, unstable, and meta-stable balance. In the first case a small displacement from the equilibrium state gives rise to forces to return to that state in due course. With an unstable balance, small displacement results in a cumulatively greater displacement usually toward some new equilibrium. In the third case, the system is stable only in the absence of a suitable catalyst which if introduced would make a ruin of the system.

The results of the analyses of the three cases could be summed up in the following way. In the first place, it seems that in all three cases the position of the rulers became questionable. Somehow they had lost their influence. Their relationship to other political leaders was no longer clear. Their religious justifications became a point of doubt. In the meantime, potential alternate leaders grew in influence. Mighty nobles got more and more power and possibly grew as influential as the ruler himself. Then, in all three cases, a suitable cataclysm took place: an accidental murder of the leader, the killing of some people, or something like that. This became the immediate reason to start the war between the followers of the king and the followers of the alternative leaders. It will be clear that in fact an unstable or even a meta-stable balance of power was disturbed. For, where the position of the ruler is unclear and ill-defined and where alternate leaders are present, the balance of power is no longer to be called stable. Corning would speak perhaps of dominance and certainty. The immediate cause only starts the war. I think it is important to underline that the occurrence of only one of the components is not sufficient to produce war. In the

Tonga Islands the balance of power was meta-stable for nearly a century. The existence of potential alternate leaders in the realm of the Incas did not produce war each time and the murdering of people in Buganda only once gave rise to a civil war. Only when there is an unstable or a meta-stable balance of power and an immediate abuse will civil war be the result.

GIVENS: Dr. Pope's summary . . .

POPE: My topic is colonialism and the Danish West Indies: present and past. The Danish West Indies from the eighteenth century on have been largely Afro-American. The islands of St. Croix, St. Thomas, and St. John became U.S. possessions in 1917, and were henceforth to be known as the "American Virgin Islands." Then and now the islands have been marked by violence. Is it purely by chance that within the past two years on St. Croix sixteen persons have been murdered: fifteen whites and almost all tourists? Can it be the pressure of ethnic stress? There are the local people, the Crusians, the Puerto Ricans, the down-islanders; there are people from the French and British islands; there are Americans and there are people of Danish extraction. Tensions are high between Crusians and down-islanders, mainly because housing and appropriations for schooling are insufficient and this pressure is coupled with remnants of past ill-feeling.

When Danish colonials ruled, it was by rigid laws. Slaves could not leave sugar estates unless they had written permission. Runaway slaves absent for three months without permission could lose a leg. Violence was built into the social structure and oftentimes it brought death. There were many ways to fight back. It was possible for a slave to ruin the sugar-refining equipment or poison the food. One sometimes wonders how the Danes ever enjoyed a meal. A complete revolution would have been difficult because the Danes aligned part of the population with them by setting up a "free colored" class. By allowing the free colored class to compete and to emulate the Danes they were able to convince them to cast their lot with the Danes.

Were the Danes more harsh than other colonial people? Cruelty, of course, is very hard to measure. Certainly, the acculturation or trans-culturation process failed for them. In formulating an acculturation continuum for Afro-Americans and Europeans in the New World, Herskovits placed the French and Spanish at the far end, signifying a greater blending of these cultures with the African cultures. Next came the English, and finally the Dutch and the Danes. Why? The French and the Spanish have generally intermarried more frequently with native populations. The French have extended citizenship, the English have even shared their honors. Catholicism for the French and the Spanish meant that they saw the black man as possessing a soul. But the Danes offered little that would make for this affiliation which is so necessary. Limited historical references reveal them to be indifferent, even to the white visitors to the island. (There are possibilities here for culture and personality research.)

I view with alarm the tensions present today in Caribbean cultures, tensions also due in part to overly glamorous, overly expensive tourist hotels. The tourist hotel may be seen as a replacement for the big plantation houses. Today, on many of these islands, you see very few big plantation houses because of the conflict and revolt. But tourism is the economic product of the Caribbean and a highly inappropriate one for people who see service to others as reminiscent of slavery. As Lowenthal thought, the geographer says, "Past is a living presence in the Caribbean."

Change is a process. Do we casually let it go on and not interfere with it? I have never really subscribed to applied anthropology, but since I have been at this conference, I have wrestled with this problem again and I suppose I must agree with Dr. Smith on the problem of evil. Do we just graciously acquiesce when we lose?

Throughout all of this, while not discussing it, I would draw attention to the value of conflict. We examine warfare in all of its forms and when we see people in the institution of slavery, and we see the fight, the battle they put up, I think that we can only come to the conclusion that there are times when there is something very positive about conflict.

GIVENS: Could we hear from Dr. Saxe-Fernández?

SAXE-FERNÁNDEZ: My paper deals with the conditions of post-industrial societies and internal war in post-industrial systems. Historical experience shows that the type of post-industrial system that we are living in is primarily characterized by a situation in which affluence is attained through a total mobilization of human and material resources. I'm dealing with the post-Vietnam situation, in which apparently the notion of internal enemies is becoming more and more crucial. An idea was suggested in a paper by Jules Henry in which he talked about the extent to which the notion of the enemy is embedded into national character. In the past, all reasonable people believed in witches or in people being possessed by demons. In the past, also, people believed in the external enemy. In great part due to the efforts of Mr. Henry Kissinger, the notion of the external enemy has been eroded and therefore, we should pay attention to the condition of the internal enemy, particularly since today all reasonable people, including many social scientists, still believe that there is such a thing as mental illness or sexual perversions or schizophrenia or juvenile delinquency or unacceptable violence.

The paper dealt basically with one of the elements that I was most shocked by in my analysis of the internal enemy, that is, psychosurgery programs. The social sciences are being used, and in improper ways, to justify programs of internal repression. Thus the program of mentally crippling by brain surgery applied to prison inmates in California was narrowly averted last year when the plan was made public. (I wonder how many of those present know about it.) Three prisoners had already been subjected to amygdalotomies in 1968, but the Department of Corrections and the University of California planned to fund new operations of this sort. Their plan was cancelled when a letter from Mr. Procunier, Director of the Department of Corrections requesting money for the new program to use psychosurgery on prison inmates, fell into the hands of the press in California. Governor Ronald Reagan announced at the beginning of this year in his "state of the state" message the formation of the new research center to be called "Center for the Reduction of Life-Threatening Behavior." The new center is to be located at the University of California's Brain Research Institute in the Department of Psychiatry and is funded by more than one million dollars this year. It is part of a resurrection of the Vacaville University of California psychosurgery project. The proposed center also seems to include a number of even more 1984-style projects. I call your attention to several points in the proposal. First, the document is the only one the existence of which the state has so far acknowledged though two legislators pressed the California criminal department (the CCJ) for information. While reluctantly delivering the document to one legislator, the same organization denied the document's existence to another legislator of California. Second, the proposal displays shocking incompetence and arrogance, straining the credulity of the reader by asserting that the center will accomplish each and all of the following, and I quote: "Explore the causation, identification, prevention, control, and reduction of violence. Define the epidemiology, cause to be tested predictors of violence, document the circumstances of violence. Develop and cause to be tested models for the detection and the prevention and control and treatment of life-threatening behavior." The study will in addition discover nothing less than the following: "Relationships between changes in society, the family structure, unrest among the poor, the changing role of religion, the impact of mass media, and gang behavior." And more: "genetic, biochemical, neurological, and neuro-physiological elements of life-threatening behavior including chromosomes, hormones, abnormal electrical activities within the brain and various forms of brain lesions." The objective is to develop and disseminate packaged programs for "detection, prevention, control and treatment, and education." The target groups whose violent behavior is to be modified include youth and rioters. The control models are to include chemical and physical controls and the preventive models are to be incorporated "into public school programs, law enforcement activities, governmental actions, and private organizations." No consideration is given to the question whether even several millions of dollars will suffice to re-invent the sciences of Biology, Pharmacology, Psychology, Sociology, Anthropology, Criminology, and Medicine as the scope of the project logically implies. Virtually nothing is said about what and who specifically are to be studied, nor can you determine what practical applications the investigators would have in mind. Nothing whatever is revealed about who is to perform this pioneering investigation. No scientists or legislators with their wits about them would contemplate committing three million dollars of the taxpayer's money to a project whose substance is so evanescent in the minds of the applicants.

GIVENS: Thank you. We have one more paper in this group, then we will take some questions. Dr. Oldfield Hayes?

OLDFIELD HAYES: The paper which I have submitted to this conference is entitled "Warfare and the disappearance of Meroe: a preliminary application of cross-cultural findings to Nile archeology."

The Meroitic civilization dated from about 850 B.C. to A.D. 350 and existed in the north of what is the modern-day Democratic Republic of Sudan. In the paper I show how warfare played a major role in the evolution and devolution of Meroe. Most relevant are the differential effects of warfare on the social body and on the overall culture. I, and others, too often have used three terms almost interchangeably when discussing Meroe and other ancient states. The terms that we use interchangeably are state, civilization, and culture. Most social science literature distinguishes at least the state from the culture when speaking of a people. I propose that it would be to our advantage to distinguish between all three, for by so doing a richer picture and more cogent questions are evoked.

For our purposes we should distinguish between the state, the civilization, and the little tradition of Meroe or other ancient states that we are considering. These, if they follow the performance of other human groups, probably changed somewhat independently; for Meroe, the state is the most fragile of the three. A particular state organization can come and go with relatively little effect on the civilization of little tradition. Witness histories of China, Egypt, and Europe. A civilization, therefore, is less fragile than a state, but if the civilization of a group disintegrates, it is almost certain that the state will go. The little tradition is most resilient. The peasant's life often may remain relatively unchanged for periods of thousands of years. Witness particularly China between 11,000 B.C. and A.D. 15, and about 5,000 years of cultural history in the Nile Valley with such states as the Old, New, and Middle Kingdoms, Meroe, and others coming and going. However, it is difficult to imagine the little tradition undergoing radical change in a short period of time with either the state or the civilization having much of a chance to survive. The little tradition can slowly change without destroying the state or civilization although they will be modified along with it. A good case in point is the Japanese little tradition which underwent considerable change between pre-Meiji times and in 1945 with the same state exercising continual sovereignty without interruption. If we speak of the disappearance of Meroe or any ancient state, of what do we speak: of the disappearance of the Meroitic state, the Meroitic civilization, or the little tradition? It seems that these three aspects of the sociocultural system possess different susceptibilities to disruption and that the susceptibility rank order is fixed. Warfare, therefore, affects them differently in both their evolution and devolution relative to special social bodies.

ESSER: I wish to address Dr. Saxe-Fernández's paper as a psychiatrist and as someone who is personally familiar with many of the people Dr. Saxe-Fernández mentioned. I am very sympathetic with Dr. Saxe-Fernández's paper, but for this moment I speak for an in-group of psychiatrists and he's attacking psychiatry. So I will say that I am sympathetic to his point of view, but I must point out that there are definite differences between those cases in psychiatry in which violence can be shown (individual violence can be shown to be part of the dysfunction of the brain) and in which the victims of this disease ask to be relieved. There are dramatic examples of the latter, including the example of the killing in Austin, Texas, and the example of a Canadian killing in which the man went over and over again to his psychiatrist and said, "I have violent outbursts; can you do something about it?" but was totally disregarded. When he finally homicided and suicided, they found a definite enlargement of the vessels in the brain which could have been removed. There are some fact and data to the contentions that are being made. What is incorrect is the elaboration used by well-identified political systems and certain directions in our country to which these scientists become maybe willing victims, but in the beginning they did not conceive this problem. (This is the same thing that the atomic scientists had when they built the atomic bomb.)

Both Dr. Saxe-Fernández and Dr. Carroll really should, in their impassioned plea for action, distinguish between two realms: the conceptual and the actual realm. In the conceptual realm, I am fully agreed with Dr. Smith. In the conceptual realm there are no objective truths. In other words, there is no such thing as evil, there is no such thing as good. Both can co-exist and I gave you the Chinese example of Yin and Yang in which there is black and white and you can never separate them easily because black is in white, and white is in black. However, in the actual realm, if you see there is oppression (in the case of Dr. Carroll, oppression in a political system and war, and in the case of Dr. Saxe-Fernández, when he sees there is oppression in any political system, trying to suppress people internally) you SHOULD speak out and fight that. That is, however, YOUR choice and your decision and that's what Dr. Smith says. She doesn't say we should just live as evil. No, if we see evil in a thing and we decide to fight this then we decide to do that but in that case we cannot decide that there will be no war anymore, because we will make war, that is our choice. Dr. Saxe-Fernández will make war on Governor Reagan, if that is possible, right? That was his choice and I'm with him. I happen to be in that corner. We have to do our best continually to see the complementarity in all actions, to perceive the way the universe is constructed by us and therefore the responsibility of our choice.

(I speak for myself: Dr. Fernández, I am with you in fighting a Reagan system and any other system, and I am glad you brought that to my attention. I speak also for myself when I say, conceptually I do not agree with you that people like Delgato, Ervin, and all the other ones whom I happen to know — and am not particularly friends with, but I've worked with some of them — are necessarily "evil.")

M. NETTLESHIP: A very small point of definition: I don't understand a term which may be a key to Dr. Saxe-Fernández's paper and that is the concept of invalidation. Could you explain that briefly for me?

SAXE-FERNÁNDEZ: I am using that term to denote the way in which one suppresses the effectiveness of social interaction of a person, or his legitimization, his legitimacy. For instance, a person defines himself or believes himself to be Jesus Christ for several reasons, which might be very valid and legitimate reasons, but we don't go into those reasons, we just label him schizophrenic or anything and therefore one doesn't deal with his problem. You just label him as such, therefore you invalidate him in his social intercourse. You can invalidate anyone with labels.

M. NETTLESHIP: Invalidation is something always done by others to someone?

SAXE-FERNÁNDEZ: Yes. I am suggesting that one of the main features of contemporary institutional psychiatry is a massive process of invalidation.

M. NETTLESHIP: Is there a complementary process of validation? Would you describe it in the same way?

SAXE-FERNÁNDEZ: Yes, it would be getting into the problem of who can define whom as such and, therefore, it is the problem of power in the last analysis. Those who do the defining for a social group can define a subgroup, as for instance "criminal" or "deviant" or whatever, and treat them as such. Therefore you are dealing with the problem of power. You can see that also in criminology. In the last analysis the criminal code is nothing but one of the best expressions of conflict, the types of conflict that occur in a society where a social group can define other social groups as "criminal" or "abnormal." If you have property and someone takes property away from you, you can label that as stealing and incorporate that into the books and then treat those who "steal" as such; then they are invalidated.

M. NETTLESHIP: Considering your definition of the two terms, I wonder if you might not be a little bit less passionately against invalidation, since it seems to be a very crucial part of the process of social living. What I am saying is that not all invalidation is evil or bad.

SAXE-FERNÁNDEZ: No, but I am referring, for instance, to medieval times when you had forms of behavior that you could not account for or understand. You could label the person a witch or in possession of witchcraft, or as being possessed by demons. Today when you do not understand certain forms of behavior you can label someone mentally ill or you can label him schizophrenic and invalidate him and treat him accordingly.

A. NETTLESHIP: As a medical scientist, I hope we are not raising again the old-fashioned bogeyman of portraying the medical scientist, the biological scientist, or any of us scientists, as evil or good people who are involved in some obscure "ism" which might in some way destroy other people, since our sworn humanitarianism is very well known. There is a point here where we must all remember that things which we do are pretty dependent on what society makes us do. I point to the fact that there was a large group of cancer researchers available during the Second World War and the military simply said, "Your funds are gone, you are now going to work on the A-bomb." I think our postures of research and our postures of productivity are those which society, predictably or not, tells us to do. Now that may be a rather limp attitude, but again, it has been pointed out here this morning that one must eat and one must live. I'm not too sure that this is a strong cross-current but it certainly is one which we must deal with.

KRAKAUER: Several papers and comments mentioned something of the same point. Dr. Tefft asked why do all values persist. Dr. Pope was talking about the fact that the problems of Danish colonialism seemed to carry on even after the Danes left and Dr. Oldfield Hayes talked about the little tradition. I'd like to tie these together a little bit. They are, after all, various levels of one of the things we know about the human species, which is that we have a tendency to hold onto values for quite a long time, long after the reasons for them are gone. Sometimes it's a relatively late level in development. For example, I happen to be a manager of a group of nine factories and I have been a manager for quite a long time. I have observed cases where a bad manager would create an attitude that lasted for ten to fifteen years after he was gone, as compared to the attitudes in another group in another factory that didn't have this original type of experience. That ten to fifteen years was rather shocking to me when it happened, but it's very, very common. I have another case, and this was a very, very serious one in which I came to the conclusion after a long time and after some psychiatric evaluation of the situation, that the attitudes of a power group in one factory were so deep and so anti-authoritarian, so deeply enculturated, that there was no choice but to close the factory. This was after twenty years of effort.

BIGELOW: I agree entirely with Dr. Pope that there is something positive about conflict or that there can be. In my opinion, some past wars and revolutions were necessary; for example Adolf Hitler had to be stopped and had to be stopped violently. However, I still believe that Dr. Smith's point is very valid and very important and that we should try to be constructive. We should try, at the same time, to minimize the frequency in our society of those psychological states which dehumanize and make evil, inhuman enemies of our opponents and hence promote violence and war. In the long run we must minimize social injustice and such things in our society.

War: Its Meaning and Its Control

Chaired by A. NETTLESHIP and R. TAMAYO Y SALMORÁN

Discussion of papers by P. HUBER, H. SIVERTS, R. W. HOWELL, S. K. TEFFT, R. TAMAYO Y SALMORÁN, R. G. SIPES, M. SHOKEID, S. ALBERT

A. NETTLESHIP: We shall start this session with Mr. Huber's summary of his paper.

HUBER: The central purpose of my paper was to relate the development of violence to its social context among a particular people located in New Guinea. In deciding to do this, I made another decision which has been vindicated to some extent. It was an arbitrary decision not to call this war because I felt that that imposed or imparted certain assumptions about the nature of the social system itself which would be inappropriate in the Anggor context. In other words, the Anggor haven't those characteristics of state-like organization that so many people want to consider to be the *sine qua non* of war, thus I decided not to call it war, but to talk about violence more generally and to try to relate it to its social context.

Anggor society focuses on the village as the basic unit, frame of reference, cosmos, or mode of existence. They have a non-corporate village; there is no formal allocation of leadership positions within this village and no formal differentiation into hierarchical kinds of structures within this village, but rather it's a bunch of people who live together and interact in terms of certain common features of their language and conceptual structures. The structures that might be considered the building blocks of this cosmos involve differentiations between people according to lineality. There is separation into patrilineages and patrilineal clans, and the transcending of those differentiations in the form of marriage. Patrilineal clans are exogamous, so that all marriages within the Anggor village unite people who are separated by birth. In that way you have a kind of objectification of the experience of difference between self and other in certain concrete and widely understood forms of the way people can be different and at the same time relate. They are different in a certain specific sense which admits of some kind of relationship at the same time.

This is the structural level at which the Anggor create this cosmos in terms of common ceremonial observances, certain kinds of exchange, and certain types of relationship that occur within the village. There is another level as well though (and I have been quite taken with the term synergy which I hadn't been familiar with before I came to this conference) which I would like to describe as synergistic. Synergy describes the Anggor very well in certain respects, because within the structural differentiations you also have a development of interpersonal relationships, so that if a particular man marries a woman and she has four or five brothers, some of them are classificatory, some of them are true, and his relationships with each of those brothers may be different even though they are all classified as the same type of relationship. The intensity, the frequency of interaction, the kinds of interaction that they engage in grow out of the relationship. They don't see clearly when the marriage is contracted just exactly what they will do together for the rest of their lives, but they create the relationship as they go on. Some affines are quite satisfied to have a very distant relationship with one another, even though there's no animus between them. Others merge their daily lives in practice; very close cooperative subsistence activity, which may happen, is simply not predictable. It depends on circumstances of each and as the circumstances change, the relationships may change as well.

This synergy creates a kind of interlocking of destinies in everyday life. People are constantly interacting with each other in the subsistence area for gardening in terms of sago (gardening and the planting of sago are long-term activities) so that personal relationships are investments in one sense. But they also have an emotional context so that within the framework of the village, these things create a dispersed but interlocking network. This is not to say within the community everybody gets along. What it does mean is that the connections between some people compensate for the animosities between others. If two affines, for any trivial or really serious reason, come into serious conflict with one another, it will then happen that the clansmen of the two disputing parties rally to the side of each. But the clansmen themselves are linked by ties of affinity which they place a great value on, so that this widening of the conflict also tends to diffuse it, to compensate for it. This works fairly well within the village, although it doesn't always work. Village schisms sometimes simply cannot be overcome in this way, and this can lead to fighting within the village and complete disruption and destruction of the community with one faction going off to live in a different area, forming a separate village. To remain as one village requires the prevalence of kinship over enmity. This is the basis of the village and the life of the village is symbolized in terms of various kinds of acts and religious observances which are appropriate. The village and kinship grow through a kind of familiarity on a personal level and also through familiarity with common meanings, common interpretations, and common committments.

However, this familiarity is always limited by the fact that people are, if nothing else, mortal and every Anggor death represents a loss of familiarity, a termination of this process of synergy. Once a kinsman, friend, agnate, or affine is dead, the relationship simply ceases and the surviving soul of the dead person becomes an anonymous and menacing presence which needs to be expelled from the village. Death results from the magical activities of unknown sorcerers from outside of the villages; thus the person who becomes a member of the community is ultimately pulled out of the community and becomes a stranger — in the sense that his actions are unpredictable, his destiny is no longer linked with the members of the community, and he becomes a threat to the community. He joins the outside world. The Anggor believe that there is nothing you can do about sorcery. By definition it is beyond social control, although it is possible to divine or expose the identity of the specific sorcerer and in that sense restore some semblance of order to the cosmos. This process is going on all the time and it doesn't necessarily lead to any kind of war or violence. Warfare arises through a process (outlined in six different case histories included in my paper) the essence of which is that some kind of violent episode triggers off a retaliation in kind. This isn't prescribed, is not part of a process of adjudication or balancing or achieving parity. It is simply a reaction, at least in the Anggor view of things. As is pointed out in the case histories, retaliation can lead to a process of escalation between villages: one person is killed, his village tries to retaliate with a massive raid on the killing village and this leads to a violent confrontation in which both sides may add men by calling in the committments of their co-villages to balance each other off in self-defense. It's not a question of who started the conflict; once it gets going, you rally together for self-defense and in this way very extensive battles get started between different villages.

In conclusion, it seems very clear to me that the Anggor don't value violence in any positive sense, they don't say that it's a good thing and something that they have to strive for. They don't use violence as an extension of policy. They don't see it as a technique of social control or action. They respond to violence as a threat by closing ranks and affirming committments within the village. This involves a paradox because in the very act of opposing outsiders and denying relationships with them one affirms one's relationship with one's own kinsmen. The whole idea of kinsmen as opposed to strangers grows out of this experience of constant tension between the villages. It's not a thing which is created or structured; it is a thing which simply cannot be controlled. It represents the limits of sociality within that society.

A. NETTLESHIP: May we hear from Dr. Siverts about his paper?

SIVERTS: The "Jívaro headhunters in a headless time" was not originally written as a contribution to a conference on warfare. It was rather intended as a piece of descriptive analysis dedicated to the theme of ethnic groups and boundary maintenance. It focuses on ceremonial headhunting as the dramatic expression of ethnicity among the Jívaro in the south Ecuadorian and Peruvian Montaña.

The fact that the Jívaro indulged in warfare with great enthusiasm brings certain bits of ethnography to the fore which are interesting in the sense that light might be thrown on fighting as a profession — so to speak — as a way of life, among people who otherwise tend to be friendly and peaceful. What I explicitly try to do in this paper is to relate intratribal raids to intertribal warfare. Analytically, this is attempted through a conceptual framework which is based on certain notions about the nature of social processes. It is a dynamic approach, as distinguished from a strictly structural-functional one. This processual way of speaking implies such underlying concepts as choices and constraints on choices and leads to discussion of the relative merits of restrictions on individual choices and decisions. These restrictions may be ecological as well as etiological.

Ceremonial headhunting was an endemic phenomenon in the area in question. It was a recurrent and expected event. Trophy hunting was considered highly rewarding as the very essence of being Jívaro. Intertribal warfare was a distinct undertaking, the primary purpose of which was the protection of Jívaro-ness rather than a protection of territory as such; that is, it was protection of the privilege to take each other's heads. Before summing up the argument, it might be proper to give a brief outline of the general ethnography. The whole Jívaro ethnic group comprises some 40,000 people in an area of 60,000 square kilometers,

approximately. Subsistence activities involve shifting horticulture combined with hunting, fishing, and collecting wild fruit and plants. The
chief garden plants are yucca or sweet manioc and various species of
plantains and bananas. Although they form a linguistic and cultural
entity and ethnic group, they do not constitute a tribe, if you take tribe
to mean a permanent political group or corporation. The Jívaro are
rather an aggregate of neighborhoods called Jívareens in Ecuador,
whose members consider each other as ceremonial foes or temporary
allies within an all-embracing kin and affinal network. As headhunters
they recognize only Jívaro heads as worth taking. These they shrink to
be displayed and celebrated at a great victory feast following a successful headhunting expedition. In other words, a Jívaro is a potential head
trophy while all others, including the white people, are just foreigners.

A. NETTLESHIP: Forgive me, I have always been curious: do they eat
the people or just take their heads?

SIVERTS: Never any cannibalism.

A. NETTLESHIP: That's kind of a pity.

SIVERTS: Although intra-tribal raids were considered an undertaking
totally different from inter-tribal warfare, the former practice consti-
tuted a basic condition for the successful execution of the latter. The
headhunting ideology and the kin and ethnic network tied all Jívaro
together in an ethnic group. This network provided the underlying
framework for the establishment of temporary corporations and ex-
pediency measures to cope with the problem of defense and the conditions of dispersed living. Since alliance formation was dependent upon
the emergence of great war leaders with limited life spans, the corporations were necessarily short lived, permitting the constant activation of
the underlying framework to form new alliances. By implication, the
limit set for fusion of traditionally hostile units is the totality of warriors recognizing each other's heads as trophies: the mobilization of the
members of the ethnic group to form a corporation. Feuding and raiding were the institutions which generated the perpetration of the corporate unit.

A. NETTLESHIP: Your summary, Dr. Howell.

HOWELL: The most popular anthropological approach to primitive
warfare today seems to be inspired by ecological considerations.
Thomas Shore, Marvin Harris, William Divale, Vayda, Rapoport, and
others have all argued one way or another that primitive warfare, including raids, is to be accounted for in terms of population pressures
and the availability of resources. I'm not going to review all of the
arguments here, except to note that very often the evidence is not all

that persuasive and the statistics sometimes are a little bit shaky. Some cases can be accounted for more easily than by going through the ecological argument.

"Wars without conflict," implies that the definition is quite important. I find conflict to be a special case of competition. Competition itself involves some sort of opposition with an approximate effective balance of forces (which doesn't need to be defined only in terms of military hardware) and all valid statements about competition will be valid for conflict. But there are a number of ways in which some kinds of competition can be distinguished from some other kinds of competition and these kinds correspond to conflict and non-conflict kinds of competition acording to my definition. For one thing there are differences in the rules for the two types. In the non-conflict types the rules are likely to be agreed upon in advance of the encounter and usually there will be some event that will be used to mark the end of the encounter and everybody understands this ahead of time. In basketball when the time is up, and there is a disparity in the score, then that's the end of the game. In the conflict kinds of encounter, the termination is more likely to be a matter of negotiation and not something that is agreed upon ahead of time. Probably more important, however, is the idea that in a conflict situation, there is a tendency toward resolution rather than a mere interruption of the encounter. In the non-conflict kind of situation, in baseball or anything like that, if we don't win this time, there is always tomorrow, or if we are in the cellar, there is always next year and we don't really want to eliminate the other team. This will apply also to certain kinds of so-called primitive warfare. What Dr. Richards called predatory competition would describe the conflict situation and the non-conflict might correspond more closely to the emulative. In a conflict situation at least one party wants out. In some cases conflict resolution is too costly (if it means using the bomb, for example), so we have to settle for attempts at conflict control or conflict avoidance. We did not use the bomb in Vietnam and we avoided Tibet.

In order to have a conflict situation, according to my idea, all of these conditions have to be met. Displaced aggression avoids conflict by disengaging the primary opposition. If there is no balance of forces then there is no contest and therefore no conflict. When the Russians moved into Czechoslovakia in 1968, we had a lot of unhappy Czechs, but no conflict according to this definition. When the Nazis swept across France in the spring offensive of 1940, it was the same kind of thing. As the move slowed down when they reached the Channel, in some practical way conflict became more a part of the encounter. Again, we had a lot of unhappy Frenchmen but no, or very little, conflict according to this definition. This is not an all or nothing affair; we could say that in these cases there is conflict to the extent that there is some sort of effective resistance. This is the kind of example that applies often to modern warfare. The other kind of situation, where there is not so likely to be any clear evidence of an attempt to achieve resolution, is more likely to be found in the so-called primitive warfare cases. Turney-High was appalled by the evident lack of military sophistication of the North American Indians and other warriors who nearly always yielded to the temptation to accomplish "useless little victories," slaughter of one man or the crushing of one small party, so that more often than not, no real advantage was acquired by the victor nor permanent injury done to the defeated. Kroeber reported that the California Indians delivered mass fire, but that the extreme range made it notably bloodless; they went so far as to take poorer arrows to war than they used in economic hunting. This inspired Turney-High to charge that most Californians were too cowardly to make fighting men, but there is no evident interest in such cases of any attempt to achieve a resolution because the purpose of the war games was to demonstrate bravado, if not courage. If one killed off the opposition then the game would be over. Fred Gearing has shown for the Cherokee (although he wasn't trying to make this point) that sometimes the tribal council would meet and in effect say, "We have a problem, how are we going to solve it?" That implies the conflict situation. Prior to about 1730 they were more likely to meet and say, when winter (the season for war) approached, "Well, we're going to go out and fight, who shall we fight this time?" That implies a non-conflict situation. Briefly, then, by not simply assuming that a conflict exists, and by trying to demonstrate the relative variables, we are led to question objectives and motivations when the definition doesn't seem to be met. In most cases it seems the objective is not to eliminate the enemy, but rather to gain individual glory. Just why we seek glory — and we seek it also through danger in automobile racing and things of this sort which have been mentioned already — is a question that remains. In some way it might well be possible to say it reflects some sort of adaptive pattern through our long history.

A. NETTLESHIP: May we have comments on the first papers? Dr. Sipes?

SIPES: Dr. Howell pointed out that in one of William Divale's papers which was a cross-cultural analysis, there were some mishandlings of data and I agree with him completely. Bill Divale shouldn't have done that, but there is something about cross-cultural correlation studies that many people don't quite understand. We may disagree with the concepts. We may think that the one element that's being checked would be better split into two or combined with something else. We may, as many do, object to pulling out of context various cultural or behavioral elements and so allegedly destroying any meaning they possess, and we spot just plain factual errors in coding. But, if the cross-cultural correlation study shows that there is a strong correlation between two or more elements then that correlation must be explained. All data errors and conceptual errors tend to lower, not raise, correlations. If we spot and point out such errors of concepts or data, then we must assume that if they were corrected and eliminated, the correlation would be even stronger than what it was in the paper. If Dr. Howell would care to comment on that again, I would appreciate it.

HOWELL: As a matter of fact, in the example I gave it turns out that if you make all the necessary corrections, it's likely that the exact opposite result would be found. In other words, if you work it out it works exactly against his argument.

TEFFT: I have an issue I would take with one of Dr. Howell's statements: he says that much of traditional primitive warfare fits into a non-conflict category. One difficulty here is that one identifies the non-conflict form of warfare, collective violence or collective engagements, without realizing that in many cases this is only a phase in the whole warfare pattern. Among the Timbaga, for example, there are so-called "nothing fights" which would fit Dr. Howell's category, but "nothing fights" serve a number of purposes, one of which is to allow the parties to evaluate the military potential of their rivals. If the enemy shows weakness, maybe runs away from the "nothing fight" in an early stage, this may escalate the fighting between the two groups into full-scale violence of the form which I imagine Dr. Howell calls conflict or which might be called predatory competition. Then the result of these fights is to lead to the acquisition of new territory and some of the effects that cultural ecologists are talking about.

Mr. Koratop, in some of his work in the Congo, has suggested that the distribution of conflict may have an effect on the relative intensity of disputes and the possibilities for resolution. He suggests that personal grudges and feuds last much longer if they are sustained by the immediate parties involved in this dispute, but if the disputes or conflicts tend to spread out and become ramified throughout a larger structure or through the formation of alliances, there is a greater likelihood that these conflicts will be resolved because there's more opportunity for mediation or intervention by neutral parties. It struck me that Mr. Huber's study, especially Case 6 versus Case 4, might serve as an illustration of that kind of possibility.

BISHOP: I am in essential agreement with Dr. Howell's paper. Concerning the cross-cultural techniques, it depends to a great extent at what period in their history you choose a particular group. I'm thinking in particular of the Dakota, who at the time of contact were living, as far as we know, in essential peace with their neighbors. Yet, after about 1680 or 1690, they became embroiled in a feud with the Ojibwa over land and land rights in Minnesota and Wisconsin and were involved in full-scale warfare. Eventually the Dakota got shoved out of this region out onto the Plains, where they adopted the horse, competition with the Ojibwa virtually ceased, and warfare, which during the eighteenth century had involved bloody battles, virtually came to an end. Then warfare became more of the non-conflict type because they weren't competing over resources anymore. They had plenty of buffalo; they didn't need beaver pelts; they could do without much of the technology they had formerly required, living in a different ecological zone. It depends at what point in their history you look at the Dakota, as well as some other groups, whether you classify them as being engaged in warfare or non-warfare.

A. NETTLESHIP: Dr. Bishop, do you feel that there is a specific time in most groups, as they grow, at which they will go to war?

BISHOP: No, I wouldn't say that. In North America at least (north of Mexico and excluding sections of the Southeast) most groups were living in a state of essential peace, and conflict, at most, involved a certain amount of feuding. It was only after Europeans came that warfare developed. Furthermore, I don't agree with Mr. Sipes' comment yesterday, when he said "It didn't matter what the size of the group was, they were all in there pitching as hard as they could." I don't believe that. I think the object of warfare was to outdo your enemy, not to kill him, but to touch him. Certainly there were cases where individuals were killed, but in most instances where warfare did exist it was on a very small scale. Where guns were introduced, the peoples without them were absolutely horrified when groups moved in and started to slaughter them. It was totally foreign to their thinking.

ROPER: I'd like to ask Mr. Huber about the business of sanctioned killing without and within. It seems to me in reading your paper that killing within the village was allowed; people weren't happy about it, and sometimes they moved away and out, but there was no punishment.

HUBER: It was allowed if you could get away with it, but killing within the village was a very dangerous thing to do. You are killing the brother or the affine of your next-door neighbor who's sitting right next to you. It's a very dangerous thing to do.

ROPER: But it's murder. You seem to say that it is murder within and without, whereas in our society we only have murder within and when you kill somebody without, that's warfare. It seems to me that this is a very big distinction between your group and most other groups.

HUBER: That's true in a sense, but the definition of murder doesn't depend so much upon the status or the category of the victim, but rather on the effect upon the solidarity of the village. In other words, a person who killed a co-villager would normally be considered reprehensible. He might be killed himself in retaliation. His act would be an act which would threaten the very solidarity of the village; it would threaten to split the village into two opposing camps of kinsmen and destroy it. There are cases in the village in which one individual comes to be identified as what they call *motowa-hopwa-nom*, which means literally a man of bad consciousness or conscience. This person through his actions over a period of time continually threatens the village, not by violence against others, but through insults and exposing the village in various ways to quarrels. Once the person is identified in that category you can, conceivably, kill him and get away with it. His death doesn't, at that point, threaten the village since the rest of the villagers are willing to see him as a danger which needs to be removed. That is a very subjective judgment on the part of the killer, and he can be wrong.

M. NETTLESHIP: We execute people we don't find socially desirable too, at various times, but we still have the category of murder and your rather vague redefinition of that category will not help our analysis at all. What do you mean by murder? Whom can a man go out and "murder"?

HUBER: If you don't want to call it murder, I don't care. What I'm talking about is the kind of moral significance they attribute to killing.

M. NETTLESHIP: I'm talking about your analysis of the situation and the use of terms which mean the same to all of us: what do you mean by murder?

HUBER: I don't think it matters.

A. NETTLESHIP: I believe on one hand we are talking about a legal definition under this name, and on the other hand you are talking about a social definition.

MIDLARSKY: I was concerned about Dr. Howell's definition of conflict. I found it a very interesting treatment because it leads us into some territories that probably have not been dealt with adequately before. At the same time, we've got a definition of conflict here which is tied to the balance of power, directly. If the offensive by the Panzers in France in 1940 is not an example of conflict I am troubled. If one asks any French resistance fighter whether in 1940 he was in a state of conflict with the advancing Panzers, I think he might give us a different answer. Of course, we cannot rely on that; it is not our final evidence. At an analytical level what I am concerned about is tying the concept of conflict into the balance of power, because the balance of power, at least in my interpretation of it, or in the field of international relations, is treated as a possible cause, or is treated as a theory, that may explain the onset of war or the onset of peace depending on who's using it. Whatever the possible validity of it, it is treated as a causal type of thing and to identify something operationally by something else which may be a cause is to create a potentially tautological situation that could be dangerous.

HOWELL: May I ask an information question? I'm not sure I understood you entirely. What would be the situation when there is an absence of a balance of power?

MIDLARSKY: The absence of a balance could mean any number of things; it could mean a dominant situation, a unipolar hierarchically organized. . . .

HOWELL: Would you describe it as a conflict situation?

MIDLARSKY: The Roman Empire?

HOWELL: Well, any place where there is absolutely nothing even approximating a balance of power.

MIDLARSKY: Well, I think I would have to know a lot more about it before I could know whether it was conflict or not.

HOWELL: I'm just trying to understand your argument. I am not sure you were really saying anything much different.

MIDLARSKY: I'm saying that there may be a relationship between the balance of power and the onset of conflict. To this extent you may have hit on something valuable. Where there is balance, there may actually be more potential for conflict. When you get closer to a balance of power, international policy would have a situation that could develop into war. But that's not the same thing as defining the conflict as consisting of violence.

HOWELL: In order to have a conflict situation you have to have a number of conditions met, only one of which is an effective balance of power. The North Vietnamese, the Viet Cong, were able to put up an effective resistance against the United States, even though we had more hardware. So you can't weigh the thing that way.

A. NETTLESHIP: We are balanced off the knife's edge, or we're balanced on the knife's edge.

MIDLARSKY: There is another aspect also in terms of the idea of asymmetric conflict that Dr. Carroll brought up earlier. To exclude the asymmetric situation from our usage of the term conflict might be to remove a potentially or actually important category.

HOWELL: This is strictly a heuristic device as far as I'm concerned. It's a way of helping to get a better understanding; it's not an all or nothing affair. Serious things can start from things that are not serious to begin with — or things differ in time. These are not immutable, permanent situations for any group or even any encounter. What started off as a supposedly non-conflict type of competitive situation in the Olympics once, for Johnson, at least, became a very traumatic conflict situation and he refused to go into the ring. He was experiencing such conflict that he withdrew from the arena without fighting when he was a middleweight.

FINK: I also wanted to respond to Dr. Howell's paper on the point of separating some terminological issues from empirical issues. He's adopted a particular definition of competition and a particular definition of conflict as a species of competition which has certain characteristics differentiated from other forms of competition. In doing that he's adopting one of three major terminological traditions in the use of the terms competition and conflict. The other two reverse the meanings. One of them reverses the meanings so that conflict is the general category in which competitive and non-competitive are the two types he has identified. Another calls conflict, what he calls conflict; and calls competition, what he calls non-conflict. There are at least three different terminological traditions which roughly represent the same conceptual distinctions. In saying you can have wars without conflict, you are speaking to one group but not the other groups in terms of terminological tradition.

The significance of what he says, however, has to be looked at in terms of whether you can have wars, given the psychological, sociological, and behavioral circumstances that he identifies as non-conflict. Can you have war without conflict of interests or opposition of interests between the parties, and can you have it without mutual harm of some sort to the parties? In other words, if you have neither mutual harm nor opposition of interests, is it sensible to call it war? In the way we've been analyzing war are we really talking about war games or ritual antagonisms — which are not the same things as the kind of war we're talking about preventing?

SCOTT: I've suggested that a lot of the animal data indicate that serious violence — destructive violence involving killing and serious injury — results from conditions of social disorganization. I have raised the possibility that perhaps this principle might apply to relationships between human societies, as well as between individuals. It would seem that what Bishop has described among the Indian tribes at the time the white man arrived on this continent might be a laboratory case of this. The Indians had apparently worked out in the past a reasonably well-organized system in which the tribes did not come into conflict and there was actually very little killing. Then the white people came in and in various ways disorganized the system, introducing the gun, pushing people out of their normal territories, etc., until the end result was a tremendous increase in conflict and the deadliness of the conflict which has probably given us quite a false picture of the Indian life.

In the evolution of animal societies there is a tendency to reduce harmful conflict to rituals of threats and avoidance rather than actual killing or anything that results in very great harm. It would seem to me that you might get a similar tendency in cultural evolution in evolving of this non-conflict type of behavior in which the harm that is done is considerably reduced.

SIPES: I would like to address myself to Dr. Bishop and Dr. Scott. I do believe that the advent of the white man in the New World increased the frequency and level of violence between Indian tribes. Still, if we see North America as a paradise before the advent of the white man, where there were infrequent and very few wars, my goodness, it was an unusual place. When we go from the Eastern woodlands to the swamps of Florida, to the deserts of the Southwest — to all of these ecosystems — we find generally peace or very little fighting, yet when we look at other aboriginal parts of the world such as South America, Meso-america, Labrador, Africa, and Southeast Asia, we sure don't find it there. I would assume that there were quite a few little wars fought over here. The statement that they do the best they can was a rather facetious statement. If we step behind the fatuity, what I meant to say is that I believe that there is no significant correlation between group population and per capita violence and warfare. If Dr. Bishop thinks that there is, he should run a cross-cultural correlation test on that; it would be a good subject for a paper, either way.

BISHOP: In response to that, I come back to what Dr. M. Nettleship said earlier about the emergence of an early state type of society with a specialized group of personnel, whose sole function (or at least one function of which) was to engage in military activity. There is no evidence of military societies among the Eskimo for instance. The conflicts between the Eskimo and the Montaignes are late historical developments as the Montaignes moved up into that northern region of Labrador. I explicitly excluded the Southeast where you did have protostates and there is some archeological evidence for warfare. I didn't include Mexico, where it obviously existed too. I was explicitly limiting my definition of feuding to small horticultural groupings or hunters and gatherers with which I am best acquainted. As far as state societies go, I don't deny that full-scale warfare did exist. Certainly among protostates, as in Polynesia and parts of Africa, you obviously had warfare.

CARROLL: I wanted to extend the comments that were made before by Dr. Fink about the conflict of interests and to explain why I think that this is not merely a terminological problem, but one which has rather serious political implications. (This is a position that was really developed primarily by Hermann Schmit of Scandinavia, who some years ago published an article called "Peace research and politics" in the *Journal of Peace Research* and subsequently published a very interesting article called "Peace research as a technology for pacification" which appeared subsequently in some IPRA proceedings.) If you exclude from conflict the conception of latent conflict, and you deal only with manifest conflict or behavioral forms of conflict (conflict which manifests itself in some kind of open hostilities and, even more narrowly, in symmetric behavioral conflict) then you exclude from vision, and from your conception of what you ought to be dealing with, the whole range of conflict of interest, asymmetric conflicts, conflicts in which structural violence may be taking place, but in which there is not yet an overt expression of the conflict. What happens in practice is that the conflict resolution people or peace researchers spend their time dealing with ways of suppressing violence — that is, suppressing the behavioral manifestations of symmetric conflict — and not with the problem of latent conflict and the asymmetric conflicts which may in fact be producing enormous quantities of violence in the structural sense.

HOWELL: I wouldn't exclude any of that and I would say that the cold war, by and large, has been a conflict situation, one which has been manifested partly through displaced aggression.

CARBY-SAMUELS: The question is the relationships of interdependence and the institutionalization of interdependence, and whether there are optimal ways to institutionalize it. We have one way which Dr.

Sieverts pointed out and another way which Mr. Huber pointed out. Fundamental to what is being said is an ontological proposition which still has to be empirically tested and it is this: Which one of you here, even the person who speaks about civil war, can categorically say that predatory competition is not a rational form of expression of interdependence? If that is the case, to what extent should the research on wars not be related to finding out the norms of ways of expressing interdependence and whether there are optimal or suboptimal modes for working out perceived interdependence?

A. NETTLESHIP: May we now hear Dr. Tefft's summary?

TEFFT: The systematic study of warfare regulation among tribal peoples has been neglected, and in order to begin some tentative movements in this direction I reviewed some peace theories which pointed toward important conditions whose presence or absence could determine possibilities for warfare regulation. My definition of war and conflict between political communities does not meet with the conceptualization on the part of many people in the Conference, and I will not defend it, except that on a pragmatic basis, it served my purposes for my research. Based on this review, I have advanced a number of hypotheses which might account for differential frequency of warfare among tribal peoples and I tested these hypotheses with a cross-cultural survey method based on a narrow sample of societies, partly from the Human Relations Area Files and partly from other sources.

Most of the hypotheses were not confirmed. Some of them were only partly confirmed insofar as certain types of warfare were concerned. For example, one hypothesis that's widespread in the literature is "Political communities whose members intermarry extensively fight less frequently than political communities who do not intermarry." This was not confirmed. This serves as an example of the kind of hypotheses that have been advanced and that don't seem to be supported by my research. One of the difficulties with the existing theories and hypotheses is that they don't provide a coherent theoretical framework by which we can predict how interrelated variations in techno-environmental and techno-economic factors, population levels, military organization and military objectives, ethos, and so forth affect warfare frequency. Future studies dealing with tribal and band peoples must deal with the study of interrelationships between these various factors over time. More studies along the lines of Dr. Bishop's examples are necessary to sort out some of the kinds of problems that we have been confronted with in this conference. The fact that my study has tended to refute some pet hypotheses about factors that might enhance warfare regulation among tribal peoples does not necessarily mean they do not operate successfully in the modern international community.

A. NETTLESHIP: One more paper before discussion: Tamayo y Salmorán, if you please.

TAMAYO Y SALMORÁN: I will point out certain features of the motivating function of law, before remarking on how acts of force, such as reprisal and war, are used by the legal order, in this case by international law. Then I will indicate why international law still uses warfare and, finally, I will indicate how warfare may disappear if we follow the evolution of the whole legal system. It is very easy to observe that the motivating function of the legal system resides in the fact that law is an order with the use of sanctions for making men behave in a certain foreseen manner. If we consider that the sanction of the legal order ought to be executed even against the will of the individual, if that individual resists by physical force, then the result is that the law uses violence to bring about the desired behavior. Acts of force appear as a principal element in the motivating function of law. There are two different sorts of acts of force affecting law: acts of coercion or force which have the character of sanctions and acts of coercion or force which lack this character. From this we can state that the violence contemplated by law appears as a sanction or has the character of sanction. We can deduce, paradoxically, that law as a coercive order regulates acts of violence by acts of violence. By determining the conditions under which an individual may use violence, the legal order establishes a system of collective security because it protects the subject against the use of violence by other individuals. By establishing a system of collective security, the legal order pacifies the community in a sense — the legal sense. The peace of law is only a relative peace because the law does not exclude the use of violence by individuals against other individuals. But, by determining the procedure by which violence is used from man to man, the legal order introduced peace in the human community, a law peace. International law performs, as national law does, a prescribing function which consists in bringing about certain behavior of the human being, the subjects of the states, or simply the states. Becoming a determining motif of reciprocal human behavior is not an easy task. To make men behave according to the wishes of another it is necessary to rely on very persuasive elements to bring about the desired behavior. In compliance with this, international law, just as municipal law, uses a certain form of behavior, the characteristics of threat, hostility, aggression, attack, or deprivation of life, health, economic values, liberty, etc., which consist of reprisals and war in the most representative forms. Just as in municipal law, there are in national law two different sorts of acts of force or coercion: the act of force or coercion which has the character of sanction and the act of force which does not have this character. In international law, reprisals and war, as acts of force or coercion, are prohibited unless they are determined as a sanction against an international delict. But the use of violence is generally prohibited unless it is determined as a sanction. How can we know whether we face an illegal use of force or the use of legal sanction? The answer to this question is immediately given in national law. In national law there exist objective authorities, law courts with compulsory jurisdiction and competence to decide whether the use of force constitutes a crime or an execution of sanction. In international law another situation occurs, and this is the cause of warfare on the international scene. There exists no authority to settle international conflicts, that is, to answer impartially the question of which of the parties to the conflict is right and which is wrong. Each state is authorized to decide for itself the question of whether the other state has violated its rights. Since the other state has the same competence to decide for itself the question of law, the fundamental legal problem remains without authoritative solution. Objective examination and the question of whether or not the law has been violated are the most important factors in legal procedure.

In the scope of national law, the existence of objective authorities competent to decide conflicts between subjects has eliminated in a high degree the use of force from man to man, at least in legal confines. The use of force has been effectively reduced and reserved for a central agency authorized to use violence only as a sanction against illegal acts. Consequently the next step on which our efforts must be concentrated is establishing an international corps endowed with compensatory jurisdiction. Reprisals and war do not disappear with installation of international law courts. On the contrary, reprisals and war have to be maintained by international law as a sanction of the international legal order. International law needs to rely on very positive motives for inducing the states to refrain from certain acts deemed illegal by the international law courts. The decision of the court must be endorsed by effective means, such as reprisals and war, so that resistance by the convicted state will be hopeless. With an international law court reprisals and war do not necessarily disappear. What WILL disappear is self-help procedure. Perhaps reprisals and war can disappear when the sanctions of international law can be addressed not to the states but to the members of the states — to the individual directly. When collective liability in the area of international law is replaced by an individual liability, then collective sanctions such as war will not be needed for the maintenance of international peace.

A. NETTLESHIP: We are rather humbled and certainly grateful to you for this brilliant thrust at the mass of seemingly unresolved areas in the international situation when it comes to legality.

KRAKAUER: We are approaching the end of this conference and part of this session is involved with the question of war and its control. Certainly we cannot expect to ever prevent conflict. I don't even think it's healthy. Is it possible that our best hope of peace is to encourage domestic conflict with poised ultimate weapons that threaten the lives of the followers and leaders on both sides? This is the situation which has existed for the last ten years or so and has worked.

TEFFT: I would like to compliment Dr. Tamayo y Salmorán in moving in the direction that may provide some solution. However, the problem still exists of inequality between the existing nation-states in terms of wealth, opportunities, industrial growth, and unequal political power to influence international decisions. I can't quite see how an international court is going to eliminate these problems. As long as they exist, there are going to be attempts by nation-states, through one form of warfare or another, to engage in "self-help" mechanisms.

ROPER: We have a World Court already and nobody pays any attention to it. It banned the French bomb testing but without effect. Dorothy Hutchinson, a former president of the Women's International League, is presenting the U.N. with the idea of a mediation board. In the U.N. there is a jump straight up to the World Court without intermediate procedures which might be less threatening to countries.

A. NETTLESHIP: We need a kind of international ombudsman so we can all talk and air out our differences.

RICHARDS: Dr. Tamayo y Salmorán has expressed very elegantly the problems that fit with the views of Hoebel about the necessity for an overriding authority to settle disputes. Hoebel starts with the family, where the family head settles disputes within the family. Then there is a lineage head to settle disputes between families, and a clan head between lineages, and so on up. A federal government settles disputes between states in the United States.

Tamayo is proposing an interesting, very logical, and necessary next step. But one of the difficulties is that this overriding authority must be accepted as legitimate by the participants. One of the things that we have learned from anthropological data is that laws that are successful (ones that work and have the fewest violations) are laws that express the general consensus of the group as to what should or should not be done. In the United States, we have had a great deal of experience by now with laws that nobody agrees with; they are not obeyed. It is almost impossible to impose laws on other people without a tremendous amount of violence and conflict. One of the difficulties with the World Court is that it has not been accepted as legitimate and its decisions have not been accepted as binding on the participants.

MIDLARSKY: Hans Kelsen defines laws as a reflection of the norms of society and herein perhaps lies the problem; the norms of international society are so wide and varied that it is difficult indeed to institutionalize them in any operative legal framework.

No, I think we have to take Tamayo's idea seriously in terms of something that has indeed worked, imperfectly so far, but at least it has worked.

Seeking a solution to war problems in terms of this poised nuclear framework is to allow that finite probability (that we have been so worried about and which has, fortunately, been working in our favor) of something happening.

PARKER: I get very disturbed when I hear a suggestion of a single approach solution to, or explanation for, war. It was proposed earlier that if we just simply let people do their thing, for instance, if they want to perpetrate evil on each other, well that is quite fine. The fact is that we don't enter wars until we see the evil or until it is forced on us. We find it very easy to ignore the fact that evil is being perpetrated on others. We do not get excited unless we feel our interests are involved at some point.

The same thing applies to the whole area of international law. There are those who think that this is the solution. You are on very touchy ground when you start trying to take what has been done on the domestic scene and try to explode that into the international level. There are complexities which operate at one level that don't at the other. The last thing that we need in this whole field is single-approach solutions to and explanations of the cause of war and conditions which might promote peace.

OLDFIELD HAYES: Law was just defined as the codified norms of society. I believe that it was Pospisiel who said that laws on books are one thing and laws in social reality are something else again and that until subgroups of societies internalize laws they are essentially meaningless. That is why we have laws on books that judges themselves ignore. It is too idealistic to think of such far-reaching laws as would come out of some such august body as a world court.

YOUNG: We have a problem of making international laws that are acceptable to people and we need to take some positive action in this way. I think we probably all agree that it is undesirable at this time to have international law with violent sanctions to uphold it, because it does not have sufficient legitimacy. The problem is to build legitimacy. For example, if this country were to submit cases to the World Court and abide by those cases that would increase the legitimacy of international law in everyone's mind.

Somebody has suggested that a group of private people get together and establish a court of mankind. Any international question could be brought before the court. The only effect the court could possibly have, of course, would be moral, but I know that the AAUP has done pretty well over the past fifty years by adjudicating issues over which they had no jurisdiction, but on which they were able to exercise a moral influence over the actions of colleges.

FINK: My first comment is on the specific assertion that nuclear stalemate has prevented war, has worked. It has not. We have had more war in the last twenty-five years than we had in the previous twenty-five years. The nuclear stalemate has only prevented nuclear war. It is a self-containing system but it certainly hasn't done anything to prevent other kinds of war.

Even thinking about operating on that level or taking that as a primary direction is extremely dangerous. In addition, the idea that international organizations, international law, or the government in general has succeeded in preventing or reducing war has got to be seriously questioned. It is conceivable that government itself is the cause of war, therefore we should be very careful and remember that war is not just international war, it is a societal phenomenon, an inter-group phenomenon.

AMSBURY: I have a release from the U.S. State Department of a few years ago, where their chief counsel discusses international law. He points out that the U.S. State Department does not take a narrow, traditional, or fixed attitude towards international law. They take a flexible attitude towards it. He pointed out that we have been able to make our point stick in Santo Domingo, but we were still working out our legal position in Vietnam. He seems to be saying that international law consists in what they will let you get away with.

TAMAYO Y SALMORÁN: I only want to remark about what Professor Young has said. Certainly when I talk about international jurisdiction I mean international jurisdiction completely, not as it now exists in international law. When we talk about an international court, we mean that it has a compulsory jurisdiction which guarantees the effectiveness of the position of the judge. Why do you pay taxes? Because you cannot avoid the sanction of the United States machinery. The next stop is international laws that have compulsory jurisdiction, not only moral influences. We need a real tribunal.

CARBY-SAMUELS: I am in total conceptual as well as empirical disagreement with the propositions embodied in a so-called world court. It presupposes what I would call uni-modal solution systems. Some people, for instance, proposed that to deal with the limited resources in the world, we need a United Nations-type body, an international body that can allocate resources. However, there is no assurance that a United Nations or a world court system will have the wisdom to find optimal solutions that are consistent with man's evolution. A world court system, especially one that has sanctions at its disposal, must be based upon the ability to monopolize the use of force. Thus it will be supported by those who can provide force and the availability of force depends very much upon the loyalty of the individuals affected to the decision unit. Yet it is possible that those peoples of the world who do not have an entree to force may in fact have the optimal solution for the evolution of mankind, but their solution will not be tried because of some sanctions of some world court system. We should try to preserve multi-polar or multi-modal approaches to human evolution and I am very much against anything like world domination by any one body that thinks it has a monopoly on truth.

A. NETTLESHIP: May we start with Dr. Sipes' summary please?

SIPES: The paper that was written for this conference summarized a previous paper in which I reported a multi-strategic investigation of the relationships between war, sports, and aggression. I used a synchronic, cross-cultural correlation test in twenty societies and then a fifty-year time series case study of the United States. In that investigation, I used these relationships to test through their predictions two rival major models of human behavior: the drive-discharge model and the culture pattern model. That paper was entitled "War, sports, and aggression and an empirical test of two rival theories." It appeared in the February 1973 issue of the *American Anthropologist*.

That research removed the culture pattern model, at least partially, from the realm of speculation and established it as a validated explanatory model and as a relatively accurate predictive instrument. Although substantiated by empirical tests, however, it was static. I therefore constructed a general dynamic processual model of cultural patterning and present that model in the paper written for this Conference. It describes how, within a given group, rules and patterns of behavior, goals, and value hierarchies most applicable to and generated in one area of behavior such as warfare diffuse into other areas of behavior and then reflexively support the original behavior. It takes a few faltering steps toward quantifying that diffusion process. The general model, of course, applies to all areas of behavior and the general effects of any culture change, whether internally or externally generated. It promises to be useful in predicting future results of changes introduced to or generated in pre-industrial countries by contact with industrialized Western societies. I also present in the paper a specific application of the processual model to warfare and combative-type sports — showing how we can account for the worldwide distribution of combative-type sports through the evolutionary selection for warlike societies. That portion of the paper most applicable to the discussion of war *per se* provides an evolutionary explanation for the current prevalence of warlike societies. It also claims that warlike behavior still has a selective advantage and suggests that war is going to be with us for a long, long time, because the steps necessary to eliminate it are impractically massive.

I am talking of evolutionary selection of cultures. I am not talking of evolutionary selection for physical, mental, or emotional characteristics of the human organism. This is cultural evolution, not biological evolution. A culture can be selected out without eliminating or even reducing the number of human individuals involved. One culture can be selected out by another group imposing its own culture on the first group, forcing them to change their language, their legal system, their marriage customs, their government structure, their subsistence base, and so on, and a subordinate group also can voluntarily emulate part or all of a dominant culture. Of course, a less successful group can be pushed back into undesirable territory where they slowly disintegrate or they can be killed which takes care of their culture quite nicely. All of these have been known to happen. A society proficient in and prepared for warfare and willing to engage in it (other things such as population, level of health, state of technology, etc. being equal) has a greater chance of survival than a society and its culture not proficient, willing, and able. This is not mere idle speculation; it has been empirically tested and verified by Naroll and Otterbein. This being so, we have selection for warlike cultures or societies. For millennia then, warfare has conferred a statistical selective advantage on the culture, on the society, proficient at it. We might as well face the fact at least for those societies which still can engage in warfare without calling for weapons which shatter the victor fully as much as the vanquished, it is still better to have warred and won than not to have warred at all. The state of Israel is surviving better and more securely today as a result of her successful military actions against her neighbors; so is the state of North Vietnam.

There still is selection for warlikeness. This could be changed. We could supply every nation on earth with advanced nuclear weapons. Then we would have an environment selecting against warlikeness. Any society would stand a greater chance of survival if it did not engage in any war, regardless of its chances for a textbook victory. We might expect warfare to disappear over the course of several hundreds of years if we do this, because the societies practicing warfare would disappear. Unfortunately, there is as good a chance that the human species would disappear first and so dissemination of nuclear weapons is not indicated.

There is another way to eliminate war, although it's not too encouraging. Massive culture change would be required. It should be possible to attenuate or even eliminate war-linked values and behaviors in any given society by: (1) eliminating the military and quasi-military organizations; (2) removing all references to war, riots, brawls, murder, and assaults from all communications media; (3) eliminating combative sports; and (4) at least minimizing zero-sum-game conditions in nations, in business, religion, government, force of law, and other social institutions. Only such an imposed, multi-strategic, and coordinated approach would do a thorough enough job, and even then the result would not be obtained until the second or third generation. If this were done by a single nation, it probably would eliminate the chance of that nation initiating war, but it also would make that nation a sheep in a world of wolves, and wolves are seldom converted to eating grass by the presence of sheep. Truly lasting peace would seem obtainable only through a politically achieved world order plus a simultaneous and massive culture change effort in all societies. The probability of this happening has yet to be computed. This is not to say that we can't influence any particular imminent or actual war. I believe we can. Rather what I wish to stress is that there will always be ANOTHER imminent or actual war with which we shall have to deal. In theory, there is a way to bring lasting peace to our planet. In fact, I cannot foresee it happening.

A. NETTLESHIP: Dr. Shokeid's summary next, please.

SHOKEID: During my field trip with people from the Atlas Mountains and for a few years afterwards, while writing about them, I was mainly impressed by the stream of dispute. It is true, I was puzzled by the many gatherings and celebrations I observed and recorded, which seemed to be a permanent failure relative to the ongoing successful disputes. I did not think that I could produce from that data a pattern of social behavior, the usual goal of our work. Therefore, it was only recently that I decided to try and understand that apparently bizarre phenomenon. Looking carefully into my records, of all gatherings and celebrations, counting all the participants on these occasions, I finally found out that there was a pattern in that apparently patternless phenomenon. Bitter opponents would meet sometimes in a more congenial atmosphere. However, opportunities for these peaceful meetings were only at parties thrown by those of a lesser status in the community or those not fiercely involved in politics. On these occasions, guests were neither committed nor indebted to the host. At these parties, influential members could show their sociability and meet their opponents in a friendly manner without offering any real concession, even if the party was given by a member of an opposing group of relatives. Other opportunities were at impromptu parties which developed on neutral territory without any preparation in advance.

Anthropologists usually consider standardized methods, dynamics, and customs of conflict avoidance and peace-making. I wonder if they haven't dismissed the apparently non-standardized forms of occasional relaxation in social relationships and, by so doing, overemphasized situations of conflict. It is in this direction of observations and analyses that we may try to answer Foster's question as to how, in spite of never-ending bitter competition and strife, do peasant villagers, and I would add other face-to-face societies, continue without flying apart from centrifugal force.

HUBER: In taking Howell's distinction between wars without conflict and wars with conflict as a distinction between confrontations without violence and confrontations with violence, several of the people who responded talked in terms of some kind of ritual combat (which had no serious intention to commit violence as part of it) as opposed to a war of conflict (which would be over some kind of resource or because of some kind of disparity in aims). But in the ethnographic papers presented in this session (Dr. Siverts' and my own), there are two cases of precisely that kind of war without conflict, without any disparity of aims between the combatant parties. Yet, even lacking "conflict," the stakes can be very high indeed, especially when such things as total annihilation of a village, at least for the Anggor, are entirely possible.

The suggestion that in wars without conflict there may be some kind of simply "going through the motions" is very misleading.

Dr. Scott was asking whether or not there might be some kind of cultural evolution that led societies to create forms of ritual confrontation which have no practical significance for the violence and killing. Here are two cases that we have in hand where it is clearly not the case. In connection with this idea of evolution of different forms of confrontation, different forms of violence, may I ask Dr. Sipes how changes occur which may then be selected for? What is the mechanism of social variation or mutation?

SIPES: Speaking off the top of my head, it is most likely that for some set of reasons or other, the opportunities or the necessity for combat would have disappeared for a period of a hundred years or so. I don't imagine it would take any longer than that to make a society peaceful in the absence of any sort of stimulus whatsoever toward warlikeness. They probably would still have the capacity; there would be residual behavior patterns and value patterns which would make them warlike again rather rapidly if the occasion demanded, but they would be in abeyance.

How does a society become warlike? This is probably an incremental thing and probably would again take place over a period of numerous generations. Human beings are born with the capacity for warlike behavior; there's no doubt about that. (Whatever human beings do, they are born with the capacity to do, obviously.) This is a capacity that apparently runs counter to very few propensities in a human being. When put under pressure, for instance, by seeing what happens when a warlike enemy comes in — they stick a spear into you — it doesn't take you too long to get the idea that maybe you can stick a spear back into him. This is, again, probably a somewhat facetious approach, but it would happen in a common sense way like that, I believe. At first a very peaceful society when confronted with a warlike society would cut and run real fast and then they might decide that perhaps they can do something about the situation and over a period of generations would develop the institutions, the techniques, and the value systems required to be rather proficient at war.

RICHARDS: We have been concerned with definitions, communications between disciplines, and so on, thus we've been arguing about what is conflict, what is war, what is violence, what is feuding: I'd like to try to play Alexander and cut the Gordian knot. We seem to have a continuum of hostile interactions with at least two dimensions or axes. One is the number of people involved, ranging from two up to millions;

the other is the intensity of the hostility, from threats and shouting up to killing. We have pinned labels at various points along this continuum and we've disagreed about just where these labels should be placed. But, at the same time what we are really trying to find out is what are the enabling or correlating conditions that prevail at these various points along the continuum. Can we perhaps identify differences in those conditions at various points? For example, decision-making processes may differ significantly from one point to another. Social institutions may differ with consequent differential effect. Technology may vary. Mobile or sedentary living may enter into these surrounding conditions, and so on. Can we, perhaps, make a scale that will enable us to predict a greater or lesser likelihood of hostile interaction occurring, depending on which of these conditions occur at specific points at each level? By this means can we perhaps identify key variables that could be manipulated to move us in a direction along the continuum that would lead to involvement of fewer people and a lower intensity of hostility? I feel, personally, that I can see a very faint light at the end of the tunnel, and feel that research problems, after this Conference, for me, are a bit more obvious, a bit more specific, a bit more concrete.

MIDLARSKY: I would like to agree with Dr. Richards on the clarification function, at least for me in finishing my book (this being at the end of a period of research). A lot of what has been said here has functioned as a sort of clarifying filter that now places some of the things I've done in better perspective. I would like to try to integrate some of the research that I know has been done, and that I've done with others, and direct a question to Dr. Sipes. He mentioned diffusion, the diffusion of violence, and I have worked on some of the mathematics of diffusion of instability (as Richardson has done in the case of war). I wonder if Dr. Sipes could comment on some of the work that he's done.

SIPES: This work, by and large, has yet to be done. I am initiating several tests of this dynamic diffusion model of mine and in two years I will be able to give it to you.

ESSER: I am a bit sorry and a bit distressed to hear that at this point, close to the end of our meeting, we are still thinking about some very simple solutions. I agree instead with those among us who have said that there will be no simple solutions. What Dr. Carroll said regarding the possibility of distinguishing good and evil causes is really not correct. You can only speak for yourself and, maybe, a couple of your friends. But it is impossible to demonstrate that there are certain good or certain evil things. Similarly I disagree with Dr. Sipes' suggestion, even if it's in jest, that we might abandon and abolish war by playing a simulation or game as if war is based on a stimulus-response theory. (He stated that when you have no stimuli for a hundred years, then by that time war will have died out.) On the contrary, the concepts which we can construct as humans will determine what we will do rather than the available so-called objective realities around us. It is the old struggle between those of us who think that there is an objective world which has natural laws, where, if we can discover them we will be in good shape, and those of us (and I believe that Tamayo and Smith join me in this) who think that WE construct this world and consequently what we want to do and what we want conceptualized may happen if we find enough to go with us. With that statement I hope we can, at least conceptually, put this matter straight.

CLAESSEN: I read with much interest the paper by Dr. Shokeid and I would like to ask him a question. You mentioned the situation in which two enemies meet each other in the neighborhood of a neutral person and have a talk with each other. In your opinion this has a possibility of lessening stress in the village. Do you think it possible, perhaps, that this situation could take place between nation-states to find a meeting ground? Could this perhaps be a help to find a solution for growing stress between nations?

SHOKEID: It's true, I found that in small-scale societies enemies COULD meet. I wouldn't say it would be very friendly but at least they would talk to each other, or at least they would sit at a table. I did not think about the possibility of trying to bring this over to nations, the meeting between nations, when I wrote it. From my little experience here at the Conference and yesterday in Chicago in a situation when I confronted an Egyptian and we were speaking about the same phenomena, we were polite. I thought we must talk, I don't know what happened: we didn't talk. If I would try to generalize from my experience of meetings in the situations between individuals on neutral grounds: we are polite but we don't talk. We should try to find out why. I notice that to some extent I don't feel terribly easy, so I wonder what that means.

A. NETTLESHIP: I think you have defined for us, very beautifully in words, that when we face someone we feel insecure with, we emote, our adrenal reticular axis pours out its enzymes and cortisone runs through our blood and our blood pressure goes up and we wonder who's going to strike, or shall we strike. We've come here in peace and I think we must practice this before we can communicate. One finds a curious thing, certainly, in the Anglo-Saxon world, that we are often fearful; you know, we sit and we sit in a railway carriage with someone for twenty years and look behind that paper and never speak to them, and then a funny thing happens. Someone drops a paper and they are friends like they could have been for twenty years. It amazes me always, what are we doing here? It's not that much of a problem; the guy wouldn't hit you if you said, "Hi," you know.

War or Peace?

Chaired by M. A. NETTLESHIP

M. NETTLESHIP: When I first thought about having this Conference, it seemed to me that what we would be talking about would be something called "war research." I believed this subject matter and the approaches to it to be of a rather different nature from what I had understood as "peace research." Indeed, the few peace researchers that I had met at that time were rather critical of what they called war research. Yet, here we "war researchers" are, and I have found myself surrounded with a hotbed of activists, any one of whom could be a fine peace researcher. The only problem with this is that we may not have too much to argue about in this session.

Our first presentation this afternoon is going to be made by Dr. Saucelo of the World Peace Academy. He's going to tell us something about the aims of his organization and what they hope to do. While this is not an academic group, it is a group which believes, with many of us, in the genuine possibility of achieving peace. I think what we might learn from Dr. Saucelo are some of his ideas as to how we might go about this. He has some very practical notions, particularly having to do with financing. I will turn the meeting over to Dr. Saucelo to make his presentation.

SAUCELO: First of all, we are really here not to give a lecture, but rather to gather more knowledge. We realize that this is not our field and we are taking the opportunity of listening to you, to the intellectual discussion of the subject of war and peace. The World Peace Academy is a non-profit organization, dedicated to the belief that the use of destructive weapons to settle international conflicts can be, and must be,

eliminated by creating a climate that would render this method unnecessary or absurd. We believe, however, that we cannot be effective
with our objectives unless we extend our activities and our philosophy
to countries around the world, including China and Russia. We believe
that unilateral disarmament would be ineffective and dangerous. Our
goal therefore is to create chapters of the World Peace Academy in
major cities all over the world. Our function will include research and
educational activities involving anthropologists, social scientists, edu-
cators, physical scientists, doctors, lawyers, writers, and other concerned
community leaders all over the world. We will also send our ambas-
sadors to different countries and sponsor international goodwill travel.

It seems to me that the greatest cause of failure and eventual death
of peace organizations is the lack of adequate financial resources.
Every year, hundreds of peace organizations around the world die out;
many of those which survive are hardly moving while relatively few
maintain a healthy existence. It is as a result of these considerations
that the World Peace Academy conceived of the World Peace Exposition, which project should really be shared by all organizations concerned with peace.

The World Peace Exposition is a permanent world's fair. First of
all, the World Peace Academy is involved or interested in research and
educational activities, but, as I said, we cannot be effective unless we
have a continuous source of income. So we thought of the World Peace
Exposition as a means by which we can have a continuous and adequate income. The World Peace Exposition is such a big undertaking
that we have tried to approach people who we thought had money and
to interest them in financing the project. Luckily, we were able to find
just such people and they have now formed International Goodwill Incorporated as a regular business corporation. This is a new concept in
contrast with the more familiar military-industrial complex. This one
will represent what might be called a commercial-peace complex which
will be interested in peace while also deriving some profit in the process. International Goodwill Incorporated will make it possible to have
the World Peace Exposition and when we have the exposition, the
World Peace Academy will become more effective and, together with
other peace organizations, we intend to help the ones whom are capable
of helping.

World's fairs are ordinarily only good for a year, but this project is
going to be a permanent one which will have an international trade
center and cultural center. It will also have a city of tomorrow with
unique transportation. I believe anthropologists would have a big op-

portunity in studying the whole population in this experimental city. It could serve as a laboratory of mankind's problems of war, crime, pollution, etc.

PARKER: While other problems threaten us—that is, pollution, crime, dwindling resources, and an energy crisis — while these other problems do exist in various degrees and threaten people to various degrees throughout the world, war — total war — threatens all mankind. It is becoming increasingly recognized that, whereas science and technology provide hope in finding solutions in some of these other areas, they are used primarily to enforce and promote the war system rather than to remove it. We don't have much confidence in science and technology in this respect.

There is simply a need for people on the job. Millions go to work each day for war and a handful for peace. There is a need to increasingly prepare, within our universities, people who can deal with peace research. Hope lies in the belief that war can be eliminated as a means of resolving international conflict not only in theory, but also in practice.

CARROLL: My organization is an umbrella organization which embodies a varied range of institutions, including programs of key studies at universities, research centers like the Center for International Studies at M.I.T., and the like. It also embodies a variety of other types of organizations such as foundations and program organizations and some, including the American Friends Service Committee, which might normally be called activist organizations. The intent and practice of this organization has been to attempt to assist the various associated members to develop their programs and resources, to communicate with each other, and to provide facilities.

RAPOPORT: I was here at the last session and I was impressed with two things. That is, two tacit or explicit assumptions are made in the context of peace research. One is that war is somehow related to aggression. Now it may very well be related to it, but it's not necessary to assume it. If you examine the history of war during the last few centuries, when the tremendous technology of war was developing, we find that it is possible to divorce war from aggression altogether. Once upon a time when a person went to war he had to kill his enemy with an axe or a sword and of course he had to be aggressive in order to do that. With the development of firearms used at a distance, when he fired at his enemy he did not have to be aggressive. With the development of aviation, artillery, the automatic battlefield which is the Utopian dream of the military, it is not necessary to be aggressive at all in order to engage in warfare. Very ordinary people are killing when engaged in warfare and they do not ever come face to face with an enemy. It's the same as the change in the type of person who is a warrior. At one time a warrior had to be fierce, he had to be bold, he had to be strong. All of this is unnecessary today. There is a serious limitation in considering that war is a by-product of aggression. It may very well be. Its very deep roots may go all the way down to the primates and beyond and there may have been only a very gradual evolution of these instinctual patterns. But, as in many other instances in evolution, it is possible to have the final product completely divorced from its origins. We know that, for example, in semantics word meanings change and come to have absolutely no relation to their origins. Institutions change and come to have absolutely no relation to their origins. For example, the functioning of a modern monarchy in Europe has absolutely nothing to do with the way a monarchy used to function. What I would like to emphasize is that one need not begin with the function or history of aggression in order to examine the role that war now plays in human affairs.

The second thing that impresses me is the tacit or explicit assumption that war is some kind of a problem. If we know enough about a problem, its etiology, its sources, and so forth, then we could arrange things in such a way as to relieve the problem. In other words there is an analogy between peace research and medical research in which the causes of some diseases have been found and it's only a matter of time until specific procedures can be developed to cope with them. But there is a very serious fallacy in the analogy; that is, whereas in the case of medicine institutions exist that are in power, willing and able to deal with the problem when and if sufficient scientific knowledge is made available to them, this is not true in the case of war. Let a cure for leukemia be found tomorrow and within months any medical institution will have available the means for coping with that situation. Institutions exist for coping with medical problems and only knowledge is lacking in order for them to cope with it successfully. I challenge anybody to point out existing institutions that are able to deal with eliminating war even if we had the knowledge of how to deal with it. On the contrary, institutions exist which prevent the creation of institutions which could possibly conquer the problem.

Peace research should undertake analysis of the war-making institutions, not merely analysis for analysis' sake, but geared to the purpose of making these institutions less effective, or perhaps making them powerless altogether. The analogy which I would like to pursue is that between the war-making institutions and organized crime. Instead of analogizing war with disease, I would say that the war-marking institutions are somewhat on the order of organized criminal syndicates. They are parasitic bodies. They implicitly support each other. Each exists and finds rationale for its existence because others exist. They cooperate with each other in promoting their own existence and development. The scientific and technological developments that strengthen one institution, of course stimulate development of the others, so that it is possible to treat these institutions in the same way that one treats the Mafia.

One of the finest pieces of peace research done in recent years was one that was sponsored by Robert McNamara. I am referring to the body of knowledge that came out in the Pentagon Papers. But that was research, was good clean research; it was factual, it was organized, and when it finally became publicized, I believe it did more to incapacitate the war machine than practically any other piece of research available. Another piece of research that contributed to the incapacity of the war machine was the Watergate investigation. It was not, perhaps, conventional research, but then it was very respectable research, and quite indirectly it made the war-making potential of the United States government less because it destroyed the image that the United States has enjoyed since World War II as the power that could do no wrong, as the guardian of democracy, decency, and prosperity around the world. It impaired the image of the United States and that helped detract from the war-making potential of at least one great power.

The directions of peace research can depend very largely upon the conception of war. There are several such conceptions. We should not for a moment disparage other conceptions of war: one is as an outlet for instinct; one is as a problem, similar to the problems of natural disaster; etc. An equally genuine conception of war is one which makes war appear, not as an abnormal state of affairs among human beings nor as a disaster that occasionally plagues humanity, but on the contrary as a normal state of affairs. I accept completely Clausewitz's definition of war as an extension of policy by other means. I accept it because it is descriptively accurate. I am not, of course, a political realist in that sense of the word because I do not approve of that conception. Therefore I was very much impressed to hear Dr. Esser say that, with respect to human behavior, we are not faced with an objectively existing world such that if we find out how that world is then we are able to cope with it. No, reality we create for ourselves. The *Realpolitik* description of nations is probably the most accurate, but it is not TRUE because it is objectively so, but because thinking about it in this way makes it so. The *Realpolitik* description of the international arena is descriptively an accurate one. I certainly do not accept it. Therefore, I believe that the thrust of peace research should be directed toward weakening this conception of international relations and national systems by weakening the loyalty to the nation-state which we have inherited for the past couple of centuries as something which was considered to be self-evident.

Patriotism is now not at all necessary to wage war. The bugle-blowing, flag-waving wars that characterized the opening of this century are perhaps a thing of the past. Wars do not happen that way anymore. However, it is impossible to keep up the war machine without the tacit support of the populations. To be prosaic about it, funds have to be obtained. In a comparative democracy such as the United States it is possible to reduce popular support by disconnecting the bonds of loyalty of the population to their government by making people more aware of the way their government functions, by exposing the shenanigans and the lies and the distortions that have gone into the conduct of wars in the past decade or so. Then peace research (or war research; I don't care which it is called) will be directed towards finding techniques of how to believe most effectively and toward uncovering the facts of the case. Take the kind of research that is being done at the Stockholm Peace Research Institute. All they do is publish yearbooks. They published a yearbook on the arms race. This is very useful, mind you; very, very useful. It's as if the entire operation of the Mafia were put in a yearbook for everyone to see. Of course it is not enough, because one must do something about it in addition to knowing. The SIPRI yearbooks, the Watergate exposures, the Pentagon Papers, are knowledge. It is not enough to have that knowledge; one must act upon it. But it is the kind of knowledge that is most useful for the sort of aims that peace research, in my opinion, should have in mind.

PARKER: If a nation does not feel secure without war-making potentials, then I doubt that a simple attack on these institutions is going to eliminate them. They have a tradition of being able to justify their existence, if in no other way, by presenting us with the old view of the enemy, the external enemy. We do need to begin to make these types of attacks on war-making machinery, but at the same time, we have to look at the function that it seems to be serving and begin to ask questions such as, are there replacements? Can we perhaps find different approaches other than through the war machinery for dealing with the kinds of things which thus far our leaders seem to feel can only be resolved through resort to these kinds of institutions?

ROPER: One of the biggest contemporary myths is that the state can now protect its citizens. Since the advent of the hydrogen bomb, this is no longer true. We have to let people know that their state can no longer protect them. If they want to be protected, then we're going to have an alternate institution like the U.N. But first we do need to see what the functions of war are in our society as separate from the causes and conditions, the immediate causes, of war. This whole business that the military has tied to itself is keeping it in existence. For example, the on-the-job training of skills for young men after high school takes place only in the military as far as I know and a lot of men are drawn in because of that. We must create alternate institutions to take over these other functions of the war system, so that war can wither away, but I don't think it will until then.

KRAKAUER: Perhaps it's not a major point, but I don't understand what Professor Rapoport is saying about flag-waving wars being a thing of the past. There's still a lot of flag-waving in this world. There are many, many countries in this world, and flag-waving evokes the greatest emotional response in human beings. There is probably still more danger of flag-waving wars than of wars by the military alone.

MIDLARSKY: Mrs. Roper's comments on the indefensibility of the territorial nation-state reminds me of John Hurd several years ago, who wrote an article on the demise of the territorial nation-state arguing that just as the walls of the feudal castle were no longer able to protect its inhabitants when gunpowder was invented, so, too, with the advent of nuclear weapons the walls of the nation-state were no longer adequate. Then, several years after that he wrote an article on the territorial nation-state revisited, in which he had to re-think his position in terms of apparently successful nationalism of North Vietnam and Israel. Dr. Rapoport is correct when he says that we have to deal with the problem of nationalism.

CARROLL: I think that Rapoport, though correct, holds too narrow a position and I fear very much that we shall discover in time that neither the Pentagon Papers nor the Ervin hearing will have an effect other than to stabilize the institutions. The Pentagon Papers were produced by the Pentagon. What we're seeing in Watergate is like what has been called among the British a crisis of the aristocracy. Ours is a crisis in the aristocracy and in terms of change in the system will have little effect. Much more attention should be devoted not to the powerful but to the powerless.

MRS. ESSER: I know what Dr. Carroll means and I feel just as she does, but one other thing has happened and this way of stopping the war machine has tested the endurance of the United States for the very first time in its history. The resulting shame and difficulty in our being able to sort out our emotions and feelings as American citizens because of this Watergate business are going to test this nation for the very first time and they might just possibly teach us to endure long enough to develop the capacity for change.

RAPOPORT: My seeking out in different directions was not meant to say that this is the way we should go. Sometimes these ways are neglected because the mainstream of peace research is techniques of conflict resolution. I have nothing against conflict resolution, but it just has limitations. The idea being: here is one nation; here is another; they quarrel about issues; how can we bring them together so they don't quarrel any more? Yes, this happens on occasion, but there are other facets of war-making that have nothing to do with it. The United States didn't quarrel with the Vietnamese people. The United States wanted to establish its control — political, economic, and strategic — over a certain geographic area, because it was a link in a chain of bases that circled around the Communist land base which at that time included both Russia and China. The chain had to be closed. This was the goal, and therefore all the technology, all the strategy, everything was mobilized in order to put bases in there. In the process, the U.S. was confronted with the people who lived in the area and who did not want this done, but Americans didn't hate the Vietnamese; they were not their enemies. In the same way the Spanish *conquistadores* did not necessarily hate the Indians when they exterminated them. Not all warfare has to do with aggression and hostility, confrontation and quarrels. There are, of course, wars that have to do with that. There are also wars that have to do with quarrels between peoples themselves, with mutual hatred between nationalities, a behavior of nationalism, but there are also other wars that have nothing to do with it whatsoever. War is not one thing. War is a great many things, and some of them I suspect are totally unrelated to others. We all use one word to describe all these phenomena. But these phenomena are widely disparate.

With regard to the nationalist, flag-waving wars, I was speaking relatively. The highest peak of that kind of war fever was probably reached in Europe at the end of the nineteenth and beginning of the twentieth century, when the brave troops marched off into battle to music. In the Second World War it didn't happen and it certainly hasn't happened in wars that are presently being conducted and will be conducted in the near future. Those are not the mechanics, and therefore it would be a mistake to think that war can be alleviated by showing that your nation is not the only one that has a right to exist.

With regard to whether such revelations as Watergate, the Pentagon Papers, and so on, can permanently incapacitate the war machine; of course, no such thing is in my mind. Sipes, earlier, indicated what had to be done over a period of a couple of centuries in order to eliminate war from the world. It is not possible at the present time to find the solution which would enable us to eliminate war quickly because there are no institutions, and neither can they be created, because there are counter institutions that prevent their creation. It is not a problem of solving the problem of war. The problem is how to fight against war and there I would not venture to say what the best way is. Nobody could say what is the best way to fight against the institution of war because nobody has had experience at this. It is safe to assume that the war-making potential of at least one great power, the United States, has been somewhat impaired by the events of the past ten or fifteen years. When a revolution starts in Brazil (and it will) I do not believe that the United States can send its ground troops, a million or a half million men, to fight a war of the sort it has fought in Vietnam.

I do not believe that the nuclear confrontation is as present a danger as it was ten years ago. That does not mean that the danger does not exist. Just as long as the institutions exist, as long as the silos exist where the warheads are aimed at each other's cities, of course the danger exists. But it is not nearly as great as it was in, let's say, 1960 to 1962. The reason for this reduction is that the notion of omnipotence that governed United States foreign policy has been undermined by the changes in public opinion.

When you consider the activities of the people that are engaged in war today, and that of course involves tremendous armies of people — not armies in the sense that they fight battles in the battlefield, but armies in the sense that they contribute to the atmosphere of the war machine — they don't do anything aggressive. On the contrary, they cooperate. The bigger the organization is that is supposed to accomplish anything, the more organizational cooperation, loyalty, efficiency, and conscientious performance of duties is required. That is what people learn in the war machine, as they do in any big organization. Psychically it provides a great deal of satisfaction. Consider the careers that are open in the war-making institutions and their adjuncts. In our culture there is hardly any other activity as satisfactory as the mastery of something, performing on a high level of ingenuity, efficiency, and so on, and that is what these opportunities are — not opportunities for aggression, but opportunities for creative work.

The thing that channels attention-getting work into destructive ways is the interest of the war machine. What is quite necessary, in addition to all the other facts, is a direct assault on the war-making institutions and the war-making states. I am even tempted to coin a term, a Latin term, *Status belagarus*, a new species. This *Status belagarus*, the war-making state, has a psychology of its own which is not related to the psychology of its components any more than the psychology of individuals relates to the psychology of the cells that compose them. When one individual fights another, it doesn't mean that every cell fights the other. The cells do their business; they do what they've always done. And so it is now with warfare. Everybody simply goes around doing his business, business as usual. The fact that it all adds up to a tremendous destructive machine is something that the individuals themselves cannot control. I would then seriously recommend the study of this emergent organism, the war-waging state; its physiology, its psychology, its anatomy. Especially important are the kinds of studies that would contribute to ways and means to effect its destruction.

Questions on the condition of humanity may be taken facetiously. It is very easy to describe "man" as the sum total of the human beings on this planet. Of course this is not what is meant. Of course, what was meant was a much more profound thing. One speaks of "something" of humanity. For example, the interests of humanity, as opposed to other interests. Isn't that what you meant, the faith of humanity?

CARBY-SAMUELS: No. The important proposition is: the human being is a perceiving being and the human being acts consistently with his perception and consistently with his goals. Now if one is going to save humanity, one has to have some objective function that includes the diversity of perception. How are YOU going to treat those who say, "Damn it, I don't like your saving technique"?

RAPOPORT: I thought that that was exactly what was meant. If one talks about saving humanity, one must have some objective. Would you agree that there are certain conditions that must be fulfilled in order for humanity to go on existing as humanity? I'll be trivial about it, but for example the atmosphere should be more or less as it is; without the atmosphere, humanity cannot possibly go on living; or perhaps you would say it is not in the interests of the forces of humanity to survive at all. Would you agree that it is good for humanity to survive?

CARBY-SAMUELS: Gentlemen, here I come to something which makes me, I don't know, kind of queer, but to my mind it is critical that when we talk about humanity we make up our minds whether we're talking about the conscious entity which is a part of the biosphere.

RAPOPORT: As to whether or not there is a consciousness of humanity, I would venture to say at the present time, no. But perhaps we can adopt one. Is this not perhaps a worthy goal? We develop an ecological imperative to become a part of the human consciousness but we do not know exactly how to work towards that end. Nevertheless it is an end that one can define.

CARBY-SAMUELS: In that case what one is doing is trying to manipulate the physical environment so that that environment is supportive of other material or physical entities. We are talking about manipulating the environment as such rather than constructing a desirable type of humanity.

TAMAYO Y SALMORÁN: In response to Rapoport: perhaps we can create another machine called a peace machine. Instead of making this warfare machine we can substitute a peace machine so that the warfare machine would no longer be necessary. Instead of deciding to throw away our arms right now, which is very stupid to do, we should try to create a climate in which these arms are no longer necessary.

RAPOPORT: There are two ways of looking at it. One is that military machines exist because conflicts exist in the world, and the machine must be used in order to safeguard the world from these conflicts. Another view is that conflicts exist in the world because there are military machines. Now, it may be that both views are correct and so one should not subscribe to inner motivation in such complex matters as behavior. When I say that the military machine must be attacked, this is a very far cry from unilateral disarmament. There is nobody that can force unilateral disarmament on the United States.

Wherever military machines exist they are parasitic bodies. They support each other in their existence because the existence of every one of them is rationalized on the basis of the existence of the others. Of that I believe we have ample evidence. Ask any American why the United States needs such weapons, you will get a very straightforward and seemingly logical answer: "Why, because the other powers — usually the Soviet Union — have a military machine which would be used against the United States if the United States did not have it." Ask the Russian the same question and you would get exactly the same answer. The way to ask the question is not one separately and then the other. The way to approach the question is about both together. Why do both military machines exist? And to this question there is only one answer. They exist because they exist. Each exists because the other exists, therefore both exist because both exist and that, I submit, is an absurd answer. It's like high school algebra; it's child's play to solve two equations simultaneously with two unknowns, but if you go about it one at a time, you can prove to yourself logically that you cannot solve it. (If you have two equations, x to y, you cannot know y until you know x and you cannot know x until you know y and therefore the problem is insoluble, though there is a very simple technique of solving the problems simultaneously.)

A number of peace researchers in Europe point out that the elimination of war tensions through some kind of agreement or collusion between the great powers today (especially among the nations of the world that comprise the so-called advanced technological societies) may very well be directed towards maintaining built-in "structural violence" by means of which the "have" nations exploit the "have-not" nations. As a result, the whole focus, the whole center of gravity of conflict in the world, may very well shift. Since World War II we have been predominantly concerned with the outbreak of total war, nuclear war, dissolution of the United States, and so on. The center of gravity of conflict may shift to that between the exploited Third World and the exploiting world of advanced nations. When and if that happens, and I do believe that is in the offing, I think that the entire problem of war and peace will have to be rethought. The techniques of conflict resolution and peace making may very well be used as techniques of suppression. Please note that the procedure which was instituted by the Nixon and Johnson Administrations in Vietnam was called pacification. (In Tzarist Russia, pacification meant that the Cossacks came out with whips and pacified the people.) We should rethink the entire problem of war and peace and conflict if it is no longer to be concerned with approximately equal, prosperous nations which confront each other as in the traditional conception of war as it was invented in the system of nation-states in Europe. All of the textbooks that deal with war deal with that kind of war. It is something else that is now brewing: a conflict between those that have and those that do not.

SMITH: Dr. Carroll said earlier that anyone could tell the difference between wars of liberation and wars of incursion.

CARROLL: I said that there were differences, and probably measurable differences, between symmetric wars, that is, wars between nations of approximately equal status and wealth and military power, and asymmetric wars, those between "have" and "have-not" nations. Between the "have" and "have-not" nations are situations of oppression and liberation: the "have" nations are very crudely characterized as oppressing nations; the "have-not" nations are very crudely characterized as ones who are fighting wars for liberation.

ROPER: I'd like to try to clarify just this point that Dr. Bigelow raised, using the Philippines as an example. We're all trying NOT to exacerbate the conflicts within these countries. What the United States is doing is exactly that. We have sent as ambassador to the Philippines William Sullivan, who was the person who planned secret warfare in Laos. He was ratified as ambassador by a vote of 12 to 3 in the Senate Foreign Relations Committee. This is why I think Rapoport is a little optimistic. Some of you may have seen the *New York Times* advertising supplement which looked exactly like the *New York Times Magazine* with Marcos on the cover. It was at least a $100,000 job and was beautifully done. Who was paying for the advertising in it? Dole Pineapple and various other transnational corporations dominated it! A marvelous teaching tool in itself. You don't have to say a word; just lay it in front of the class. We are trying not to have these things happen, and if there are problems within countries, for them to work it out. But the problem is that we are playing footsie with the oligarchies in these countries and we are causing the problems that are causing the people to have to revolt.

JACOBS: I think it appropriate to read into the record a statement by the President of the Institution which is our host. Father Hesburgh said that the problem of peace can't be separated from the problem of justice, and I think that we will not be able to develop alternative institutions to war without providing some way of having justice in the world.

MIDLARSKY: I don't think that one has to necessarily see oneself in either one camp or the other on this. I don't entirely agree with the proponents of either view that we need peace at any cost, or we need justice at any cost. Any kind of activity or inactivity involves a cost and this has to be assessed no matter what the alternative chosen. The concept of structural violence can be integrated very well with the normal kinds of violence, and the concept of symmetric and asymmetric wars can be seen as coming out of the same framework, Galtung's framework, the one of top dog and underdog. These things can be integrated within the same theoretical view and, possibly, even certain kinds of actions can be taken which are not necessarily either in one camp or the other.

PARKER: It was asked earlier, "How do peace researchers define humanity?" We were not that successful in defining humanity and I think that the anthropologists came to the rescue. This points out one thing about peace research: I think as a new field of research we haven't taken the time to lay the foundations — that is, to assess the tools that we have available and determine where we should be going and deter-mine the kind of questions we should be asking and what, in fact, should be studied.

One of the things that has impressed me particularly about the Con-ference is not that we have the solutions to the problem, because I don't think we do, but that we have a discipline, anthropology, which can make a contribution to our research. I have come to feel that this whole area, beginning with war and peace, is one which is by its nature multi-disciplinary. And the thing that has impressed me most is that people have been willing to sit as a group for four days, and not to simply deal with the puberty rites or religious mores of various socie-ties and groups, but in fact to begin to ask, as anthropologists within the confines of our interests and our knowledge and our focus, what kinds of questions can we begin to deal with which are relevant to the whole area of war and peace. To me this is a profound thing, for before coming here I would have thought 75 percent of you had very little interest in the subject and very little commitment. You have studied war but in a similar manner you have studied religion. You have seen your work as related to other societies, I'm sure, but many never have really thought of its application in dealing with what I call a problem (I don't know what else to call it). And so I have to say that other people may have different expectations as to what this thing should have come to.

SMITH: Maybe we can control war with a world peace movement, a world government, but to talk about eliminating warfare, a cultural pattern that has characterized man's evolution for millions of years, is absolutely naive.

POPE: In cultural anthropology we say that a person is not worth his salt unless he does fieldwork. If we want to know about the war machine, then we need to study it as an institution. We need to become very well acquainted with its participants and this is extremely difficult. Now and then I suggest to my students that they really ought to get out and study American insurance companies. You might also try to study government and this means that you have to make your way up into the inner circle and this is hard to do when you are out in the Caribbean or Africa. But it's frightening to my students and on second thought, they would sooner go to New Guinea.

JOSEPH SZALAY (Supporting member, World Peace Academy): I am very sorry, but I feel that I have to say something. I lived through the Second War; I lived through the Nazi dictators. I lived through the Communists. I was seven years in a concentration camp. What I want to say is this. I am really grateful for you people taking time and the intelligence to do something. I have lived through torture and hating. There is no difference between Communists and Nazis. I know only one way — one way we can stop war — through educational means, and I have to really praise you and thank you for all of you who are really doing a wonderful job. God bless you. War is no way, no way to solve mankind's problems.

Biographical Notes

STUART ALBERT (U.S.A.) is Professor in Psychology at the City University of New York.

CLIFTON AMSBURY (1910, U.S.A.) was educated at the Universities of California and Nebraska, and California State University, Hayward. He is now teaching at Contra Costa College. His Master's thesis was an in-depth analysis of an anthropological argument: "Peasant-based societies and the Foster controversy."

GHAUS ANSARI (1929, India) was educated under Wilhelm Koppers at Vienna University. He is currently Professor of Cultural Anthropology at Kuwait University and is author of numerous articles and books on the caste system among Muslims in India and on theoretical growth in cultural anthropology.

ROBERT BIGELOW (1918, Canada) was educated at McGill University and now is Reader in Zoology at the University of Canterbury, Christchurch, New Zealand. He is author of *The dawn warriors* and articles on human evolution.

CHARLES A. BISHOP (1935, Canada) was educated at the University of Toronto and the State University of New York at Buffalo. He is now Professor of Anthropology at the State University of New York College at Oswego and Associate of the Royal Ontario Museum, Toronto. He is author of *The northern Ojibwa and the fur trade* and papers in professional journals and books dealing with Northern Algonkian land tenure, ecology, social organization, and the fur trade from late prehistoric times to the present.

ROBERT CANCRO (1932, U.S.A.) was educated at Fordham University and the State University of New York, and he is currently Professor of Psychiatry at the University of Connecticut Health Center. He is the editor of seven books and numerous articles.

HORACE R. CARBY-SAMUELS (1933, Jamaica) is a development economist. He was educated at the Universities of Toronto, British Columbia, and Chicago. In 1971–1974, he was Visiting Assistant Professor, University of Notre Dame (Indiana). The author is primarily a research economist specializing in the study of the policy elements that accrue to using an emphasis on the norms of the market and of market development as the framework and instrument for the development of man as mind. Analyzing the impact of this emphasis on "technical assistance" schemes is his current area of research and publication.

BERENICE A. CARROLL (1932, U.S.A.) studied at Brown University. She now teaches political science at the University of Illinois at Urbana, and is an editor of *Peace and Change: A Journal of Peace Research.* She is author of *Design for total war: arms and economics in the Third Reich* (Mouton, 1968) and numerous articles in the fields of peace research and women's history and editor of a forthcoming anthology, *Liberating women's history: theoretical and critical essays.*

HENRI J. M. CLAESSEN (1930, The Netherlands) studied at the University of Amsterdam. He is now Associate Professor in Anthropology at the National University of Leiden. He is author of *Van vorsten en volken* and several articles on political anthropology and Polynesia.

KENNETH COOPER (1922, U.S.A.) was educated in Engineering (B.S.), Philosophy (M.A.), and Anthropology (Ph.D.) at Stanford University. He now teaches and works with foreign scholars on long-range nation-planning at Stanford University. He is author of articles and director of conferences on "Third World Development Alternatives," and "Prospects for Human Survival."

PETER A. CORNING (1935, U.S.A.) was educated at Brown University and New York University and is now Lecturer in the Human Biology Program and in the Department of Political Science at Stanford University.

He has held post-doctoral fellowships at the Institute for Behavioral Genetics, University of Colorado, and, currently, at the Hoover Institution on War, Revolution, and Peace. Among his publications are several on aggression, including "Human violence: some causes and implications," "Toward a general theory of violent aggression," and "Collective aggression."

IRENÄUS EIBL-EIBESFELDT (1928, Austria) was a former student of Konrad Lorenz. He is now head of the Max-Planck-Institute for Human Ethology in Percha, West Germany, and since 1963 he has been Professor at the University of Munich. He is author of numerous scientific articles and books, including *Love and hate* and *Ethology: biology of behavior.*

ADA REIF ESSER (1926, Germany), composer, was educated privately in Berlin and New York and at the Juilliard School of Music. She obtained her degree in English and German literature at Brooklyn College. Since 1943, her main interest has been in the development of an observation on beat unit behavior in humans, and she is continuing research in this area with her husband, Aristide H. Esser.

ARISTIDE H. (HANS) ESSER (1930, Indonesia) is a psychiatrist educated at the Universities of Amsterdam and Leiden, and is presently Director of the Central Bergen Community Mental Health Center. He has edited several books, is President of the Association for the Study on Man-Environment Relations, Inc. Orangeburg, N.Y., and edits this Association's journal, *Man-Environment Systems.*

CLINTON F. FINK (1933, U.S.A.) studied at Swarthmore College and the University of Michigan, and is now visiting Research Associate in Communications Research at the University of Illinois, on leave from the University of Michigan. He is author of numerous articles on small groups, social conflict, and the history of peace research, and he is a former editor of the *Journal of Conflict Resolution.*

S. I. GHABBOUR. No biographical data available.

R. DALE GIVENS (1928, U.S.A.) studied at the Universities of Texas, California (U.C.L.A.), and Kentucky and is currently Associate Professor of Anthropology at California State College, Dominguez Hills. He is author of numerous articles in the areas of biological anthropology, psychological anthropology, and biocultural theory.

EDWARD E. GRAHAM (1942, U.S.A.) was educated at the University of California, Davis, and at the Universities of Oklahoma and Utah and is now a research analyst at the University of Utah Research Institute.

RICHARD W. HOWELL (1926, U.S.A.) studied at the Universities of California and Hawaii, The George Washington University, and Kyūshū Daigaku (in Japan), and is currently Associate Professor of Anthropology with the University of Hawaii at Hilo. He is author of numerous articles and co-author (with Harold J. Vetter) of *Language in behavior*.

PETER HUBER (1945, U.S.A.) was educated at Duke University and is currently Assistant Professor of Anthropology at Princeton University. Previously, he taught at Chatham College and was Visiting Assistant Professor in the Department of Theology of Notre Dame University.

RUTH HARRIET JACOBS (1924, U.S.A.) was educated at Boston and Brandeis Universities, and is now Associate Professor of Sociology at Boston University. She is author of numerous papers in sociology, education, and gerontology. She is a member of the American Sociological Association's Committee on World Conflicts and chaired the World Conflict session at its 1974 meeting. She teaches a course on the sociology of war and peace.

ADRIAAN KORTLANDT (1918, the Netherlands) was trained as a geographer and a psychologist at the Universities of Utrecht and Amsterdam. His publications focus on the concept of instinct and ethological theory (1940–1959), on the dehumanization hypothesis of African ape evolution (since 1959), and on ape and human evolution in general fieldwork on birds and chimpanzees. He is author of *New perspectives on ape and human evolution* (Stichting voor Psychobiologie, Amsterdam, 1972).

DANIEL KRAKAUER (1915, U.S.A.) studied zoology at Cornell University and Johns Hopkins and dynamic psychology at Brooklyn College and as well as psychoanalysis. He is currently president of a manufacturing organization. His major professional interest is the management and motivation of human beings and a related interest is the evolution and nature of human nature.

ANTHONY LEEDS (1925, U.S.A.) studied at Columbia University and is now Professor of Anthropology at Boston University. He has edited two books, *Social structure, stratification, and mobility* and *Man, culture and animals: the role of animals in human subsistence* (with A. P. Vayda), and has written numerous articles on ecology, social organization of complex societies, and the history and philosophy of anthropology.

NORMAN MACDONALD (1911–1973, Scotland) was educated at Edinburgh University and was a Chest Consultant at Clare Hall Hospital, near London. He is author of medical journal articles on ethics and the social responsibility of doctors. He was a founder member and was recently Chairman of The Medical Association for the Prevention of War.

MATTHEW MELKO (1930, U.S.A.) was educated in international relations at the London School of Economics and Political Science and is author of *The nature of civilizations* and *52 peaceful societies*. He is currently Associate Dean of Breadford College.

MANUS I. MIDLARSKY (1937, U.S.A.) was educated at Northwestern University and is now Professor of Political Science and Project Director at the Institute of Behavioral Science of the University of Colorado, Boulder. He is author of the book *On war: political violence in the international system* and has authored articles and chapters of edited volumes dealing with the problem of political violence.

ANDERSON NETTLESHIP, M. D. (1910, U.S.A.) was educated at Johns Hopkins University, Cornell, and Duke University and is now Director of the Antaeus Institute, Fayetteville, Arkansas. Formerly he was chairman of the Department of Pathology at the University of Arkansas Medical Center in Little Rock, Arkansas. He is an international lecturer on medicine, history of medicine, etiology of ear, and the author of a book on cancer. He is a sculptor and a published poet.

MARTIN A. NETTLESHIP (1936, U.S.A.) received his academic education at the University of Chicago and the London School of Economics and Political Science. He is now an Institute Associate at Antaeus Lineal Research Associates 1948, Fayetteville, Arkansas. He is author of various papers and books on arts, crafts, and applied anthropology including: *Cheng Yu-lin, a creative woodcarver*, "A unique Southeast Asian loom," "Chinese-Aborigine relations on Taiwan," and *The Atayal: mountain people in contact and change.*

ROSE OLDFIELD HAYES (1936, U.S.A.) was educated at State University of New York/Buffalo. She lectured at the University of Khartoum and has authored articles on prehistoric warfare and women's roles and population growth in Nile Valley cultures. Her publications include "Meroitic archer's rings: an outline of political boundaries" and "Female genitial mutilation, fertility control, women's roles, and the patrilineage in modern Sudan: a functional analysis." She is currently conducting research on the Shinnecock Indian Reservation.

RICHARD PARKER (1946, U.S.A.) was educated at Colorado State University and George Washington University. He is presently a graduate student in Peace Research at St. Louis University and a part-time faculty and staff member of the Institute for the Study of Peace, St. Louis University. His special research interest is in international conflict and conflict resolution.

POLLY POPE (U.S.A.) was educated at the University of California and the University of Southern California in anthropology and journalism. She is now an Associate Professor and Chairperson of the Department of Anthropology, California State College, Dominguez Hills. She is author of several papers on folklore and warfare.

IRWIN PRESS (1937, U.S.A.) was educated at Northwestern University and the University of Chicago and is now Associate Professor of Anthropology at the University of Notre Dame. He is author of various articles on peasant society, social-cultural change, and urban folk-medicine.

ANATOL RAPOPORT (1911, Russia) was educated at the University of Chicago and is presently Professor of Psychology and Mathematics at the University of Toronto. He is author of books on conflict and international relations: *Fights, games and debates* (1960), *Strategy and conscience* (1964), *The big two* (1971), and *Conflict in man-made environment* (1974).

CARA E. RICHARDS (U.S.A.) received her Ph.D. in 1957 from Cornell University. She is currently Associate Professor at Transylvania University, Lexington, Kentucky. She has done research principally with applied anthropology, directed social change, and minority groups. Her publications include "Presumed behavior: modification of the ideal-real dichotomy" (*American Anthropologist*, 1969) and *Man in perspective* (Random House, 1972).

MARILYN KEYES ROPER (1935, U.S.A.) studied at Bryn Mawr College, George Washington University, and the University of Pennsylvania. She is now Coordinator of War or Peace, a 1967 project based at the University Museum in Philadelphia. She is the author of "A survey of the evidence for intrahuman killing in the Pleistocene," *Current Anthropology* 10(4).

BART M. SAUCELO (U.S.A.) is President of the World Peace Academy, South Bend, Indiana.

JOHN SAXE-FERNÁNDEZ (1940, Costa Rica) was educated at Brandeis University, Massachussetts, and Washington University, St. Louis. He is now Professor of Sociology and Latin American Affairs at the School of Social and Political Science, National Autonomous University of Mexico. He is author of *Hemispheric projections of Pax Americana*. He has written numerous articles dealing with U.S. counterinsurgency and counterintelligence, social science for national security and, more recently, articles on thermonuclear strategy which have been published in France, Peru, Cuba, Mexico, Brazil, Costa Rica, Argentina, and the United States. He is also Director for the Project on Internal War in the Western Hemisphere, for the Latin American Center at the National University of Mexico.

BARBARA G. SCANDALIS (1917, U.S.A.) was educated at California State University, Los Angeles. She has been a lecturer on Psychological Anthropology at California State College, Dominguez Hills, California, and at present teaches Anthropology at San Gabriel Evening School, San Gabriel, California. She is author of several papers and articles on cross-cultural medical practice and co-author (with Maurice N. Walsh) of papers on psycho-anthropology.

JOHN PAUL SCOTT (1909, U.S.A.) was educated at the University of Wyoming, Oxford University, and the University of Chicago where he received his Ph.D. in genetics in 1935. He has been chairman of the Department of Zoology at Wabash College, chairman of the Division of Behavior Studies at the Jackson Laboratory in Bar Harbor, Maine, and is currently Regent's Professor of Psychology and Director of the Center for Research on Social Behavior at Bowling Green State University. He is the author of a book, *Aggression*, as well as numerous scientific articles on the subject. He is now President of the International Society for Research on Aggression.

MOSHE SHOKEID (1936, Israel) was educated at The Hebrew University of

Jerusalem and the University of Manchester, U.K. He is now Chairman of the Department of Sociology and Anthropology at Tel Aviv University. He is author of *The dual heritage: immigrants from the Atlas Mountains in an Israeli village* and co-author (with S. Deshen) of *The predicament of homecoming: social and cultural life of North African immigrants in Israel.*

RICHARD GREY SIPES (1928, U.S.A.) studied at the Universidad de las Americas, Pennsylvania State University, and State University of New York at Buffalo and is now Assistant Professor of Anthropology at Long Island University, Southampton. He is a cross-cultural correlation methodologist and has authored several articles on that subject, as well as on warfare and aggression, including "Rating hologeistic method" and "War, sports, and aggression: an empirical test of two rival theories." He is currently engaged in research on the cultural determinants of population growth.

HENNING SIVERTS (Norway) received his doctorate in 1959 at the University of Oslo and is now Senior Curator at the University of Bergen. In 1953–1954, 1961–1962, and 1964, he did fieldwork in Tzeltal and Trotzil of the Highland Chiapas, Mexico, and in 1970–1971, he worked among the Jívaro (Aguaruna) of the Montaña in north Peru. His other research interests include political systems, ethnicity, ecology and human adaptability in tropical forest regions, and language in society (cognitive systems and ethnographic procedures). His publications on the above topics include "The Aguaruna Jívaro of Peru: a preliminary report" and *Tribal survival in the Alto Marañon: the Aguaruna case.*

M. ESTELLIE SMITH (1935, U.S.A.) was educated at the University of Buffalo (now SUNY-Buffalo) and is presently on the faculty of the SUNY-College at Brockport. She is also on the editorial boards of *Urban Anthropology, Studies in European Society*, and *Journal of Political Anthropology.* She is also editor of the Festschrift *Studies in linguistics: in honor of Georg L. Trager* and author of *Governing at Taos Pueblo*, as well as other short papers.

JOSEPH SZALAY (U.S.A.) is a Supporting Member of the World Peace Academy, South Bend, Indiana.

ROLANDO TAMAYO Y SALMORÁN (1944, Mexico) was educated at the Universidad Nacional Autónoma de México and the Université de Paris. He is now Associate Research Fellow at Institute for Legal Studies (Instituto de Investigaciones — Jurídicas) at the Universidad Nacional Autónoma de México and Professor of General Theory of the State at its School of Law. He is author of several papers on the theory of law and political philosophy.

STANTON TEFFT (1930, U.S.A.) was educated at Michigan State University, University of Wisconsin, and the University of Minnesota. He is now Associate Professor of Anthropology at Wake Forest University. He is author of several papers on political anthropology, culture change, and value systems of the American Indian.

UMAR ROLF VON EHRENFELS (1901, Austria) was educated at Prague and Vienna universities. He lived in India and did field research there for over three decades. Since 1949, he has been Head of the Department of Anthropology at the University of Madras. In 1962 he joined the South Asia Institute of the University of Heidelberg. A specialist in matrilineal societies, he has written numerous articles, books (among others: *Mother-right in India, Kadar of Cochin, Innere Entwicklungshilfe*) and has contributed to compendia (such as *Epistemology in anthropology* and *German scholars on India*).

MAURICE N. WALSH (1950, U.S.A.) was educated at Wayne State University and the University of Minnesota. He is currently Associate Clinical Professor of Psychiatry at University of California, Los Angeles and is author of several papers on psycholinguistics, leadership, and psychoanthropology. He is editor of *War and the human race, University of California, Los Angeles, Faculty Lecture Series of 1968.*

CLARENCE W. YOUNG (1902, U.S.A.) was educated in psychology at Stanford University and the University of Iowa. He taught psychology at Colgate University for 42 years and is author of a variety of papers and reports and co-author with G. Ledyard Stebbins and others of *The human organism and the world of life.*

Index of Names

Index of Subjects